praise for cindy waszak geary

In this captivating memoir, Cindy seeks and finds her ancestors' footprints within their European homelands as well as the lands they eventually occupied on Turtle Island. With candor, honesty, and empathy, she explores the stories of her family, herself, *and* the Indigenous Peoples her ancestors displaced. Her exploration illuminates the legacies of settler colonialism that are often silenced, ignored, and erased. *Ancestral Landscapes* shows us how the past actively shapes our relationships with land, water, food, climate, and each other throughout our lifetimes and in future generations.

Hilary Giovale, author of the award-winning book
Becoming a Good Relative: Calling White Settlers toward Truth, Healing, and Repair

Ancestral Landscapes is a flowing tributary arriving at "whatever edge of liberation we can get ourselves." Cindy Waszak Geary offers a delicate but purposeful lens for excavating what it means to arrive in any homeland, to arrive in any homeplace unraveling the sacredness of boundaries inside the liminal spaces of researcher, historian, documentarian, activist, lineage, and inhabitant. . . . Geary offers us the gift of understanding that we are all nothing more than the echoes of our ancestors when we humbly howl and whisper their names or that the soles of our feet understand that the history of a land is never separate from the social or political histories of that place, any place.

Jaki Shelton Green, North Carolina Poet Laureate

Ancestral Landscapes brilliantly dissolves the notion that people with diverse European ancestry can not reconnect with their homelands. . . . Through graceful prose and haunting photographs, Geary wrestles with the impact these routes have had, not only on our country, but also on her family and herself.

Nora Murphy, author of *White Birch, Red Hawthorn: A Memoir*

Geary weaves a story of landscapes, following four branches of her family as they immigrate at different times from locations of hardship in northern Europe. Her careful explorations and elegant photographs take us not just to her ancestors' original homelands but to the places they settled or later called home in what is now the United States. These heartfelt stories begin to fill in the map of colonization we citizens did not learn in school—the Eastern Shore of Virginia in the 1620s, the Hudson River Valley slightly later, Iowa along the Mississippi in the 1880s, and western North Carolina from the brutal destruction of the Cherokee Middle Towns to the present day. With careful attention to the harm dealt to First People and the land itself, Geary yet manages to help us touch the humanity of her settler ancestors.

Louise Dunlap, author of *Inherited Silence: Listening to the Land, Healing the Colonizer Mind*

A lyrical, honest, searching account that invites each of us to consider diverse landscapes and people as well as our own place in history.

Kate H. Rademacher, author of *Reclaiming Rest: The Promise of Sabbath, Solitude, and Stillness in a Restless World*

A needed story of claiming ancestral accountability with both honesty and compassion. *Ancestral Landscapes* tutors us in the essential self-understandings that can emerge when Euro-Americans turn to genealogy to grapple with the settler colonialism of their ancestors.

Mary Watkins, liberation psychologist and author of
*White Work and Reparative Genealogy: Reckoning with
Ancestral Debt as a Path to Racial Reparations*

An intimately self-reflective memoir of a woman who, in discovering her ancestral past, gained life-changing insights about identity and belonging.

Nadia Dean, author, *Demand of Blood*

ancestral landscapes

ancestral landscapes

searching for my place in the world

Cindy Waszak Geary

Torchflame Books
Vista, CA

ISBN: 978-1-61153-713-0 (hardcover)

ISBN: 978-1-61153-708-6 (paperback)

ISBN: 978-1-61153-709-3 (ebook)

ISBN: 978-1-61153-710-9 (large print)

Library of Congress Control Number: 2025918617

Ancestral Landscapes is published by: Torchflame Books, an imprint of Top Reads Publishing, LLC, 1035 E. Vista Way, Suite 205, Vista, CA 92084, USA

Cover design and interior layout by Jori Hanna

Map drawings by Frederick M. Marine

Family tree illustrations and map borders and labels by Denise Todloski Design

All photographs by Cynthia Wasak Geary

To my brother, Greg, and to my descendants,
Emily, Max, and Daisy Starlight,
and those yet to come.

"To become aware of the possibility of the search is to be onto something."

Walker Percy, *The Moviegoer*

" . . . the significance of past events appears in these ordinary moments experienced by people whose names we rarely know. That's why the quotidian becomes the limit for speaking about the past. The unknown is more than an occasion for possibilities. It is a provocation that propels us on a journey, a route of unknowing, in which we experience the ways in which we do not know something."

Matthew Cunningham, *Everything has a name*

"The lands of the planet call to humankind for redemption. But it is a redemption of sanity, not a supernatural reclamation project at the end of history. The planet itself calls to the other living species for relief . . . Who will find peace with the lands? The future of human-kind lies waiting for those who will come to understand their lives and take up their responsibilities to all living things. Who will listen to the trees, the animals and birds, the voices of the places of the land? As the long-forgotten peoples of the respective continents rise and begin to reclaim their ancient heritage, they will discover the lands of their ancestors."

Vine Deloria, Jr., *God Is Red*

contents

land acknowledgement

I did not know, when I began searching for my ancestral past, it would be my ancestors' homelands that would guide my journey. I didn't expect to uncover, buried under the upheaval of modern life, both love and resentment for ancestors I knew—parents, grandparents, and great-grandparents—or to find cause for digging deeply into how their lives shaped my own. As I reached further back in my families' histories, I had little prior inkling of the extent to which my ancestors were colonial settlers. Until I went to investigate their lives on both sides of the Atlantic Ocean, I knew little about the conditions of their lives in Europe or America. Nor did I know of how the dire consequences of European settlement and America's westward expansion live on into the present in the lives of Indigenous people, settler descendants, and the planet itself. But I know now.

As I wrote about the history of the lands now known as America, I was aware that these lands have had many other names, and the rights to these lands continue to be contested by descendants of those who were here before Europeans first made contact. Wherever I could tell you the history of names of places I wrote about, I did. When I wrote about places as I was traveling through them, I used current names. And I have provided maps to situate the reader in time and space.

Within this book, I have described the people who were living during and before colonial settlement on the ancestral lands I visited. The place I am living and where I have written most of this book, now called Chapel Hill, North Carolina, is part of the traditional territory of the Saponi people, whose descendants include the Occaneechi Band of the Saponi Nation, who still thrive in this region and are officially recognized by the state of North Carolina. I am grateful that I am able to live here; simultaneously, I recognize the harms caused by the unjust acquisition of these and all Indigenous lands through acts of racism, violence, dispossession, displacement, and erasure of cultures by settlers as part of the larger, land-centered project of settler colonialism. There is a continual need for healing. This book is dedicated to a new understanding of the past and the process of repair.

preface

At a time in my life when I was feeling dislocated and out of touch with loved ones, my ancestors came calling me to come find them. That was not the way I thought about it at the time, nor would I have shared such a mystical notion with others even if I had. When I first logged on to Geni.com, I approached my search as research, leaning into my more comfortable identity and training as a social scientist. I wasn't trying to prove that I was descended from royalty. I wasn't even looking for absolute certainty about the bloodlines between me and particular individuals thought to be in my lineage. My objective was to find in my ancestors' lives an explanation of my own socio-demographical, historical, and cultural standing. I began writing about my ancestors as if I could pinpoint the reality of their lives at the confluence of historical and sociological abstractions—that I could analyze the reasons they did what they did from a distance. Safely abstract. Cerebral. Intellectual.

Even though understanding the world through a social science lens was my comfort zone, I eventually found myself wandering through speculative, lyrical territories of their lives and mine that stretched my abilities to describe them in words. I wanted to find my *Genius loci,* what poet David Whyte[1] calls the metaphorical place where all our experiences and influences come together to create the circumstances of our present lives. It is inside each of us, and it is held in the land under our feet. I was looking for my place in the world.

Intrigued as I was by all the bigger picture knowledge I was gathering, my messier, more human self kept tripping over their ordinary troubles, so like my own. I tried to find explanations of why my own life had rolled out the way it did. What I mean to say here is that, in imagining their anxieties and their struggles, my own anxieties and struggles rose up inside me. And so, I found myself everywhere in their stories.

Seeing them as real people caught up, like me, in the times they lived, freed me to love them, even in their morally complicated world of settler colonialism. I was able to see that I also find myself caught up in a life where there may be few alternative ethical choices, with none of them being perfect. If I look closely at my decisions, I know there is always collateral damage for someone, sometimes even people I love. I came to understand the need for grace for ancestors I knew and those I did not, and for myself, as well—for the times I hurt people even when I never intended to.

Words that come to mind as I think back over the journey my ancestors called me toward: mystery, revelation, and redemption. Sparks of light in the darkness and grace manifested made me ever glad for this journey, for my ancestors' love, and for the life they made possible for me.

———— ∞ ————

Perhaps you have come to this book because of your own deep yearnings to know your ancestors, even if you don't know exactly why. Maybe reading the story of my search will give you the feeling that you yourself are "onto something" that is calling out to you, whatever that might be. Maybe you are looking for a way to understand in your own family history the roots of some current entanglement or misunderstanding. Maybe you have never thought about any of that before, but now you feel beckoned to know more.

As you read these essays, you might feel moved to consider visiting the geographic and social landscapes of your own ancestors. You might feel a nudge to learn more about the lives that flowed from them. Are my family stories in any way similar to yours, sparking either joy, regret, or both, over what you didn't know or understand previously? I hope that the story of my journey will inspire you to take the first step, or the next step, on a similar journey guided by the lands of your ancestors.

September 2023

The stories of my ancestors are also my stories.
The land holds our stories.
We can create new stories with the land.

part one
the beckoning

time out of time

MY INITIAL CERTAINTY about what was real and what was not began to fray one bright summer afternoon over thirty years ago when I first felt time stand still. It happened as I was sitting on my maternal grandfather's front porch in the mountains of western North Carolina in the middle of a conversation with him and my first husband, John. It was, until then, just like any other summer day.

That porch and the tall, tree-covered elevations around us I knew intimately from many childhood visits. It was the geography where, because of my itinerant early life, I had deeper roots than any other place on earth. John and I were in our early thirties. I was already the mother of two children and in graduate school studying social psychology. My ninety-something grandfather was vigorous enough to grow his own vegetables. But I heard the tremble of his voice, saw the shakiness of his hands, and the deepening creases in his farmer-tanned face. Even with fading short-term memory, he could still recite verbatim conversations from decades ago. He loved to talk, and this day was no exception.

The day of this memory, we were making slow, quiet small talk—how tolerable the weather had been, cousins getting married or moving away or having babies, and, as always, my grandfather wishing the cars and trucks that whizzed by too fast on the narrow two-lane highway at the end of his front yard would slow down before someone got hurt. From that perch, we could see my aunt Dorothy's house across the road and the familiar hills behind it. Clear blue sky.

Then amid that ordinariness, the usually-firm borders of the material world around me shimmered and softened. Like a dream, but not a dream. Sounds were not distorted but were now distant. All I could see was essence. Everyone else's world seemed to move forward, but for just a hair's breadth of a moment, mine did not. John and Granddaddy continued to talk, but I was not part of it. It was not just a shift in attention, it was something else. I had no words for it, nor did I attempt to tell others about it—this felt too fragile, too likely to be misunderstood or dismissed as inconsequential. A silent jolt, only inside me.

This small, personal moment stayed with me in my body and in my mind. Accounts of mystical-like experiences offered by non-mystics such as biologist Jane Goodall, resonate with my experience that day— barely noticeable shifts in perception of short duration that are mostly indescribable to others, but offering flashes of insight described by Goodall as "heightened awareness" and something "that would stay with me for the rest of my life."[1]

I might have understood this inner event while it was happening as the presence of God if I had not been on an extended hiatus from spiritual practice. Terms from other religious traditions that I had never heard before that day, like "unified field" and "ground of being," ring true to what I remember of that experience. Until that moment on Granddaddy's porch, time seemed as real to me as anything I could touch, even if its passing was discernable only as the forward movement of clock hands, pages ripped off a calendar, aging bodies, taller children, or rusted pipes. In the early years of adulthood, juggling the competing responsibilities of family and work lives, time was a vise grip that held me tight. And then, for an instant, I felt this small rip in time that leaked out the possibility that my sense of reality could be out of sync, even momentarily, from that of those around me.

This opening into another consciousness zipped itself back up fairly quickly as I went back to my day-to-day life, but it left a physical and mental impression on me, and the confusing notion that time might not be the absolute certainty I had thought it was. It was now a mystery to be pondered. And if time was not what I thought it was, what else might I have been wrong about—and how might it change my life to find out?

Several years afterward, and not too many feet away from my grandfather's front porch, I was walking in the woods on the edge of my parents' nearby vacation home. The energetic presence of a half dozen of my cousins and me, as children from the past, rushed by me, through the grass in the meadow, up the hill and into the woods. Not as ghosts or hallucinations, but they were there. I flashed through their journeys into adult lives, and as I did, I had the thought that it wasn't only famous people who were worth writing about; even my own family had interesting stories to tell. I wished I could write that story.

꧁ꕥ꧂

Decades later, memories of these fleeting moments of wonder came back to me as my ancestors started whispering in my ear. Until then, they had not been of much interest to me. My only notion of ancestors was what I knew of my old and frail great-grandparents—my mother's grandparents—still alive while I was a child. They were in poor health with poor memories, crinkly skin and crackly voices. I loved them, but I could not imagine them as ever having been vital people worthy of my taking interest in their earlier lives.

In a pivotal moment, however, my elders became less like background scenery to my family story and more like people with rich lives worthy of my attention. I found a photograph of one of my aunts as a young adult, much younger in the picture than I was when I was looking at her photograph. I knew the hard times ahead that she had no inkling were coming for her—a difficult marriage, a son's mental illness and murder. A sob caught in my throat; tears burned in my eyes. I felt profound sympathy for her that I had never felt before— this new compassion born out of my own family struggles.

This spark of insight into the real people I had not yet imagined my ancestors to be was followed by others—as I listened to an oral history recording of my grandfather telling another aunt about the hardships of getting through the Great Depression, as I read my uncle's college journal written in the three years leading up to the United States entering World War II, and as I read letters between family members filled with poignant details of money concerns, sick children, and missing home and each other.

I had now lived long enough to know that sometimes we try as hard as we can to do what we believe is right, yet we still find ourselves in need of grace. Affection, empathy, grief, and regret rose up inside me as I got to know these people in their fuller humanity, creating the desire to go back further and learn even more.

Where do we come from? What are we? Where are we going?/The gathering depicts the communion I have felt with people in this photo since I began the project of investigating how my ancestors' lives live on in mine. Through my research and travel, I found a new respect and love for these people I had not paid much attention to previously. Their stories showed the difficulties of raising a family in a complicated world. This image is an homage to the lives that made mine possible. The ancestors in this image are from left to right: my great-grandparents, William and Bertha Lindemann; my paternal grandparents, Augusta Lindemann Stock and William Stock; my father, Rudolph Stock; my great-grandmother, Wilhelmine Stock; great-grandparents Joeberry and Bertha Kuykendall (seated); my mother Norma York Stock (standing next to them); great-great-grandparents Thomas and Margaret Deaver (seated); grandparents Ethel Kuykendall York and D.D. York; great-grandparents William York and Annie Leonie Miller York, and great-great-grandparents John Wesley Miller and Nancy Burnett Miller.

setting out and moving forward

"We can only begin
with what has happened. We owe the future
the past, the long knowledge
that is the potency of time to come."

Wendell Berry, "At a Country Funeral"

BEFORE ANSWERING the call of my ancestors, I worked for nearly 30 years as a social scientist at an international reproductive health organization whose mission was to improve the health and well-being of women and their families in poorly resourced countries. I worked there to make the world a just and good place for human beings. Research was a good fit for my abilities and sensibilities, but its methodologies are necessarily slow and emotionally detached. This left me impatient and looking for a more direct way to influence social change. I wanted to call out injustice directly when I saw it and to do something about it from a more personal heart-space.

All my writing as a social scientist was published in peer-reviewed journals and purely academic. To learn to write differently—that is, to unlearn abstraction and passive voice—I took classes in creative non-fiction. For an assignment in one of them, I wrote an essay about growing up White in the South in the 1960s and '70s. This became a book I co-authored with LaHoma Smith Romocki, *Going to School in Black and White: A Dual Memoir of Desegregation.*

What I experienced in a racial equity workshop a few months before that writing assignment likely inspired my essay's focus on race. The impetus for the book, however, was the discovery—after reading the essay in my writing group one day—that LaHoma, a member of that group, and I had unknowingly crossed paths in high school. And we each had a story to tell from opposite sides of the racial divide about our experiences going to a newly-integrated but formerly all-Black high school in Durham, North Carolina in the early 1970s.

Through writing that book, I came to understand not only the influence of my high school experience in my life, but also, a harder truth to bear—my unconscious racial biases. Sometimes discussing these with LaHoma was uncomfortable, but our guiding principles of honesty and respect made it possible to write the book together—and to become close friends. We believed that our stories, told in conversation with each other, could facilitate public discussions about the role of race in education. Its publication in 2017 gave us a chance to meet with many groups of people with whom we did indeed have those kinds of exchanges.

<hr>

About the time LaHoma and I were making final edits and looking for a publisher, I started noticing my ancestors beckoning me into their lives. I can't pin down one precise moment when I decided to undertake what I began calling the Ancestor Project, but it came at a time when I also was feeling a certain wistfulness for a previous closeness to my mothers' mountain family, with whom I had grown up spending summers and holidays.

One memory tugged at me: Thanksgiving dinner at my Grandmother York's house, the kitchen thick with women shoulder-to-shoulder cooking and cleaning, and children swarming in and out and up and down the stairs while we waited for dinner. The men showed up in my reminiscence sitting around the table after dinner had been served. The invisible force field of kinship held us together. I felt steadfastly accepted and loved without doubt or question. These were my people. Though my family lived in many different places around the southeastern United States when I was growing up, this place was my home as much as it was my mother's. It belonged to everyone in it, and we all belonged to it.

Many years on, I longed to be in that sweet dream and feel that way again. Everyone in this extended family loved each other, hard and strong, but over the years, feelings were hurt, ways parted, unbreachable walls were erected. The stresses of our lives, too much distance, not enough time, the judgments people who love each other feel entitled to make about the others—how they spend their money or raise their children—and the deaths of my grandparents, aunts, and uncles, unraveled many of the ties that bound us together so long ago.

The story of my marital family had not lived up to my idealized version of family togetherness, either. We had been separated by emotional tidal waves of divorce and remarriage, by my adult children's choices to live in distant places and lead lives isolated from mine. My father's death from Parkinson's disease and my mother's dementia added to my yearning for connection. My brother and I enjoyed each other's company, but we lived almost a continent away from each other. Much of my feeling of disconnection stemmed from a world beyond my control, but I couldn't help but ask myself if there wasn't something I could do to feel less alone.

My hope for renewed family ties heightened the sadness and the sweetness I felt as I sorted through photographs, letters, and journals —passed down to me from my parents' emptying closets. Could going back further and finding more family stories quench my desire for whatever I believed at the time I was missing? I wasn't sure that those idealized memories could ever be reconstituted in real life, but, as I searched deep and wide into my family histories—the story of this book—my world became bigger through their lives. I found paths linking their personal narratives and a larger history that also had created the conditions of my own life.

I spent hundreds of hours on genealogy sites finding ancestors I previously had not known of.[1] Genealogy is not an exact science, and it was not the destination of my search, but it was a useful guide. I began constructing a family tree. Sometimes I could get large swaths of the picture put together rather quickly, but sometimes it took forever to find one small part. Like putting together a jigsaw puzzle found at someone's beach house, it had missing pieces that I'd never find, but I didn't know which ones were missing, so I just kept looking for them.

I started with what I knew about both my parents' families, going back to my great-grandparents. I knew all these people except for my father's grandparents, the Stocks and the Lindemanns. My father's father immigrated to Iowa in the early 1900s from Germany, and he married a woman whose family, the Lindemanns, had also immigrated there from Germany, but a generation earlier. Mother's family, I knew, had come from Europe before the American War for Independence. I did not know much else, except that her father's family, the Yorks, were of English descent and her mother's father's family, the Kuykendalls, were of Dutch descent. Both families had lived in the mountains of Haywood County, North Carolina for more than a century before my mother was born there.

I called a cousin on my mother's side, Nadia, one spring morning as I was beginning this quest; I asked her to help me start my search into our two maternal lines. She graciously passed on to me much of what she had found before the advent of all the fancy online sources. I took notes on what she verbally downloaded from memory, beginning with the Kuykendalls.

I started with an internet search for Jacob Luursen, who Nadia told me was the first Kuykendall[2] to come to America. Through several genealogy sites, I found that he was born in the Dutch town of Wageningen in 1616. He married Stynte Douwes in Amsterdam in 1638, and they sailed to New Netherlands around 1640. They had several daughters and one son, Luur. Over a dozen generations later, the number of Jacob and Stynte's descendants in the United States and Canada is now estimated to be more than 10,000.[3] It is from Luur that I am directly descended.

With so many descendants, much genealogy research had been done on this family before I started my own. Working back from my great-grandfather Joeberry Columbus Kuykendall to these index ancestors, I was quickly able to fill in a whole branch of the tree, from their coming to America onward. It was with much satisfaction that I was able to trace a generation or two back into the Netherlands before Jacob and Stynte were born.

The profiles I found for Jacob and Stynte on different websites varied a bit but were mostly consistent, according to work done by many different people. Most of them related to me in some distant way. Not all the information I found along the way has proven accurate, however. I often came across contradictory information about the same person between and even within sites.[4] In the midst of so much easy access to information, I learned to be discerning.

As I followed the Kuykendall family branch from the past toward the present, I found a website with lists of kin, parents and children, photographs and stories, and links to blogs and newsletters. My maternal grandmother was listed as Sophronie Ethel, my great-grandfather Kuykendall's first child. I had only ever heard her called Ethel. When I mentioned this surprise to my mother, she told me that I had never heard it because my grandmother hated the name Sophronie. A small detail, but, after thinking I already knew everything about these people and finding out I didn't even know my grandmother's real name, how could I not go on with my search? What else had I missed?

Poet Jane Hirshfield called a discovery that portends further mysteries the "experience of the keyhole"[5]. Of her own similar encounters, she wrote, "I could look through and see that more life, more worlds were out there, beyond the edges of my own knowing . . . if one thing can be hidden, then shown, then more will surely be hidden beyond it. And so, in turning toward the mystery, we begin to feel ourselves part of infinitude and immensity."

As I went deeper into my family's histories, I became addicted to the thrill of finding a new piece of relevant information. My life became wrapped up in finding out as much as I could about the lives of these people who created mine. I believe this is a common experience among people engaged in genealogical research. Sometimes it feels like we are bordering on obsession, like we can do nothing else but follow Alice down the rabbit hole. And we get a bit of a dopamine rush when we find pieces of Wonderland.

—⁓—

Assembling the names of all the new ancestors I was finding into one big family tree was more challenging than I had anticipated. I began first by putting each name on 3" x 5" cards and then taping them to the wall, but I ran out of wall. On-line templates got so big I couldn't see enough at one time on the screen. Finally, I drew, in pencil, a many-branched tree on a 24" x 30" piece of manila card stock. Piecing together this information into one picture gave me great satisfaction, for it is a beautiful thing, but this drawing was not the stopping place for my search. In fact, it triggered a set of new questions.

When I visualized my ancestry like this, I realized just how many of my ancestors had migrated from Europe to North America. The first had been Thomas Blacklocke coming from England sometime before 1620, preceding Stynte and Jacob's move from the Netherlands by at least 20 years. Over the next two centuries, more than a hundred others followed. When I saw this, I knew I needed to spend more time thinking about my ancestors on both sides of the Atlantic and why those who left Europe did so.

It was in these migrations that I found resonances with them in my life of movement from one home to another as a child, and among continents and cultures in my adult travel. Knowing the difficulties of moving and traveling even in modern times, I wanted to know why they would undertake arduous journeys on ships powered by wind and steam to leave the lands that their ancestors had inhabited for centuries for places relatively unknown to them.

My social scientist-self wanted to know the political and social forces causing their exodus. I read whatever I could find that might provide answers to my questions about their migrations. And before too long, my genealogy research took me on the road to learn more about my ancestors in Europe and in America. And in physically standing in these places, I knew it was the land that held their stories.

⎯⎯ ⚬⚬⚬ ⎯⎯

I traveled to the Eastern Shore of Virginia because it was there, in a public library genealogy reading room, that I could get more information about Thomas Blacklocke, an ancestor from a maternal lineage. And while there, I wanted to see with my eyes what I had imagined when reading anthropologist Helen Rountree's[6] books that enchanted me with descriptions of the physical geography of the early English settlement there—the same books that also unsettled me with stories of the Accomac people, whose lives were forever changed by the arrival of people like Thomas.

Everything I learned in Virginia pulled me toward other ancestral landscapes. I felt the gentle push from my forebears to leave my home again and again so that I could understand them through an embodied experience in the physical places where they had stood before.

Knowing I could not visit every migration destination showing up in my family tree, I devised a plan to visit the places of leaving and arriving for three migrations—England to Virginia, the Netherlands to New York, and Germany to Iowa—that encompassed the greatest number of ancestors. I loved that my metaphorical journey would become a literal one. I synthesized what I learned during each trip through writing and further desk research to answer questions raised during my travel. And what I learned in and from each place informed how I approached my next destination.

The summer after I visited the Eastern Shore, I went to the Netherlands to find Stynte and Jacob, whose family became known as the Kuykendalls of my maternal grandmother's lineage. And then directly afterward, I went to Fehmarn, Germany, to find my paternal grandfather, who left there for Iowa at age 15. The next summer I went to Iowa to find out about this German grandfather's life there and the German family he married into, but especially, to learn about my father.

Next, I traveled to New York's Hudson River Valley to see where Jacob and Stynte started their family, and then to northern England to find out about the family Thomas Blacklocke left behind for Virginia.

Finally, I added a trip to Haywood County, North Carolina—the site of my sentimental memories. It was where I felt time stop for an instant and my cousins visited me from childhood, my mother's birthplace, and where so many in my maternal lineage had lived since the eighteenth century. After my other travels, I thought I might see this familiar place in new ways; I was right.

Everywhere I traveled, I soaked up what the land offered me. I walked down streets and through fields where I knew my ancestors had been, found churches and other structures that had existed in their lifetimes, left physical tokens of my life and collected stones and botanical specimens from theirs. I recorded birdsong and church bells.

I kept a journal, and I took many photographs—eventually giving these photographs a more central role in this project. I planned my schedule loosely at each destination. There were twists and turns and going off in one direction only to double back to take another one.

Wandering and wondering deeply satisfied me. I learned so much that made the world more fascinating to me as part of my ancestors' lives and thus, mine. Standing where I knew my ancestors had stood led me into reveries where I saw layers of time expose themselves. I imagined specific relatives in each place encountering me from the future—liminal spaces where veils between worlds were torn.

———— ≈≈≈ ————

I was now completely intrigued by what happened in the places where any of my ancestors lived. Even the smallest details made me feel like I was part of a greater arc of time and existence. Because I read so much history as part of this journey, I saw my life in a bigger context that made more sense. This ancestor journey was a bit of a roller coaster ride. There was joy, sometimes a feeling of magic when, all of a sudden, some missing piece of the puzzle fell into place. Sometimes there was frustration and sorrow as I learned of difficult circumstances in my ancestors' lives. I intermittently stepped off the travel path to write stories generated by my memories of the family I knew. This created through-lines from past to present, and I began to understand parts of my personal history better than I had before.

It soon became clear to me I must not only explore the geography, but also the natural histories of these ancestral homes to fully comprehend their lives on both continents. Without much background in geology, climatology, and biology, this was a bit of a learning curve for me, but one that fed my love of knowledge and opened new ways of thinking about the environment. My love for our planet Earth deepened because of what I learned while writing this book, even as my grief for the evolving ecological crisis intensified my desire to work with others to slow it down. I began to see more clearly than I ever had that natural history—the history of the land—is never separate from the social or political histories of a place.

⤞⧫⤝

Almost immediately after seeing how many of my ancestors had migrated from Europe, I came to the uncomfortable realization that over a hundred ancestors had come to live in places already inhabited by people for millennia before they got here—people whose lives and beliefs about the world and nature were very different from theirs. My mother's people came as Dutch and English colonists. These colonists wanted the land and were willing to steal it and kill for it if necessary. Exterminating the "merciless Indian savages" was written into the young nation's Declaration of Independence from England a century after they began arriving. My father's family came from Germany a century after that to live in territories previously cleared of Indigenous people by military force.

As a child, I had not heard these stories about European colonization of Indigenous people. I can only remember Thanksgiving and the French and Indian War. Beyond that, Indians were viewed as "problems" as Americans moved westward. And the first Indians I ever saw in person were on reservations—Seminoles in Florida and Cherokees in North Carolina, and perhaps Navajos in Arizona. I remember them as different, maybe exotic. And I can't say I thought much about them one way or the other, except as separate from my own life. I vaguely remember the activism of AIM (the American Indian Movement) when I was in high school.

My understanding of the difficult reality of Native life in America opened a bit in graduate school in Flagstaff, Arizona in the late 1970s. It has only been through the conscious investigation of my ancestors' first contact with Indigenous people and Indigenous history on this continent, however, that I have learned of the unrelenting horrors of colonization that continue as systems of white supremacy in the present,[7] causing pain for descendants of both Indigenous people and

White settlers. Learning these stories became part of my ancestor journey; I came to believe that sharing them with others is the first step in healing this pain.

Louise Dunlap in her book *Inherited Silence*[8] tells of her investigation of her family's settlement in California at great cost to the indigenous Wappo people there—and her spiritual work to heal ongoing wounds. She cautions us that stories of settler and Indigenous conflict carry trauma with them, and care should be taken to tell them, within the context of reconciliation and healing. I have sought to follow her counsel in this matter.

⊂⊃⊂⊃⊂

Humans constantly change their understanding of reality. Every generation sees the world differently. I do not know what my settler ancestors believed about their rights to the lands they inhabited. Settler colonialism was part of their story, a fact to be reckoned with, but it was not their whole story. As I learned about my ancestors as flesh and blood people, I could relate to their complicated circumstances. I felt admiration and love for them as they made their way in an always-complex world, even as I grieved the pain and suffering caused by their presence on others' lands.

⊂⊃⊂⊃⊂

The project of all my ancestors was to create and maintain a better world for their descendants. This is the evolutionary task of all life forms: to create conditions for survival of their species. Each person in our family trees left some of their DNA behind in their descendants, but they did more than that. The worldviews of my ancestors were specific to the times and places in which they lived and were the boundaries of their destinies. As I have found, they lived according to whatever information they had available at the time. Sometimes this might have felt like making a conscious choice among two or more possible ones; sometimes it was a path they followed because they comprehended no other choice. All these thoughts and actions that ended up in births and deaths, marriages and migrations, were brought to bear on the life I now live.

A fraught past must be mourned but also turned into a gateway into reconciliation and repair. I seek to move forward into the possibility of a better future in which I can use gifts my ancestors left for me to make a new way, to use what I have learned to promote a new consciousness, leading to acts of reconciliation. And to that end I share stories about my ancestors, organized by lineage, as an act of compassionate revelation and reckoning. I offer this as an example for others who might want to find strength in the lives their ancestors made possible for them—and be moved toward a healing grace.

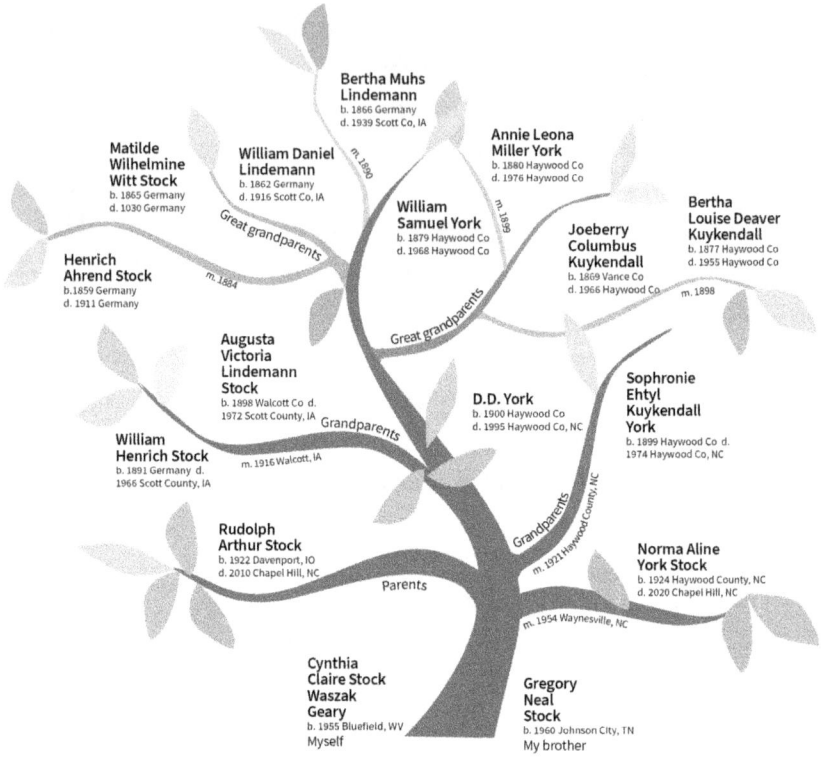

Bertha Muhs Lindemann
b. 1866 Germany
d. 1939 Scott Co, IA

Annie Leona Miller York
b. 1880 Haywood Co
d. 1976 Haywood Co

Matilde Wilhelmine Witt Stock
b. 1865 Germany
d. 1030 Germany

William Daniel Lindemann
b. 1862 Germany
d. 1916 Scott Co, IA

m. 1890

William Samuel York
b. 1879 Haywood Co
d. 1968 Haywood Co

m. 1899

Joeberry Columbus Kuykendall
b. 1869 Vance Co
d. 1966 Haywood Co

Bertha Louise Deaver Kuykendall
b. 1877 Haywood Co
d. 1955 Haywood Co

m. 1898

Henrich Ahrend Stock
b.1859 Germany
d. 1911 Germany

m. 1684

Great grandparents

Great grandparents

Augusta Victoria Lindemann Stock
b. 1898 Walcott Co d.
1972 Scott County, IA

D.D. York
b. 1900 Haywood Co
d. 1995 Haywood Co, NC

Sophronie Ehtyl Kuykendall York
b. 1899 Haywood Co d.
1974 Haywood Co, NC

Grandparents

William Henrich Stock
b. 1891 Germany d.
1966 Scott County, IA

m. 1916 Walcott, IA

Rudolph Arthur Stock
b. 1922 Davenport, IO
d. 2010 Chapel Hill, NC

Grandparents

m. 1921 Haywood County, NC

Norma Aline York Stock
b. 1924 Haywood County, NC
d. 2020 Chapel Hill, NC

Parents

m. 1954 Waynesville, NC

Cynthia Claire Stock Waszak Geary
b. 1955 Bluefield, WV
Myself

Gregory Neal Stock
b. 1960 Johnson City, TN
My brother

My family tree back three generations.

what it means
to leave a place

MY CHILDHOOD WAS a merry-go-round of never-ending hellos and good-byes. We moved dozens of times because of my father's job as a telephone equipment installer. Leaving and arriving were the most constant realities of my young life. The depth of migration experience I found in my ancestors' lives was a siren call from my own memories to search for clues about how movement across time and space shaped their lives and mine.

I found myself imagining my ancestors leaving under duress and arriving desperately homesick, feelings I soon realized I was projecting from my own story—a story that I, perhaps, needed to re-examine. As I contemplated my peripatetic childhood, I found new appreciation for the good in my experiences of moving from one place to another that I had previously thought of as only hardship. I begin this reflection with the story of the people who orchestrated the adventure of my life.

⸎

My parents—Rudy Stock and Norma York Stock—each lived in just one place until they graduated from high school in the 1940s.

Mother's roots were deep in North Carolina's Appalachian Mountains. Daddy's life was lived on the Mississippi River farther north and west, in Davenport, Iowa. For non-Southerners reading this, I should note, "Mother" and "Daddy" are what Southern women of a certain age and social class (like me and my mother) call their parents.

I don't know if leaving was in their individual destinies or if the Great Depression, followed by a world war, created a desire in them for more than what they had, but they both left home after high school. Mother got on a bus for Berea College in Kentucky. Daddy headed out to find his fortune in Illinois, one state over from Iowa, and eventually became a Merchant Marine during World War II, after a minor physical problem kept him out of the armed forces.

───❧───

My parents' paths crossed around 1952 in a small town in North Carolina, just north of Greensboro. My mother was the superintendent of the school lunch program in the local public school district, and my father was in town for a few months to install equipment for the telephone exchange. Daddy was renting an apartment owned by the couple who introduced him to Mother at a bridge party. Something was kindled between them that night, and they were married a couple of years later. In between these two events, Daddy's job sent him back on the road, but they kept in touch via affectionate letters. Mother left friends and a good job because she loved Daddy and wanted to be a wife and mother. In 1954, this meant she had to make the choice between family and work, and she chose family.

They married in my mother's hometown in western North Carolina, and after the reception they got in their aqua Buick and drove straight to Lorraine, Ohio, where Daddy had to be at work on Monday morning. I was born about 10 months later, in 1955 in Bluefield, West Virginia, one or two moves after Lorraine. I will write West Virginia as my place of birth forever afterward, but I only lived there for a couple of months before Daddy was transferred somewhere else. I, thus, began my nomadic destiny.

In each place where Daddy was assigned to work, we'd move into a rented apartment—Norma and Rudy and I. We'd unpack everything from the car. We'd settle in a bit, but not too much. Mother found a church. Daddy went to work every morning. Mother and I stayed around the house most of the time; we probably watched some TV. Mother cleaned house, sewed, and wrote letters, and I played alone or with my dolls. Daddy came home at five. We had dinner, watched TV, went to bed, and then started all over again. Saturdays, we went to parks or shopping as a family, and Sundays, Mother and I went to church, often with Daddy. After some months, Daddy would get transferred to a different job, and then they would pack it all up again and we'd move to a different rented furnished apartment in a different town without much discussion.

⁂

When I was four, we moved to Johnson City, Tennessee, where I went to kindergarten and had two good friends, Wendy and Jimmy. My brother, Greg, was born there in the spring of 1960, but we were gone by the end of that summer. And then we moved ten times that year, a blur of packing and unpacking. One of our stops was a motel, where we stayed for only a week or two. I remember a front casement window covered with draperies in bleak shades of brownish tan. Mother was holding Greg wrapped up in blankets because it was cold —probably February. Along with this visual memory, I experience the tension and anxiety I felt in my young body when I knew she was unhappy.

⁂

When I started elementary school in 1961, Daddy's company intentionally slowed down the pace of our moves, but I still changed schools more often than most kids went to the dentist. We lived in Bradenton, Florida, when I went to first grade. I began school a week after the semester started because I had a staph infection and had been hospitalized so they could give me a shot of penicillin every four hours.[1] Because I showed up late, I missed information about when I could or should talk in class that left me quite anxious about how to behave correctly in class. I stayed quiet to avoid saying or doing the wrong thing. This behavior served me well in some ways over my lifetime, but not in others.

Other anxieties made their way into the classroom as well. The Cold War was the backdrop of my childhood. At age six, I absorbed the grown-ups' fear of a nuclear attack, especially there in Florida, so close to Cuba. At school, we practiced ducking under our desks and covering our heads with our hands, as if one could mitigate injury from atomic bombs and hurricanes in the same way. The school held a mock evacuation drill just in case we were forewarned of a missile launch. My bus driver forgot my stop during this practice, and it took me twice as long to get home as it normally did. I was in a panic that I would not get to my mother before the world ended.

My greatest joy of first grade was learning to read. We always had tons of books at home—we moved with a lot of books but also frequented libraries and used bookstores. I got to be the angel in the Christmas pageant at school and wear a beautiful white robe with wings and a halo because I could read well and memorized the long speech. A few months later, my reading skills also impressed the pastor of our church, who judged my readiness for baptism by my ability to read scripture. Baptism was an important rite of passage in my mother's family, and being baptized upgraded my status in the eyes of my grandmother, aunts, and cousins.

We moved to Sarasota the summer after first grade, placing me in a different school for second grade. That year we watched astronaut John Glenn's spacecraft launch into space on television. I also remember our Thanksgiving dinner at our house on Morrill Street. Daddy invited several Cuban men on his work crew to join us. It was very exciting to have people in my house from another country. Their wives wore bright red lipstick, bright red fingernail polish, and shoes with very high heels. I was mesmerized. Why my mother did not dress like that was beyond me, and I decided I could not wait until I was in charge of my own fashion decisions.

This was also the year of Kennedy's assassination. We were kept in our classes a few minutes later than usual one November Friday afternoon and told that something had happened to the president, but I didn't really understand what the commotion was about. Mother met me at the door in tears and told me that Kennedy had died, but I still felt confused. Two days later, soon after we got home from church, Daddy turned on the television, and we all saw, in real time, Jack Ruby shoot Lee Harvey Oswald. I was still wearing my church dress. The world had not ended in nuclear holocaust, but it was turning upside down.

The first time I changed schools in the middle of the school year was a few months afterward when Daddy was transferred to St. Petersburg. I felt embarrassed and nervous to be met with curious stares as I entered the class in-progress. To make matters worse, my new teacher made it clear to me that she was unhappy about having an extra student to teach. She rarely spoke to me and sighed loudly whenever I asked a question about something I had not yet learned at my school in Sarasota. I steeled my heart against her rebuff and willed myself to become invisible. I continued to use this tactic to protect myself in unfamiliar situations, but as an adult I recognized that it was not always beneficial.

The highlight of that year was the school talent show. It was the year the Beatles first appeared on the Ed Sullivan Show, and I was drafted into a Beatles skit to lip-sync "She Loves Me." I was John, I think, or maybe George, but I hope it was John. Some boys performed a song and dance act for the talent show in black face. I cannot remember what the song was, nor that anyone was horrified by it.

These once- or twice-a-year moves to a new school continued throughout elementary school. We left St. Petersburg for the mountains of North Carolina while Daddy was working in Greenville, Tennessee. For a few months, Mother, Greg, and I lived not far away with Mother's parents while Mother and Daddy built a vacation house on land given to them by my grandfather. For those few months I attended fourth grade at Bethel Elementary School, the same school that Mother attended as a child and several of my cousins now attended. I was happy to be riding the bus and hanging out at recess with my childhood best friend, my cousin Donna.

We moved during the school year to be with Daddy in Greenville. The next year we returned to St. Petersburg, Florida, but to a different school than before.

Fifth grade was a golden year for me, with a kind teacher who made me feel smart and appreciated. Age ten—on the cusp of adolescence but not quite there yet—is a good age for girls. Stars aligned for me. I had an attentive teacher who appreciated my academic skills and encouraged me to come out of my shell a bit. We lived in a neighborhood full of kids to hang out with, including some classmates. The TV shows "I Spy" and "Man from U.N.C.L.E." were all the rage, and we spent time coming up with elaborate cloak-and-dagger games. Daddy bought me a used bicycle and fixed it up, and I learned to ride it. We went to the church where we had gone the first time we lived in St. Pete, and I had a crush on the associate pastor's very cute son. We were at church Sunday morning, Sunday evening, and Wednesday night—as we always had been. I was as outgoing and self-confident and connected as I ever felt with a peer group.

Despite this positive school experience, I had to change schools again for sixth grade. Though these ups and downs in my elementary schools seem so clear to me, I wonder how much my parents were paying attention to my emotional life. This time I had to go to a different school, not because Daddy's job was taking us to a different town. We moved just across town into a different school district because Mother did not like the house we had been renting. I protested weakly, without effect. I can only believe they thought it was no big deal, or I'd get over it. No doubt they thought changing schools wasn't as hard as growing up hungry in the Great Depression. But it felt hard at the time.

I stayed only a few months of my sixth-grade year at this new school and had little time to make new friends before we learned we would be moving to Durham, North Carolina. Mother was excited about this move; she would be closer to her family in the mountains, and she had fond memories of driving to Durham to visit Duke Gardens when she was teaching school.

To my surprise and delight, the sixth graders in my new rural elementary school in Durham's outskirts welcomed me mid-year with open arms, as if they had been waiting for someone new to relieve them of their boredom. Florida, as it turned out, was an exotic place to be from. Who knew? I found myself the object of attention in a way I generally was not. I played up how cool it was to live close to the beach and have palm trees in my yard. Outsider-ness was finally working to my advantage. The self-esteem I experienced in fifth grade returned.

And then, the people who owned the house we rented wanted it back at the end of that school year, necessitating a move across town and the end of my newfound cool as I started junior high school. Our new house on Nation Avenue was in town, relatively close to Duke University. This *new* new group of people, comprised of professors' children or heirs to old Durham money, was not so easily impressed by my past. At best, I went unnoticed.

As I think back, I wonder how different the adult I grew up to be would have been if I had not moved to new places so often. How much of who we are and how happy or contented we are is dictated by something immutable inside ourselves, regardless of situations that arise in our lives? Of course, what happens outside us matters, gives us the foundation for what is possible, but how much does something inside ourselves make us who we are and mediate the effect of events?

———⬲———

Most of my immigrant ancestors were adults when they crossed the ocean, but a few came with their parents as children. I can imagine ways in which moving as a child made it easier to find one's way in a new place, but harder in other ways—leaving a social safety net of extended family behind, and of course the physical hardship of the journey itself was treacherous. No doubt each circumstance was different, and it depended on why they left and where they found themselves.

The child-ancestor-immigrant I found most information about was my 8th great-grandmother, Marretje (pronounced similarly to the English "Mary") van Noordstrandt Westphal. She came to the Dutch colony of New Netherlands at age six with her German family after escaping a flood that left their entire island under water. Marretje's early life in America was difficult—her mother died when she was young, and she had to work as a servant for a time. While she was working, however, she met and married another settler from Germany, with whom she owned farmland and begat many children. One of her many generations of descendants includes me.

———⬲———

Having lived a life of frequent moving, and believing that I wished it to stop, I was surprised when it actually did seem to stop in junior high school. And I was surprised again to find myself a bit antsy for a move. Leaving had become a rhythm I was used to, even if I thought I did not want it. Sometime around eighth grade there was a moment when Daddy was told that he might be transferred, and we all got into our very familiar "getting ready to move" mode. But then it didn't happen, and I felt a little disappointed. Frequent moving had cut a groove of expectation of change into my psyche and created an affection for going someplace else.

And even as I desperately thought I didn't want to have to make new friends yet again, I realized I was not so good at the emotional maintenance required of long-term friendships either. I had practice making new friends but almost none in working through sticky situations with old ones. I wasn't sure what to do when my feelings were hurt or when I hurt someone else's, and I had no escape plan. Before I got to junior high school, when something uncomfortable happened in a relationship, I had learned how to pretend that nothing had happened, my invisibility strategy begun with a difficult teacher in the third grade. We had moved so often, I figured I could wait it out until we left, and then it wouldn't matter. I have spent a lifetime unlearning this tendency to wall-off potential conflict.

My ambivalent feelings about staying versus leaving continued into adulthood and linger even now. I met my first husband in 1975 at the University of North Carolina at Chapel Hill (not so far from Durham). He grew up as an army brat and we shared the experience of moving around as children. After we had been in one place for a while, we were both eager for a move. We went to Flagstaff, Arizona, where I studied for a master's degree at Northern Arizona University. We came back to Chapel Hill when we started our family, to be close to our parents, and so our children could be close to their grandparents.

We approached parenthood with the idea that we would rear our children in one place, so they wouldn't have to change schools or doctors or dentists or playmates as often as we had had to. Staying put in one place was harder to do than I anticipated, however. We made our home geographically stable, but the job that I would have in reproductive health research eventually required frequent international travel. I didn't go looking for travel, but it found me.

My job took me to places like Bangladesh and Indonesia. My husband taught school and took care of our daughter while I was gone. I did another stint in graduate school—this time just down the road at UNC. We had another child, a son. We moved to Washington,

DC, for two years then came back to John's teaching career and my public health work—and much more travel.

It was hard and it was exhilarating. Always both. Not wanting to be away from my children but needing this work to support our family. Feeling less connected to my community at home than in the field. The tensions of playing out gender roles that were even slightly non-traditional were more than I would have imagined at first feminist blush. That marriage did not survive the stresses inherent in my being gone so much. I married again, this time to someone I met while traveling for work. Leaving and arriving was woven into our relationship from the beginning.

⸎

My immigrant ancestors' decisions to leave Europe and come to America, were, I believe, made with no less ambivalence than I felt about staying put or being pulled somewhere else. I can imagine the loved ones they did not want to leave, who did not want them to leave. I also can imagine fraught relationships and situations they felt relieved to escape. On the western side of the ocean, some of them were reunited with loved ones who had left before them—like my great-great-grandparents Catarina and Wilhelm Muhs, who joined their daughter, my great-grandmother Bertha, in Walcott, Iowa. Though they missed loved ones back home, most found themselves part of an immigrant community in the new place, with whom they developed close new ties in their support of one another.

The shock of the new is something I always wonder about when thinking of my ancestors coming to a new continent, because that was what was unsettling for me as a child. After spending most of their lives in just one place, they found themselves on very different terrain. So many adjustments to make. But I can believe they also had an appreciation of what was strange and beautiful in the new land, and of the adventure of it. Did what made them happy in the new place make them feel guilty because of the people they left behind? Or is this just what I project onto them?

What did they learn about themselves in this new place? Did they find new fears and weaknesses? New talents and strengths? As I have mentally revisited my childhood relocations while thinking about my ancestors' migrations, I see that I experienced both the difficulties and the gifts, learning much I might not have otherwise, even as I yearned for another way. It seems so much of life is learning to live in this in-between space.

My ancestors who arrived here in the seventeenth century, like Thomas Blacklocke from England and Jacob and Stynte from the Netherlands, lived among people indigenous to this continent who looked and lived differently. Thinking about their experiences, I have so many questions that there are no answers to: What had they expected? What was their experience like for them? How did they understand their own right to live on this land? Was it taken for granted? Did they understand themselves as friends or adversaries of these people, or something else?

How might I have reacted in similar situations? If it had been me who came face-to-face with the ways in which these people were mistreated, even annihilated, how would I have processed those feelings? Would I have believed that it was the right of the colonial government to take land and lives away from Native people? Would I not have seen them as people, only as "savages"? Would I have looked away from the Native people killed and driven from their lands? Pretended like it never happened?

I think about alternate histories as a way of understanding what part of my psyche is constant and what part is mutable in the face of outside forces. How would I be different if I had lived my fantasy of living in one place all the time? Would I have felt stuck? Would that be better than dislocated? I can't imagine myself as the person who I am, the person that I know and like myself to be (at least most of the time), without everything that happened to me as I moved from one place to another, difficult or not. I can see how the twists and turns of my ancestors' lives contributed to this singular person that I know as myself.

My ancestors' reasons for leaving Europe and coming to America arose from conditions that made their decisions to do so seem inevitable when considered decades and centuries later. And the sum of all their actions led up to the marriage of my parents and my birth. Certain boundaries of my life followed on from what I inherited from all these people, and some followed from decisions I made within the life I was given. And the inevitability of my life followed from theirs, as it followed inevitably from each move my parents made, not knowing where it would lead. Something left behind, something new to be found.

On the move, along for the ride. Norma, Greg, Rudy, and I stand in front of our 1956 Buick, packed with tarpaulin-covered belongings attached to the car roof. The photograph was taken during Greg's first year (1960-61), on our way to the next move. I had just turned six years old. We moved ten times before I started elementary school in

Bradenton, Florida, where we are headed in this photograph, judging from our warmer weather clothing. We are in my grandparents' (Mother's parents, the Yorks) driveway in Waynesville, NC. The house that shows up in the background belonged to my Aunt Dorothy (Mother's younger sister) and Uncle Gay and was where I spent hundreds of hours playing with my cousin Donna—my best friend in childhood. I don't know who clicked the shutter of my father's camera, but I'm guessing it was Mother's brother Lamar.

part two
motherlands

the good daughter

ON NEW YEAR'S Eve 2018, I got a call from an ER doctor asking for my permission to operate on my ninety-four-year-old mother who had fractured her hip after a fall at her memory care facility a few hours earlier. She could die in surgery, yes, but with no surgery she would be in pain, would probably not walk again, and might die from what staying in bed might bring. I made a quick decision but spent the rest of the night wondering if my choice was better for her or for me. What should a good daughter do? A question I'm sure more than one of my ancestral grandmothers asked themselves in any number of situations.

———⸙———

I didn't feel like a good daughter at that moment—not the selfless, patient, uncomplaining daughter I grew up believing I was supposed to be, supposed to want to be. Mother's long-term dementia had been anguishing. The complicated reality of our relationship was that I felt many contradictory emotions. I loved my mother. I fulfilled my obligation to take care of her in this painful circumstance. *And I wished I did not have to. I had been ready to lay that burden down for a long time.* Those were words a good daughter should not voice—or even feel. The crazy-making double-bind I learned growing up is that women should not let their true feelings surface. This reinforced my tendencies toward pretending that things that made me feel uncomfortable didn't really happen.

My mother, Norma, was a good daughter, possibly the best daughter. She was the third child of six and the second daughter, born in 1924 in the Appalachian Mountains near Waynesville, North Carolina. The mountains where she grew up were part of her identity. And she loved her family, especially her mother, intensely. Her letters to her family after she left for school and then work, and marriage were filled with longing to be home. Visiting her mother was her priority whenever there was an opportunity for travel. She always wanted more time alone with her mother than she could get with three other sisters wanting the same. She spoke of her anguish about being away from home as proof of her love for her mother. I never felt the same kind of homesickness or jealousy about being away from Norma. It did not mean I did not love her, but she may have thought so at times.

As a middle child in a large family, Mother had to compete for attention. She needed more attention than she ever got. It was no deliberate slight on her mother's part; it was just that Mother grew up in hard times and in a hard place, one among many. I grew up in very different circumstances from hers. I always thought this was part of our disconnect. As the first child of only two, I wanted *less* attention from my mother and wanted my presence to be less critical to her happiness.

The times we were each born into also contributed to our differing notions of what being a good daughter meant, very much aligned with the notion of ideal womanhood. I was born in the White world of the 1950s, barely a decade after World War II. The country was focused on getting back to the way things should be after the war's displacements: women at home with kids, men working. Television shows dramatized what was acceptable for women and men's lives, women's magazines published articles about how women could keep men happy, and policies and legislation gave husbands more legal rights than wives.

Mother's mother, my Grandmother York, was the first child of ten, born a year shy of the twentieth century. That was more than two decades before women had the right to vote in this country. She lived all her life in the mountains, first as a farmer's daughter and then as a farmer's wife. She and my grandfather raised six children through the Great Depression by love and sheer determination.

From my childhood view of the world, my grandmother wielded more authority than my granddaddy. She oversaw the feminine circle of my mother, her sisters, and my female cousins. I was around her more than any other adult when I was growing up, except my own parents. Still, I wouldn't say I knew her particularly well. I had a strong, physical, grandmother sense of her though, and even now I can hear her low, gentle, slightly raspy Southern accent. She and I shared space—family space. I watched her working alongside my grandfather in the field, hoeing, or weeding, or picking vegetables; sitting on the porch, capping strawberries or stringing beans; or doing the inside work of women: cooking and cleaning. I went to church with her and ate her cooking and understood her role as the family's matriarch.

Grandmother York and I talked sometimes, but never for very long at a time or in much depth. I felt that she was, like me, a bit shy and happy not to talk when she did not need to. The usual silence between us may have been a gift we gave to each other in a family of so much neediness. I never questioned her love for me, nor felt like I needed more of her. As a witness to her care for me, I understood that I belonged in her clan.

⌘

Food was central to how I knew Mother and her female family members. The kitchen was the most feminine space in the house—my school for Southern womanhood. The Sunday mid-day meal after church—Sunday *dinner*—was unarguably the most important family gathering of the week. The grown women in the family prepared this meal together. As they did, I was able to I hear what was on their minds. Even if they were just talking about the meal they were preparing, they weren't just talking about the meal they were preparing; they were negotiating relationships with each other. And they were also talking about everything else—what they thought of the sermon and what Mrs. So-and-so was wearing and which of their neighbors was in the hospital for what ailment.

During Sunday dinner preparation, I learned from this family of women the basics of femininity as they understood them. These were: hard work (to the point of martyrdom if necessary); looking pretty (but being modest); the need for good housewife skills (cooking, cleaning, sewing); the importance of motherhood; and the prohibition from asking aloud for (or even knowing) what you really want. These were the criteria by which they judged other women—and each other. They were rarely intentionally mean in their judgements—good daughters in this family were not mean. Critiques were subtle, often delivered as a back-handed compliment: "Oh, honey, your hands are so soft; you are lucky you don't have to do as much housework as I do."

Cleaning up my grandmother's kitchen after Sunday dinner, or any other time, was never a quick chore. Grandmother York was a mess in the kitchen. When she finished making a meal, flour covered the countertops and everything on them; dirty, greasy pots and pans were everywhere else. She also broke a lot of dishes while she was working in the kitchen, and I don't know why or how. There was not one full set of good dishes in her kitchen cabinets, but stacks of mismatched ones.

While I was cleaning up the post-supper kitchen chaos one summer evening during my early adolescence, I must have sighed and rolled my eyes one too many times. When she asked, "Honey, you don't like cleaning up the kitchen very much, do you?"

I naïvely thought she could take the truth, though I had no illusions it would set me free from the job. I said, "Not much" and did not follow it with, "but of course I'm happy to do it; after all, you spent so much time making such a great meal." I thought if grown-ups ask me to help around the house, fine, I'll do it but if they ask me if I like to do it, why lie?

Well, because. Hiding resentment was as much a part of being a good granddaughter as doing the chore. I learned this because soon after this exchange my grandmother said to my mother, "I don't think Cindy likes to help clean up the kitchen."

My mother lied, "Of course she does."

And my grandmother said, "Well, I asked her, and she said she didn't." (She didn't say, however, that she was going to stop asking me to help.)

And shortly thereafter, my mother confronted me about this conversation with my grandmother, which I did not deny. I thought that honesty was the greater virtue (something I'd heard in Sunday School), but I was immediately set straight on this matter.

In my mother's mind, I had hurt her mother's feelings. I caused

Mother embarrassment and damaged her delicate relationship with her mother. Adding to my mother's shame, and attempting to create mine by telling me this, was her belief that the other girl cousins, daughters of the sisters she fiercely loved and envied, had never been so blunt and in fact, they probably truly *looovvvved* doing my grandmother's dishes. In my mind I had just answered a question. I learned from this conversation, however, that good daughters *say what they think others want to hear,* and in fact, if possible, *learn to feel something else. They don't tell an inconvenient truth. They aren't selfish.*

We were all female in this mini drama. I wasn't told outright that girls cannot voice their real feelings. I was told that I couldn't voice mine, and I was a girl, so there you go. I think of all the mothers in my lineages and how their feelings may have been silenced to make it easier for everyone to get along. This was just another step along the path I was taking to deny my feelings. Now I was learning to hide them not just to make myself feel less embarrassed or guilty, but to make others feel more comfortable at my expense. The question is, of course, whether a reckoning will need to be made with the truth at some point. But for whose benefit would this be? For one's own mental health, at the expense of others' happiness? And there's the rub. There's always a reckoning to be made sometime, somewhere.

At the time, I wasn't mad at my grandmother. She said nothing to make me feel guilty in the initial conversation, and I had felt it was a moment of connection we didn't often have. At the time, I didn't interpret her talking to my mother as "telling on me." Rather, I felt *my mother* had overreacted.

Grandmother York *had* told on me, however; she thought it necessary that my mother teach me this lesson. She did not check back with me privately to process Mother's reaction, nor did I apologize to my grandmother. I was fine with pretending I didn't know I'd upset her. I continued to do kitchen clean-up, checked my eyerolls and sighs at the kitchen door—and possibly some of my feelings of affection as well.

———◦∞◦———

In Mother's family everything began and ended with Jesus. Being a good daughter was wrapped up in no small part with being a good Christian. Both these grandparents were active in the small country church named for the Bethel community in which they lived. My grandfather had a literal come-to-Jesus experience at a revival he was invited to near the sawmill where he was working at the time. He was eighteen years old. When he started courting my grandmother, she was not a Christian, and this troubled him, so much so that he found himself outside on his hands and knees during a snowstorm praying for her conversion. She was so taken with Granddaddy's desire for her salvation that she answered the altar call at her next opportunity. She was baptized soon afterward in the Pigeon River, along with fourteen other white-clad young women who my grandfather later described as "looking like angels."

My grandmother learned to read and write after her conversion so that she could read the Bible. And because she could read, she thought it was important that all her children go to school. And not just finish high school, and not just the boys. When my grandmother learned that a girl in their community had gotten a scholarship to the rural, Appalachia-focused, co-ed Berea College in Kentucky, she encouraged and enabled all her daughters to go. Not to stay home and help with the farm, not to get married and have children right away, but to go to college. Mother's college education meant that she had a different life than if she had stayed in Waynesville after high school graduation.

It has only recently dawned on me that this was a generational shift in the definition of what a good daughter could be and do. I never heard my grandmother say a word about women's rights, but she wanted a different life—a more prosperous life for her children. She saw their potential and encouraged them to do other things; she did not stand in their way. Even the girls. The girls, Mother and my aunts, lived in a changing world for women; their life choices were still constrained compared with those of the boys, but their education was not constrained by their mother.

With this new window to the world, Mother and her sisters (and brothers) all lived in places other than Waynesville for at least part of their lives after college graduation—perhaps an unanticipated sorrow for my grandmother. In the letters from my grandmother to Mother, she always writes how much she misses her and wishes she could come home. It made my mother's own heart ache that she could not say "yes" more often—that her liberation from farm life meant separation from this family. Toward the end of her life when she was living with dementia, my mother regularly asked me if she could "go home to see Mother."

Mother's college education allowed her to experience what it was like to have a job, to have professional standing, to be considered smart and independent. She had her own car and paid her own expenses. But she still wanted a family. By her late 20s, she felt time was running short. In 1954, she gave up her profession and part of her identity to have one.

She played her traditional woman script perfectly. She quit her job, sold her car, married my dad, moved wherever his blue-collar job took them, had a baby (me), stayed at home all day with that baby, cleaned and cooked and wrote letters to her family and friends, went to church on Sunday, and had another baby.

If a man had made these decisions in the 1950s, everyone would immediately conclude that his education and intellectual potential were wasted by following his wife around and staying home with a baby. No one said *that* about my mother, except maybe me, ungraciously, as a teenager. *She* did not say it, either, or even think it, because if she had, the chasm between who she was and who she could have been would have been too painful to contemplate. Tantamount to self-annihilation. She was silently bored and frustrated. She became a textbook case of "the problem with no name," described by Betty Friedan in *The Feminine Mystique*[1]—depression and existential dread from not being able to live into one's full potential. As I think about this as an adult, I believe we were all pretending she wasn't unhappy. We colluded to sweep her discontent under the rug because we were afraid of what might happen if we didn't.

My miserable mother found the attention she needed through seeking help for her physical ailments—fatigue, heart palpitations, headaches, sleeplessness. As I was growing up, and especially while I was a teenager, she experienced a continuing malaise for which there seemed to be no adequate medical diagnosis. Now, it seems obvious to me that she was anxious or depressed or both. At the time, it would have been unthinkable to tell us she needed to go to a shrink, so she went to doctors—many of them. One prescribed valium for her problem with no name. She decided, after a short time, to stop taking them; she had already developed a weak dependency that required medical assistance.

During this same time, I was listening with great interest to teachers and women I was babysitting for whose lives were being transformed by a new feminist consciousness, raising mine in the process. I borrowed their books; I went to teach-ins. However, I thought the lives of these women who had moved down one path, only later to see other possible paths, to be a bit of a mess. I planned to make conscious feminist choices from the *beginning* that would make a later 'do-over' unnecessary. I hope you are smiling sympathetically as you read this confession of naivety.

I now see the trap Mother was in and that she could not release herself from it. I get this—she was caught in a web of forces that she had little ability to resist—but I wished it had been otherwise. I wished she had been reading the books all the ladies I babysat for had been reading and had had her consciousness raised.

What would have happened if she had, though? Certainly it would have taken some pressure off me and my brother to meet her emotional needs. But would it have benefitted her? Would there have been room in her relationship with Daddy for her to grow into herself more wholeheartedly? She tried to use her talents at work in a couple of jobs, ostensibly to add to our income, but the requirements for being a good wife and mother came into sharp conflict with her outside work. It was too exhausting and stressful. Daddy was not very supportive; it was out of his script. Neither job lasted more than a year. Any attempt to understand and fulfill her own needs would have been perceived as selfish and at a cost to others, even though she had born the cost of maintaining the status quo.

⎯⎯ ✿ ⎯⎯

Mother, at age forty-eight, was devastated when her seventy-four-year-old mother died of breast cancer. Mother and her sisters had been with my grandmother after surgery the summer before, providing company for her around-the-clock. This became forever etched in my mind as the way good daughters care for loved ones. Always daughters, not sons. When my grandmother was hospitalized the second and final time, I traveled with Mother on the five-hour car trip from our home in Durham, North Carolina, to see her. To be a good granddaughter, I took several hospital shifts. I went home alone on the bus after a week so I wouldn't miss too much school.

Grandmother York died soon after I left, with Mother still there. My father did not feel he could spare the time from work to come up with my brother and me to Waynesville for the funeral. I was fine with this because I had been there when she was alive, but Mother and her family didn't see it this way. Points were taken off on my good (grand)daughter score card, but I pretended not to notice.

I was seventeen at the time. I could not understand what seemed like my mother's never-ending grief. I was sad, but Mother was inconsolable. She lost weight and part of her mind. She went around the house singing all my grandmother's favorite hymns. I couldn't comprehend her inability to let go, but I also went through a scary period of free-floating anxiety at the same time. I had no other name for it then and never spoke of it until decades later. I was relieved when it eventually lifted. Now, I might call it guilt.

⚭

My father, Rudy, was from Davenport, Iowa. By all indications, his mother, my Grandmother Stock, welcomed Mother into her family. But Mother was not so comfortable amid Daddy's reserved, less-educated, secular, urban, Midwestern family. To make my mother as happy as was possible (without addressing the root causes of her unhappiness), we spent much less time in the flatlands of Iowa than in the mountains of North Carolina when I was growing up. Nevertheless, I can still conjure up a feeling of what it was like to be around Daddy's mother's calm energy—warm and solid—into which I was welcomed *as I was*.

When we did visit my paternal grandparents' small house on Thornwood Avenue, my German grandfather did not talk much, and my grandmother took on the job of keeping the dinner conversation going. She was also the communicator when we were not there, writing us frequent letters. She wrote the way she talked: encouragingly and affectionately. Always on my birthday with a couple of "leaves of lettuce" (dollar bills)—but also, sometimes even not on my birthday, the letters were for me. And I wrote back.

She made quilts—gorgeous quilts with intricate patterns that still keep me warm at night. The designs were perfectly executed in precise, tight stitches made by hand. I started making quilts while I was in high school. Her design and technical skill were superior to mine, but I found kinship with her in making my own.

I couldn't help but notice the differences between Daddy's mother and Mother's mother. Daddy's mother's German-laced Midwestern accent was slightly foreign to my ears. Her voice was deep and her smile was broad and honest. She wore knee-length shirtwaist dresses like my other grandmother but worn with thick stockings and sturdy shoes for indoor wear only. I have few memories of eating at this grandmother's table and fewer of what we actually ate. I imagine it was typical German fare—meat and potatoes—my father's preferred meal.

I never heard Grandmother Stock or any other family member talk about religion. Neither Daddy nor any of his siblings went to school beyond high school, and I'm not sure if his sisters actually finished high school. I never was asked to do chores at this grandmother's house, never went to church with her, never felt the obligation to say or do a thing I did not want to, or pretend I felt a way I did not.

I learned the difference between what it meant to be a good son versus a good daughter by noticing the way each of my parents related to their parents, particularly their mothers. That my father loved his mother I never questioned, but it was not something said aloud. I never heard him criticize her, or express guilt in his relationship to her, or verbalize, much less belabor, any kinds of emotional entanglements with her or any of his family. Their love and respect for each other was just a fact of life and a cool counterpoint to the drama of my mother's family's more fraught love. I found this a relief; Mother found it a void. She needed more engagement to feel loved.

—————癸癸——————

That men ruled the world *out there* was a surprise to me when this reality first hit me. When I was a young child, I thought of Mother as the powerful one. Because I didn't understand her lack of true agency, I interpreted what I was seeing as her getting what she wanted most of the time, starting with how much more time we spent with Mother's family compared with Daddy's. Mother often told me that daughters needed their families more than sons did, worrying me a bit. I had no idea at the time all she had given up to marry my father or how powerless she felt. Her evident unhappiness was confusing to me in the face of her power as I experienced it. The unspoken reasons for her sadness stayed locked away in her disappointed heart—until my father died, and the walls constructed in her mind crumbled under the ravages of dementia.

I don't know whether my early misunderstanding about women's power in the world made it easier or harder for me when I began to grasp the truth of it. I made vocational plans as if I knew no gender barriers. They were there, but they were deceptively subtle. No absolutes about what I could study or be, but it was the everyday details that stumped me while trying to combine a profession and parenthood —the expectation that I was the one who got the kids to school or stayed home when they were sick, the raised eyebrows when I didn't have time for PTA committees because I had a job or was out of town traveling for that job. No one gave me a pass for being a breadwinner; in fact, I felt the opposite. I had to do more to prove myself a good mother.

How much weight did women's desires carry in my ancestors' decisions to leave Europe for this continent? Stynte Douwes from the Netherlands came as a married woman, as did Anne Christian, wife of the younger Thomas Blacklocke. I want to imagine these as strong women who had a say in whom they married and where they would live, but given the gender politics in the seventeenth century, it is likely they (and other women in my lineage) did not have a say.

I expect that they learned to conceal their feelings until they believed they had none, as many women do, as my mother did, as I did. What I do know about Stynte and Anne Christian in particular, however, is that they came to America and made a life, had children and grandchildren, and because they did, I live.

While I was a teenager, my father argued with me that sex roles were just a logical division of labor with nothing inherently unequal in them. Except, I knew that making money meant you had more power, and having a job meant you had a purpose outside in the world. Everything was unequal in those gendered scripts. I know he loved me and wanted everything good for me, it was just his perspective of what that meant was narrower than mine.

Changes in technology upended the social order at the time of second wave feminism (feminism without any racial analysis) in the 1960s and 70s. Contraception gave women the potential to control their fertility and thus, control a much larger portion of how they spent their time and lived their lives. I took for granted not having to choose between career and family in a way that even my college-educated mother did not.

The world was slower to change, however, than I was ready for it to; I was frustrated with gender politics in the workplace and challenges for working moms (Working dads were just dads). Eventually, inertia set in. I became numb to the continuing inequities women experienced. It took too much energy to call out sexism every time I felt it. It was too scary to let myself see systems of patriarchy at work in my life. I didn't want to be "that woman," perceived as angry all the time.

I tried to do it all. I didn't lack meaning in my life; I lacked time and energy. My problem most definitely had a name—it was stress. I was angry about the reasons for the stress, but why? Wasn't I getting everything I wanted? The disconnect between opportunity and support was confusing. I blamed myself. I kept trying to make myself believe I wasn't angry because it was too scary to contemplate what to do if I was. To protect myself, I hid my rage in an emotional fog, only sometimes lifted for a moment. Eventually, however, it was too much; I left my first marriage, but because I had kept the hard, confusing feelings tamped down for so long, it took a long time to sort them out for myself and explain them to others.

The crazy part of my good daughter upbringing was that at the same time Mother and Daddy were encouraging me to make good grades and go to college so that I could get a job and *also* live a fulfilled life as wife and mother, they seemed to have no awareness about Mother's own unhappiness and anger born of these same conflicting expectations. There were limits, of course, in what they thought I could or should do with my education compared with what they thought my brother could or should do. Being a schoolteacher, for example, would be a good fit for me as a wife and mother. And that is what I thought, too, until the world got bigger for me, and I pursued a research career that made demands at-odds with being a good mother. What was a good daughter to do?

What I now see, however, is that though I made work and family life choices Mother might not have thought would be easy for me to live into, she gave me the tools to make them. As my grandmother had done for my mother. Even though they were both unhappy because of how it separated them and us from each other. And my choices to continue to pursue a career while my children were still young shifted gender boundaries that had been previously shifted before me—like my grandmother ensuring that her daughters would go to college. These choices came with some cost—even more than I knew at the time—but also brought satisfaction and joy from family and career and in my eventual realization that selflessness is not always love, and martyrdom never is.

And even as I write this, I find myself on the other side of the question I asked earlier about what would have happened if my mother had found her own voice within her marriage. How much pain would there have been if I had stayed in my first marriage for the sake of my relationship with my children? What would be the consequences for myself and everyone else had I just kept pushing down anger born of self-denial? I imagine other people feel the same uncertainty of whether they made the correct decision when both choices were painful.

The only answer I have found in contemplating these nagging questions is that I can never know the outcome had I made the opposite choice. Because I can never know and because I cannot change it now, I must learn to live consciously with the tension of these unanswered questions, acknowledging and apologizing for the pain it may have caused, and moving on with my life as it is, finding joy and purpose in what I can, and having hope for an eventual greater understanding on the part of my children as they grow older.

———⊶⊷———

I said "yes" to the doctor the night my mother broke her hip; yes, he could schedule my mother's hip replacement operation the next day. She survived, but her complicated recovery posed new and never-ending questions for me about how to best manage her care in the hospital and rehab center, made more complicated by her dementia. As the good daughter trying to take care of her, I felt overwhelmed and alone and raw. Choices between length and quality of life crushed my heart. I worked through tangled feelings to choose quality over quantity as an act of love for both Mother and me. As it turned out, enrolling her in hospice care after rehab opened the way for better day-to-day care, and this brought relief to both of us. The time I spent with my mother, when she was settled back into her memory care residence with this mechanism in place, was better for it.

———⊶⊷———

I, too, am the mother of a daughter. Was I a good *mother*? I am sure my daughter felt she got less of what she needed because of how I handled the conflicts between working and motherhood.

What did my life teach her about being a good daughter? That is her story to tell, but I will say this: she looks away from the contradictions in women's choices less often than I did, leaves herself more vulnerable to the pain of it, and has a stronger voice than I do. I wish I had protected her better, and I am also proud of her greater resistance.

The lessons we learn about how to be good daughters—and good mothers—can be a tool of maintaining the status quo or the antidote to it. My grandmothers and my mother loved their families fiercely, if imperfectly, and lived within whatever constraints they experienced as women to make a good life for their children. As a good daughter, I feel compassion for them and myself and my own daughter as we all, at whatever edge of liberation we can get ourselves to, speak our own truths.

We are born of many mothers. These are mothers and grandmothers from maternal and paternal lineages. From top to bottom and left to right they are: Bertha Deaver Kuykendall (my mother's maternal grandmother); Margaret Blalock Deaver (my maternal grandmother's grandmother); Nancy Burnett Miller (my maternal grandfather's maternal grandmother); Ethel Kuykendall York (my maternal grandmother); Norma York Stock (my mother); Alona Miller York (my mother's paternal grandmother); Bertha Muhs Lindemann (my father's maternal grandmother); (her daughter) Augusta Lindemann Stock (my paternal grandmother); and Wilhelmine Witt Stock (my father's paternal grandmother).

borderlands (england)

BEFORE HE SAILED to the Eastern Shore of Virginia in the early seventeenth century, my ancestor Thomas Blacklocke was born and lived in the contested border area between northern England and Scotland, now known as Cumbria. He was born in 1581 and baptized in the small St. John the Evangelist church in the village of Crosby-on-Eden; this was four miles east of the ancient town of Carlisle, steps away from the remnants of Roman emperor Hadrian's famous wall, built eight centuries earlier to deter invasion by unconquerable Scots tribes. Blacklocke's father, also named Thomas, died at the young age of 25, and was buried in the same churchyard only a year after his son's birth. Father and son are related to me through my mother's mother's *mother's* family.

Few traces of the lives of Thomas or his ancestors remain, but I looked for him by immersing myself in the rich history of his birthplace. I found him in the shapeshifting edges of the British Empire where he lived his early life. How did young Thomas find it in his destiny to cross political, social, and cultural borders into a different life in England's Virginia colony? How did learning the history of this ancestral homeland influence my perception of how I should live in the world?

⸺❧⸺

Before traveling to Thomas' birthplace, I scoured history books for clues about why Thomas might have left Carlisle. Initially, I focused on what was going on in Elizabethan England around the time of Thomas' life, which was when my own limited knowledge of English history began and ended. English exploration of the "New World" began about fifty years before Thomas was born. In 1584, Thomas Harriot was invited by Sir Walter Raleigh, along with John White and 600 English troops, to join his efforts to create an English colony on the American continent. Harriot and White were hired to document what they saw on what is now called Roanoke Island, along North Carolina's Outer Banks. Harriot took notes, and White made sketches; both were amazed and charmed by a world so new to them. Poor planning for the needs of so many soldiers and the English military's disrespectful behavior toward the Indigenous people, however, led to irredeemable conflict, death, and destruction, ending that colonization effort.[1]

Harriot and White, fortunately, were rescued from the fracas by the swashbuckling (as I imagine him) Sir Francis Drake and returned to England where they began writing and illustrating an account of their year there. Their widely read *Briefe and True Report* captured the romantic imagination of its readers and gave a boost to Sir Walter Raleigh's colonization promotion efforts. In 1590, when my ancestor Thomas Blacklocke was nine years old, German engraver Theodor de

Bry published a third edition of Harriot's treatise. De Bry modified the engravings of White's watercolors to make the faces of the Indigenous people, and the landscapes behind them, look more European. What was not altered, however, were their more exotic muscular arms and legs, and their dreamy visages, signifying a blithe coexistence with the natural world.

Even if young Thomas was illiterate and could not read this tract, he likely saw these illustrations, which no doubt fed his imagination about who was on the other side of the ocean. My own perceptions of America's Indigenous people were formed before I met any in person. Popular culture promoted images of "Indians"—Western movies and television shows that rarely cast real Native persons as Indians; animated Disney movies such as *Peter Pan*; children's books about Thanksgiving; and commercial logos of companies that used Native names in their brand, such as Pontiac cars or the Cleveland Indians baseball team.

But it was not only images of Indigenous people that caught the fancy of the would-be adventurers; it was the pairing of them with portraits of ancient Britons, meant to convey similarities between them, both labelled "savages." The marketing strategy exploited the mythos of the civilizing effect of the Roman invasion on the Iron Age Celts, bestowing the gifts of law, religion, and civility, for which the late sixteenth century English were eternally grateful.

The logical implication was that Englishmen had a moral imperative to pay their debt forward. They must civilize these "savages" in America, so like their ancient ancestors, lest the Indigenous Americans remain in their current primitive (and, it went without saying, hell-bent) state. Investors could do good and make money at the same time, easing any guilt they may have felt about a "tough love" approach to colonization.[2] I'm not so sure my ancestor Thomas went to Virginia to save the souls of Indigenous people, but the idea of "doing well while doing good" fueled investments by the elite and a growing yeoman class in England, which made his voyage as an indentured servant possible. And it put a softer spin on the country's empire-building.

But wait, English people were grateful for their conquest by the Romans? This I found hard to believe. I had never read or heard any living Indigenous author on this side of the Atlantic—or the other— say they were grateful for the "civilization" that invaders brought with them. This curious notion that seventeenth century English women and men appreciated the Roman conquest of their ancestors made me curious about the Indigenous Britons in a way that I had not thought about the aboriginal people in my other ancestral homelands of the Netherlands and Germany.

From my investigation into the more-complicated-than-I-imagined history of Britain, I discovered that it is a country created from migrations and invasions from multiple ethnic groups and places over millennia of time, not unlike the continent to which Thomas himself migrated. I explored the parallels between the two worlds and considered Thomas' life as a bridge between them.

⎯⎯ ⊗⊗⊗ ⎯⎯

What happened when Europeans landed, and continued to land in America was, to my mind, a continuation, or maybe an inevitable outcome of the history of Roman imperialism, millennia earlier.[3] Going deeper into this history here can open portals of understanding of the historical backdrop of Thomas Blacklocke's life in England and America, but it is the context not only for his life but the lives of all my European settler ancestors—those whom I have written about and those I have not. It will suffice, I think, to focus here on the Romans in Britain.

In 55 BCE Julius Caesar arrived in Britain with the intention of expanding Rome's empire and solidifying his personal power base. After two summers of battles complicated by stormy weather, he had to leave before he attained a full victory over the Britons because of trouble in Gaul that required his return. His Roman troops had displayed enough advantage over the opposing Celtic military alliance, however, so that he could take captives and negotiate an annual tribute from the hostile tribes.[4]

In the 90 intervening years before the more successful invasion by Rome, Celtic tribes in the southeast took sides both for and against Rome. In 43 CE, the Roman Emperor Claudius ordered the invasion of Britain to finish what Julius Caesar started. Forty thousand soldiers on a thousand ships quickly secured a foothold in the south. Rome's continued military advance across the island, however, was incremental and sometimes met with strong resistance.[5]

The Roman army reached the site of present-day Carlisle around 70 CE. They built a fort there at the junction of two rivers—the Caldew and the Eden River—and the meeting place of several roads that go north to Scotland and east across England's northern mountains.[6] By 83 CE they had conquered tribes in the west where Wales is now and in the north all the way into Scotland.

The Scots tribes could not be held, however, and the Romans fell back to a more defensible frontier across the center of the island where Emperor Hadrian ordered a wall built to protect Rome's holdings. This wall, now in ruins, was built just steps away from where my ancestor Thomas was baptized 1,400 years later. *Luguvalium* was the Roman name for the prosperous town that grew up around the fort, its reason for being, primarily to serve the troops there.

The northern Celtic tribe of people living in this area before the Roman invasion were the Carvetii, or people of the deer or stag. They worshiped the horned god, Belatucadras. The Eden River Valley was the heart of their territory that extended west across a plain to the Solway Firth, an inlet that opens to the Irish Sea. The Carvetii likely were a sect of the larger tribe of the Brigantes, worshippers of the goddess Brigantia, and inhabitants of most of the north of England.[7]

In 407 CE, the Emperor Constantine withdrew the Roman military forces back across the channel to Gaul (France). Britons and Gauls revolted against a weakened Roman rule, weakened further after the Visigoth sack of Rome in 410 CE. Britons reverted to something like their pre-Roman cultures, though they were not unchanged by the more than 400-year colonization.[8]

———— ∞ ————

Celtic tribes in England before the invasion of Rome worshipped local deities living directly in nature. Their common gods were in the form of stags and bears, and trees. They worshipped in temples, shrines, springs, and groves. The ancient Celts buried their dead with grave goods, indicating a belief in life after death in the "other world." They also made votive offerings, objects displayed or deposited, usually in a watery place for the gods, meant to be recovered at a later time. I think here of the Arthurian legend of the Sword in the Stone, which has ties to Celtic mysticism. Druids were the priesthood of the ancient Celts, serving as sorcerers, shamans, poets, or bards. There is so much speculation about whether King Arthur's Merlin was a Druid priest that one could easily get lost in the internet conversation about it.[9]

Neither pre-Christian Roman colonizers, nor later Christian Romans, were tolerant of Celtic paganism, reminding me of the same way that the English did not tolerate Native American spiritual beliefs. Romans forbade the worship of Celtic gods and savagely destroyed the Celts sacred groves as they sought to destroy the Celts as a people and a culture. The English, when they got to America centuries later, like children with unprocessed trauma, passed on the brutality of their ancestral memories to Native people in the name of their god and of civilization.

———— ∞ ————

From the departure of the Romans until the colonization of America, British history continued to be a story of ongoing invasion and adaptation between the newcomers and those who were there before them. Various Germanic tribes known as the Saxons took control of Britain during the fifth to eighth centuries, transforming post-Roman Briton into what became England, with a near total shift in culture and language.[10]

The elite who came to rule over the eventual four kingdoms of Anglo-Saxon England—Mercia, Northumbria, Wessex, and East Anglia—had diverse continental origins but a common Germanic cultural and linguistic identity.[11] Carlisle found itself in the Anglo-Saxon kingdom of Northumbria.

What happened to the Carvetii? Historian John Higham believes that they continued to live there as a separate culture after the arrival of Anglo-Saxons in Northumbria. The new aristocracy needed a servile labor force. As the lowest and largest status group, the Carvetii provided cultural stability and continuity during the several-century transition to Saxon rule. Recent DNA research is consistent with this presumption; modern blood group distribution shows similarities between Cumbrian residents and people in central Wales thought to be from the same ethnicity as Carvetii.[12] Were the Carvettis ancestors of Thomas's and, therefore, my people? Possibly, but also, possibly not.

The Vikings eventually came for the Saxons from Denmark, but their rule was not long-lived. Carlisle was overrun by them in the ninth century. The town was left in ruin for nearly *two centuries*. This is a length of time that sounds substantial to me, but in cosmic time, is short. William the Conqueror invaded southern England on behalf of the Normans in 1066. His son William (II) Rufus arrived with troops in Carlisle in 1092, reviving the fort's role as protectorate against the tribes of Scotland. A wooden castle was built where the Roman one had been. William Rufus sent troops to the castle and ordered peasants from farther south to inhabit the vacant town.[13] Were these new people my ancestors, or were my ancestors the surviving Carvetii, already there?

Thirty years later, still threatened by possible attacks by Scotland, William Rufus's younger brother, Henry I, ordered a stone wall and towers to be constructed to fortify the castle. Carlisle and its castle became a pawn in the chess game between England and Scotland as battles between the two countries shifted borders back and forth over the next several centuries.

⊶⊷

I skip forward now through several hundred years of Norman monarchy to Thomas's personal story which begins during Elizabeth's reign. Elizabeth held on to Britain's position as a European power through military might, but the picture on the home front was not so rosy. Domestic unrest had been several centuries in the making. Four waves of plague spanning the fourteenth century killed half the population. The plague created greater wealth, however, among the surviving elite, who got unexpected inheritances, and among the surviving peasantry, whose wages soared because of the resulting labor shortage. A new yeoman class rose up with its members occupying a status somewhere between gentry and laborer, better educated and more politicized than peasants. They became a politically and religiously conservative source of investment in industrialization, urbanization, and imperialism.[14]

Rural communities began collapsing; with them went the social support woven into local norms of obligations and care. Europe was experiencing a cold spell known as the "Little Ice Age," making the environment a difficult one in which to grow food. Also, the land's capacity to sustain England's growing poor population was further reduced by policy changes that allowed people with enough money to enclose lands for private use that previously had been commonly shared. Common land had allowed peasants to grow food and keep an animal or two for their own subsistence needs.

Previously common lands enclosed as private property were being used for cash crops, including pasturelands to graze sheep for wool. Fewer laborers were required for herding sheep compared with growing food, and landowner costs were lowered. Speculators artificially increased the prices of food by buying up produce to create scarcity—while common people starved to death.[15]

Peasants without access to land moved to urban areas to find jobs to pay for food grown as cash crops. This happened, not coincidentally, in tandem with the beginning of the Industrial Age and the building of factories that needed cheap labor. Peasants who rebelled were slain to keep a lid on the social order.[16] The center was barely holding. If you think this sounds familiar, I agree with you.

English elites began to see the "New World" as a much-needed escape valve to avert domestic disaster. Landless peasants were so desperate they were willing to settle in an unknown world, filling investors' needs for labor. In the first half of the seventeenth century, fifty thousand English people immigrated to America out of a population of four million, most of them as indentured servants.[17] One of them was Thomas Blacklocke.

The border area between England and Scotland during this time was a bastion of lawlessness that would have affected Thomas's life in Crosby-on-Eden one way or another. Outlaw clans called Border Reivers ("reive" means "to raid") considered themselves answerable to neither country's laws and took advantage of a lack of cooperation between the two. Reivers stole cattle and goods from both English and Scots alike. The hilly geography of the pastureland around them made it easy to take what they wanted without notice of others.[18]

The Reivers, quite a thorn in the side of the governments of both England and Scotland, elicited strong, detailed curses made against them by both laity and clergy.[19] The political chaos between Elizabeth I's death in 1603 and the naming of James VI of Scotland as James I of England the next year created an upsurge in mayhem by the Reivers. James, now ruler of both countries, made it a priority to rid both England and Scotland of them, by any means necessary. Many were arrested and hanged.

Thomas and his family, for generations, had lived in the vortex of Reiver activities, though "Blacklocke" is not on any of the lists of

Reiver clans I have found. One scenario I can image for Thomas is that his father's early death, more than a decade before James I's crack-down, was somehow related to the violence of the Reivers. Another is that Thomas left his Eden River village as a young man to avoid being caught up in the danger of it, whether that meant being asked to take sides or the consequences of getting arrested. Most settlers from the northern part of England who immigrated to America did so later than Thomas did. Perhaps Thomas left the north initially to go south to London or Plymouth to get away from Reiver activities. Once there, he would have heard more about America, and his wanderlust took him even farther away to Virginia.

⸺ ∞ ⸺

My visit to Thomas's birthplace began in Edinburgh, where my husband and I were able to visit my son and his family living there. We took a train from there for Carlisle. The train was easy to book—inexpensive, and comfortable—making me wish, not for the first time, that train travel was easier in the US. As I looked out the window, I saw a blur of lush, green grass being grazed on by countless sheep.

We arrived in Carlisle about an hour before we could check in to our Airbnb, so we wandered around the city center to find a quiet place to sit for tea. Once we got to our accommodations, we continued sorting ourselves out and then went looking for dinner. All the nicest restaurants were overbooked, but we finally found a pub. I never go to the UK for the cuisine, and fish and chips were just fine after my glass of white wine.

We were up early the next day to see the Carlisle Cathedral. It was a gray day, damp. Clouds smudged the sky. It was not cool, not warm, and just a bit humid. I packed a couple of cameras and thought the overcast atmosphere would saturate the colors in my photographs.

The cathedral, built in 1133 in the middle of the small town, is magnificent. The flower-lined walkway that runs beside the brick wall of archways led us to the entryway. At the entryway we were met by the protector of this spirit house, an older man who seemed to be as much a fixture of the church as the stone columns holding up the starry ceiling. We walked through the antique pews of the sanctuary, took in the kaleidoscopic colors in the fifty-foot-tall medieval stained-glass images of saints and angels, and were spellbound by the celestial ceiling of gilt stars against a deep blue. The open space that flows through the main body of this place of worship is surrounded by columns and statues and numerous architectural details that reflect its enduring presence amid centuries of human upheaval.

⁂

After we visited the cathedral, we headed off to Thomas Blacklocke's village, a place I had viewed obsessively on Google maps since I learned of his birth there. The Eden River flows below a bridge we crossed in Rickerby Park. "Rickerby" comes from the name of the west gate of fortified Carlisle in the twelfth century. The name of the river is an English version of its similar sounding Roman/Celtic names, "Itouna/Ituna," meaning water or rushing water. It was not named for the Garden of Eden, but it is as beautiful to me as the image I conjure when I think of that mythical place of creation.

We followed a path to Crosby-on-Eden along a two-lane road, followed then, according to our map, by a bike path. The two-lane road took us past lovely residences, but then the sidewalk ended. We walked through tall grasses on narrow shoulders, fast cars whizzing by, for a scary half hour before the bike path appeared and our walk became pleasant again.

We came up on the village proper. My map showed a pub and a place for visitors to stay overnight. A few homes remained, but the businesses had closed down, except for an equestrian school head-quarters. My initial destination was St. John the Evangelist Church, where I knew my ancestors were baptized and buried. The current structure had been rebuilt since they lived there, but the location of the church, home to a still-active congregation, and adjacent centuries-old burial grounds is unchanged. A brick schoolhouse with a brightly painted playground sat next to the church.

I was relieved to arrive after our long walk. I circled the grounds several times, taking photographs with multiple cameras. The unevenly graded yard was packed tightly with vertical stone slabs—many of them rose slanted out of the ground, pushed this way or that by the snaking roots of mature trees that kept watch over this garden of the dead. A path curved through the centuries-old grave-markers, the words too time-worn to identify those of my ancestors.

The front door was locked, so I could not see what was inside. The morning's glum sky had turned into a happier, bluer one that contrasted with bright, verdant foliage everywhere. Yellow-green grass carpeted the ground under our feet. Fields and meadows surrounded the church and stretched farther than I could see. The Eden River flowed through those distant fields somewhere beyond our line of sight.

I was ready for a cup of tea, but without a café in sight, I decided instead to find the river. We walked on a narrow, paved road, lined with huge trees that I imagined had been young when Thomas lived nearby. The river, when we found it, ran along the edge of a golf course. I was a little disappointed about this, but my husband was delighted.

We walked down the footpaths separated from the river by stands of grasses and lavender wildflowers. The water moving past us mellowed my mood as we stood and watched it meditatively for some minutes. I thought of the many rivers and creeks that show up in the stories of my various ancestors, and of my great-grandmother Bertha, a direct descendant of Thomas, who kept spring waters in North Carolina flowing for her family. She so carefully tended the bubbling water source near her house that the road close to it is named Bertha's Spring Road.

After communing with Thomas's river, wondering how far away from here he and his family had actually lived and what their house might have looked like, we found the clubhouse at the golf course and got something to drink. We thought it would be easy to get a taxi from the golf course, but taxis were in high demand because of crowds of people flooding into city center bars to watch an important local football match. We finally found a taxi; our driver listened to the game intently as he drove us the short twenty minutes back into town. I was glad we were able to ride back to town, but also glad we walked there initially to get an idea of how long it would have taken Thomas to walk into Carlisle.

As we drove through town, people spilled out of bars into the street in various stages of inebriation and sexually suggestive attire— many of them looking like they were looking for love in all the wrong places. I wondered what revelry would have looked like in Thomas's time, maybe a few roads over, closer to the market square nearer to the Cathedral and Castle. Would he have wandered through it during his youth? What about his father and his father's father? So close to a military outpost, so close to the action of the Reivers, I easily imagined a Saturday night in the sixteenth century would have been a bit wild. But I still had so many unanswerable other questions about Thomas' life.

We planned to eat dinner at a small restaurant near our lodging to keep us out of the fray, but that place was as loud and crowded and chaotic as everywhere else—no service to be had—so we made our way toward town hoping for a miracle. And we found one—a small vegan restaurant squeezed in between two massive and tightly packed chain restaurants. An oasis of relatively sober people sitting at appropriate social distances listening to American R&B music eating vegan burgers and pizza. I ordered a large glass of red wine and table-danced to Aretha, the Temptations, and Gladys Knight to ease out the kinks after a long day of walking.

———❦———

After a good night's sleep, I was ready to see the Carlisle Castle of myth and legend, so enmeshed in the history of England and Scotland.

Its red sandstone façade imposed itself on my view as I walked toward it and away from the city center. The most famous post-Norman conquest story told about the castle is that in May 1568 it was used to house Mary Queen of Scots, and her numerous attendants, after she had been defeated by rebellious subjects and fled to England. The castle warden was in perpetual fear of her escape, and eventually she was persuaded to leave for Bolton Castle in Yorkshire.[20]

Thomas's father would have been eleven years old and his mother eight at the time. Queen Mary was executed in 1587, when Thomas was a small child. No doubt he must have heard the story of her time in the castle from his mother.

Even after Carlisle was no longer thought to be in danger of attack from the Scots, the castle was used as a base from which to maintain order over the unruly Reivers, and as a prison for these cattle thieves once caught. The most notorious of these, William Armstrong of Kinmount, broke out of his castle prison cell in April 1596 and was rescued by a band of Scots. A famous ballad of his escape was perhaps heard and sung by Thomas, a teenager when it happened. King James I visited Carlisle in 1617 on his way back to England from Scotland and noted its disrepair but did nothing much to change this matter.[21] Thomas may have already had left his village, if not England itself, before James's visit.

At the castle, we went first into the history museum. I walked through display after display of weapons and uniforms used by the British military to invade and colonize the world. This acclamation of Britain's conquests made me groan, even if silently, but I knew I shouldn't be throwing stones, considering the glass house of the country where I live. The middle-aged man at the front desk, likely ex-military himself, disarmed me, however, when he saw my camera and said, "Film cameras, they're the best, aren't they?"

"Yes, they are." I smiled.

He continued, "There is something different about a photograph taken using film. I don't know how to describe it, but there is just more feeling about it."

I agreed. I told him, "Digital makes it easy to get a technically good image, but I love the feel of film, especially black and white. I'm lucky that I live near a place in the States that still processes film." Two people who both love film photography. No geo-politics. No empire building.

When my husband, Ron, and I got to the castle proper, I started up the main stairwell. The walls closed in on me and my claustrophobia; I couldn't breathe. I heard myself say to Ron, "You go on. This is too narrow for me." Back in the courtyard, I found stairs outside the tower, walked around the top of the fort, and viewed the full expanse of the city from there. A wide field of bright green grass extended out from the castle complex. From this panoramic distance, I saw for myself its protective position over Carlisle and the elusive border it was built to secure.

It is a short walk from the castle to the Eden River. I looked forward to a second visit, this time staying closer to Carlisle. We joined the footpath from Rickerby Park where we had first seen the river the day before from over the bridge. The Eden flows through wide meadows and intermittent stands of large trees and past sports fields busy with football matches, and most unexpectedly, to us, small herds of unfenced cows. The river moves at a steady pace around time-worn curves. It is an easy walk, and we could go on forever, but there was rain coming down—and then there was the matter of getting back. We crossed a bridge and returned from the other side.

I enthusiastically took many photographs, wondering which were going to be the ones I most liked when I got home. Did Thomas walk these foot paths along the river on his way to town? How much has the river's path changed in 400 years? Perhaps he took a small boat—

we do see a few kayakers. Carlisle was a much smaller town in those days with nothing else surrounding it. Thomas must have seen the castle looming ahead for miles as he neared the town. What did it mean to him—protection or antagonism? Friend or foe?

⟳

After our river walk, we made a second visit to the cathedral. On the way we stopped at a coffeeshop in the same building as the Town Hall. A line of women and men wearing bright purple robes and caps— town officials, we assumed—began leaving the main entrance, down some nearby stairs. They walked *en masse* toward the cathedral while loud music peeled from the bell tower announcing the event they were leaving to attend.

"Can you imagine our town council walking to church together in purple robes?" I asked Ron.

"But more importantly, do you think I can still visit the cathedral while they are there?"

He didn't think it would be a problem, but I was not sure of my social boundaries. We followed them, and I waited around a bit until after they all went in. Other tourists went in, so I did too. I told the same rumpled man from yesterday that I would stay in the back away from the service.

"Please join us," he offered, but I declined.

I overheard the service in the main chapel, however. The speakers were recognizing the military careers of those who were in Afghanistan, this event somehow tied to the recent military with-drawal there. My chest tightened. Feelings about the military museum propaganda resurfaced. Enough of God and country. I silently asked these people, "You believe God wants you to kill people?"

And then the ball drops. Yes, they did. Not just here, but everywhere.

This is what I can never understand.

Separation of church and state is a relatively new idea, and in many people's minds nationalism is entwined with religious overtones; imperialism clothed as the will of God. This cathedral was built shortly after the Normans rebuilt the old Roman fort. It served a military population over the course of multiple sieges and occupations by the Scots. During the English Civil War, in fact, a portion of the nave of the cathedral was demolished by the Scottish Presbyterian Army to use the stone to reinforce the castle. After unification of the two countries in 1707, the British military continued to utilize the castle to achieve their expansionist goals beyond the island.[22]

Even before the Norman conquest, this cathedral space held the tension between good and evil, spirit and flesh. Roman temples were built here while the Romans were garrisoned at the fort to protect their colony from the Scots tribes. Monasteries located nearby during the Anglo-Saxon middle ages were eventually overrun by Vikings. These grounds I had been walking on around the castle and the cathedral had been walked over by so many people who had gone there as soldiers and warriors, and it had been itself the scene of violent battle sieges. I became acutely aware of so much pain born over this terrain. How do people so easily forget? I ask again, how can they ever believe killing is the will of a God of love?

———— ⊱※⊰ ————

Saturday night's post-football match frenzy was now Sunday evening's calm respite. We found a brewpub for dinner. We took one last walk, this time through an almost empty town. We were up early the next day for a train back to Edinburgh and then left the next day for the US.

———— ⊱※⊰ ————

What did I find out about myself as a result of visiting Thomas' birthplace and delving into its history? I found a story of relatively constant human migration and invasion, a story I knew little about beforehand, so complicated and so full of possibilities. Without sophisticated genetic testing it is impossible to know which streams of migration carried Thomas's DNA to that place where he was born. For me, then, it is the whole of English history that led up to his being born in that particular time and to his migration away from it and onward across the Atlantic and through the lives of his descendants that connects his life to mine.

⸙

Robert Frost's poem *Mending Wall*[23] kept intruding into my thoughts as I wrote about the contested borderland of Thomas's birthplace, and the enclosure movement that took common land away from peasants to make it economically productive for the gentry. The dual functions of walls will continue to show up in my ancestor stories; they keep people in and they keep people out.

Two seemingly contradictory phrases from Frost's poem define our psychological attraction to, and repulsion by the barriers we erect between each other. A neighbors' admonition that "Good walls make good neighbors" rings true in a psychological sense. Good boundaries make better relationships; a certain clarity about what constitutes acceptable interpersonal behavior makes it easier for everyone to interact with others.

But there is also this from the poem's narrator: "Something there is that doesn't love a wall." A barrier placed between human beings is a provocation, almost an invitation to "cross a line." And aren't walls usually built by the perpetrator? People who have come to take something away, so they themselves need protection? I'm thinking here not only of the Roman Hadrian's wall, but of the settlers in the American colonies who erected palisades to protect themselves from the people whose land they invaded. This tension in the poem makes us question our own position on the appropriate use of walls. Doubt and uncertainty give us a way into a humanistic conversation about walls, and maybe the space to talk about fear and anger.

Conditions created by economic injustices and the worsening climate crisis are making it necessary for large numbers of people to move from their homelands to safer, higher ground. "Whatever it is that doesn't love a wall" needs to be lifted and made sacred for us to prepare a welcome for them.

When borders are crossed, one's old life is changed, as are the lives of the people already there. Something new is created in the "space between." This can be a cause of fear or of celebration. My ancestor Thomas left economic and political challenges of England and Scotland to make a new life for himself on a continent previously inhabited by people with a very different worldview. He left to make a life for himself when there were no borders to stop him from moving in, no "papers" needing to be filed. I'm not defending English settlement and colonization. The fact of it remains. But in my mind, this only adds to a moral imperative for America to welcome *all* people into a new space of acceptance.

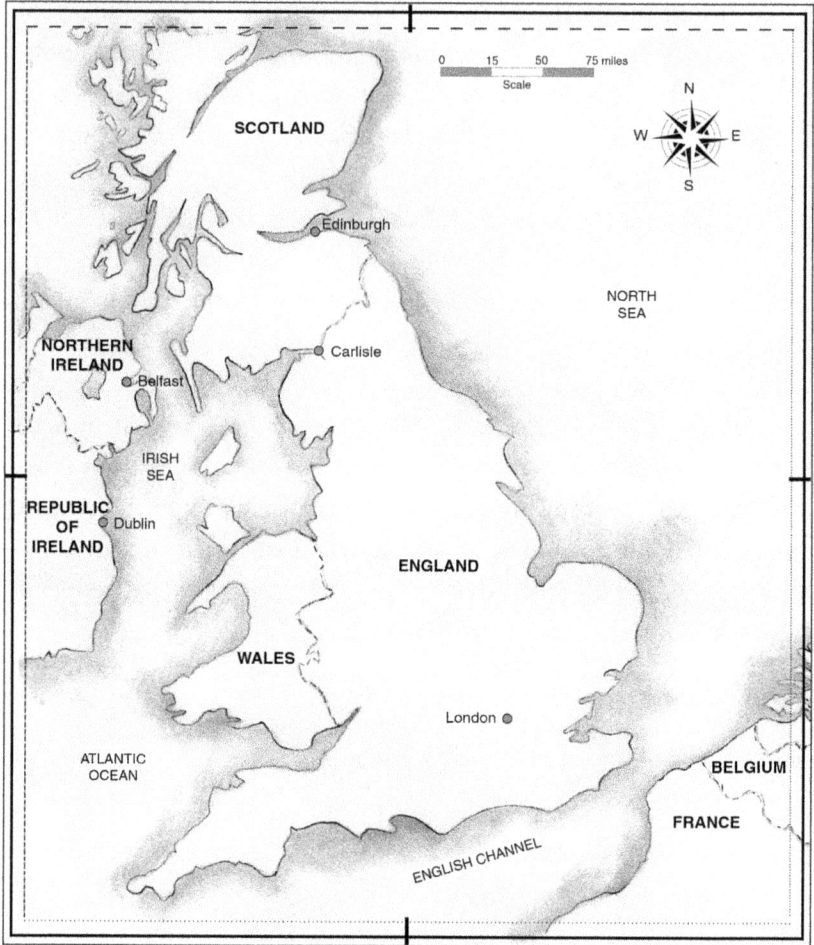

Map of England, Scotland, Wales and Ireland

The castle and the river. Carlisle Castle superimposed over the River Eden. The castle was built over an old Roman fort from the first century CE—on the contested border between England and Scotland, close to the River Eden and about four miles from Thomas Blacklocke's birthplace of Crosby-on-Eden.

finding thomas blacklocke
on virginia's eastern shore

THOMAS BLACKLOCKE WAS my first ancestor to alight the shores of America. He arrived from England at the Chesapeake Bay area sometime before 1622, as a newcomer to the struggling Jamestown Colony. His presence on the Eastern Shore was first documented on page 54 of *Lists of the Living and the Dead in Virginia, February 16, 1623*, as being among the living on a small plantation across the bay after surviving the Powhatan Nation uprising known as the Massacre of 1622.[1]

It was Thomas's name on that list that first drew me into his story. Though I was able to track down some facts of his life through land deeds and county records, conflicting opinions remain among his descendants about parts of his story. I confess that gaps in this history persisted for me when I could find no name on a passenger list, no marriage certificate, no portrait, nor letters to verify our relationship. As I pieced together what I could of his personal life, I searched history books for historical context.

I decided to go in person to the Eastern Shore's Accomac Public Library to see what else I might learn about him from their vast collection of local records of this early English colony. My trip took me north on Highway 13, crossing the long bridge over the Chesapeake Bay, up the middle of Virginia's Eastern Shore, closing in on the town of Accomac, named for the Indigenous nation that once lived there.

What I wanted, also, was to find the natural world he inhabited there—a world I fell in love with while reading the late anthropologist Helen Rountree's vibrant writing about the natural history of the Chesapeake Bay area and how the physical environment of this place shaped its social, cultural, and political histories.[2]

I went to the Eastern Shore to experience the lush beauty and natural abundance borne of a multitude of bio-networks arising from the mix of fresh and saltwater that characterize its proximity to the Atlantic Ocean and the many rivers and creeks that open into the bay, each opening an estuary—a place where a river or stream meets the bay to rise and fall each day with the tides. Shifting fresh and salt waters provide habitat to diverse species of living things that find their specific niches around the bay according to their tolerance to salt—manifesting a tight ecosystem of survival that evolved over a cosmic timeline.

The Chesapeake Bay follows the form of an underwater crater caused by a meteor that crashed into Earth thirty-five million years ago. The bay was created from a slow process of geologic and meteorological changes—including multiple ice ages—that stabilized around 3,000 years ago as its shoreline. The ancient bowl at the bottom of the bay was discovered by humans only a few decades ago, using seismic profiling technology. New knowledge of the crater's existence, shape, and depth cleared up previous scientific mysteries, like why groundwater near the bay is unusually salty and why the York and James Rivers flow backward from the bay.[3] This recent discovery explaining previously unexplainable phenomena reminded me that conditions in my own life were set in motion through the lives of ancestors, even in the absence of my awareness of them. I came to excavate my own family history to find out what I've known without knowing why.

The history of European settlement on the Eastern Shore of Virginia is critical to the story of my ancestor Thomas. It begins, however, with the English settlement of Jamestown on the western shore of the Chesapeake Bay. Three ships landed in 1607, financed by the Virginia Company as part of an ambitious attempt of English noblemen to find gold and a fast passage to China.[4] They settled as far up on the James River as possible to keep themselves safe from the Spanish. In every other way they chose possibly the worst place. It was swampy and lacked drainage for sewage, creating optimal conditions for rampant spread of disease. Crop failure, drought, poor soil, lack of labor and technical expertise, poor leadership, poor supply chain planning, starvation, in-fighting, and arrogance also characterized this endeavor.

Arguably, the colonists who survived long enough to ensure the survival of the colony did so only because the indigenous Powhatan people, whose land they invaded, shared food with the English. The Powhatan leader, called "Powhatan" by the English, did not believe the colony would last and, therefore, was not enough of a threat to defend against. He was also interested in what the English had to trade, so he let things play out for a while. His brother and advisor, Opechancanough, however, wanted to get rid of the intruders as quickly as possible.[5] As events unfolded, Opechancanough was right to worry. Reading the history of the European colonization and settlement in America is heartbreaking. I know how it ends for the Indigenous people, yet I keep wishing at every plot point something different will happen.

The Eastern Shore peninsula, just across the bay from Jamestown, was more hospitable to outsiders. With four centuries of hindsight, it is hard for me to believe the English waited a decade to settle it. Jamestown colonists who went there looking for a place to put a saltworks found a more temperate climate than where they were living. Fine, sandy soil made for richer farmland and larger corn yields than they had on the other side of the bay; a greater abundance of fish swam its many clear streams.

The English exploring the Eastern Shore also found the Accomac nation. The Accomac leader, Esmy Sichans, considered the English across the bay even less of a threat than did Powhatan, and was actually drawn to the English as lucrative customers for their corn surpluses. Thus, the Accomacs had a friendlier relationship with the English than did the Powhatans. The English found the Accomacs, I feel sad to report, "tractable."[6]

Jamestown colonists began growing tobacco to export, seizing on the high demand for tobacco in England. A steady stream of English men and women sailed and settled around the western shores of the Chesapeake, crowding out the Powhatan nation and threatening their survival. English leaders escalated their violent aggression to control the Powhatans; the Powhatans often retaliated, but the deck was stacked against them. Even after being helped by Powhatan, the English abducted and murdered Powhatan people to take land and food away from them. When they gained control of Powhatan land, English colonists ignored traditional land use practices in favor of English farming methods, damaging the local ecology.[7] Starvation and illness made it impossible for Powhatans to defend themselves against the never-ending invasion of English settlers.

By 1621, the English colony had not only survived despite so much that had gone wrong, but were a thousand people strong, inhabiting multiple settlements fanning out from the original fort.[8]

Meanwhile, Opechancanough took on the leadership of a somewhat destabilized Powhatan empire. Tired of the constant conflict with the English, he began plans for a large-scale assault to remove them all from the Chesapeake's western shores. Opechancanough asked his Eastern Shore Accomac allies to supply him with poisonous plants that grew there—probably spotted cowbane—to make their arrows deadlier. The Accomac leader, wanting to maintain the amicable relationship he had with a small English settlement now living on the Eastern Shore, refused Opechancanough's request, breaking his tenuous ties with the Powhatan empire. He also warned the English on both sides of the bay of the impending attack.[9]

When he found out the English had been warned, Opechancanough delayed the assault and changed his attack strategy, feigning a new friendliness with his enemies. On March 22, 1622, his warriors walked into English settlements and knocked on doors, unarmed—a common occurrence. Settlers invited them in and offered them food and drink, which they accepted. Then, with whatever heavy or sharp object they could find at hand, they killed the members of the house. Whole families were murdered and homes were burned down. About a third of the thousand settlers were killed, and many more died afterward from starvation or disease because of the disruption of spring planting.[10]

In the end, the colony survived because so many new immigrants continued to arrive, hungry to own their own land, paid for by the starvation and eventual demise of Indigenous nations living there before them. Thomas' life was spared because he was living on the safe side of the bay, making my eventual existence possible.

How do I feel about that? How could I not feel grateful on one hand, and sorrowful on the other? My stomach churns when I read about innocent children and their parents dying this way. I feel equal revulsion at the English brutalization of the Powhatans that motivated this assault. I hold these conflicting feelings in tension with one another when I hear this story, and every other one I encounter throughout my ancestor journey. I know there is trauma in the telling of them, and I do so cautiously and for the purpose of giving air to the festering wounds that their exposure to the air may heal.

When I first read this story, it worried me that the Accomacs, by not selling the Powhatans the cowbane, and by warning the English, had sold out their Indigenous brothers and sisters. However, the political reality was more complex than the usual "us versus them" narrative about Europeans and Indigenous people. The nations already living in America did not see themselves as all one people any more than the British, French, Spanish and Dutch saw themselves, on either side of the Atlantic, as one people. European and Indigenous nations continually shifted alliances among themselves and with each other.

The Accomac leader believed he was doing the right thing. His experience with the English was different from the Powhatans'. Not as many English people were living where he was living—yet; they were not encroaching so far into his lands—yet; or demanding stores of food at gunpoint or stealing his kin—yet. The English were useful to him. Getting along was a good idea—initially.

⤳⤳⤳

Not long after the Powhatan assault, my ancestor Thomas married a woman named Rachel. Thomas and Rachel had a son in 1628, also named Thomas—the first of my ancestors born on American soil. The younger Thomas traveled to England in his teens or twenties, possibly for schooling. There he met, married, and had a child with Anne Christian. Land grants given to Southey Littleton for providing their passages back to the Eastern Shore are documented in Accomac County records. Thomas and Christian eventually held deed to land themselves. Thomas Jr. was an active citizen. He did jury duty once a year for many years; periodically he was required to provide services as a road surveyor.[11]

These two generations of Blacklockes were tobacco farmers like their colonial Eastern Shore neighbors. Thomas Jr. and Anne Christian had several children, one of whom was also named Thomas. But it was another son, John William, born in 1671, from whom I am descended. At some unknown date, John William changed his last name to Blaylock and moved across the Chesapeake Bay to Louisa County, Virginia.

Perhaps, not being the oldest son and not in line to inherit land, he may have left the Eastern Shore for more open spaces. Several generations of farmers down John William's line, Blaylock became "Blalock," and a son was born in the mountains of (what is now called) North Carolina and named Etheldred Blalock. He served in the Confederate army in the US Civil War. One of his many children was a daughter named Margaret Louise Blalock. She married Thomas Bryson Deaver in Haywood County, and they had a daughter, Bertha Louise. Bertha married Joeberry Columbus Kuykendall. Bertha was my mother's maternal grandmother, my great-grandmother. Her firstborn, a daughter, Sophronie Ethel, was my maternal grandmother. Bertha and Joeberry grew tobacco themselves on their farm near Dix Creek and the Pigeon River, on the backside of Cold Mountain.

<hr />

Farm households on the newly settled Eastern Shore often included several stages of blended families resulting from remarriage after the death of a mother in childbirth or from smallpox. Tobacco was a labor-intensive crop on the Eastern Shore, and the need for additional help was constant. An indentured servant or two and their families might also have lived within the same household. Accomac people resisted English attempts to hire them as farmhands because the English were too harsh with their laborers and had poor hygiene. The Accomacs were also not comfortable with the settlers' living arrangements with non-family members.[12]

Despite their beliefs about the English, the Accomac nation sought to coexist peacefully with these farmers on the Eastern Shore. A mutually respectful and equitable relationship never became a reality, however. With the 1622 assault fresh in their memories, colonial settlers generally mistrusted all Indigenous peoples, unable to differentiate among Native nations. The Accomacs were never extended the trust by the English that their leader, Esmy Sichans, believed he had earned with his warning about the assault.[13]

A land rush on the Eastern Shore created intense pressure for Accomac people to sell land, sometimes in response to threats of violence. White settlers exploited the generally peaceful intentions of the Accomacs and used any excuse to override previous promises, pushing themselves beyond the boundaries into which they had been welcomed. The numbers of Accomacs dwindled from deaths due to starvation, illness,[14] and I can imagine, broken hearts. Their genocide was caused not by large-scale, bloody, violent attacks but by a slow death from disrespect, neglect, and abuse. All coming to a sorrowful end. And once gone, it was easy for the settlers to pretend the Native people had never been there, that it had always been the settlers' land. No guilt, and no one to apologize to.

I feel the weight of this history. My ancestors the Blacklocke's farmed land originally inhabited by the Accomac nation. I imagine the Blacklockes gave little thought to the pressure their presence put on the productive capacity of the land or how their farming practices, radically different from those of the Accomacs, rendered the land less fertile. They were part of an English colony. The English elite wanted them to be there to take pressure off their nation's boiling pot of troubles.

Thomas and his family took what they wanted for themselves. No doubt they felt that they had worked hard for it, made sacrifices for it, and deserved what they had. This continues to be a common sentiment in our country. In childhood memories, I can hear my father's often repeated refrain, "I worked hard for every penny I've ever had," reflecting beliefs of relatives on both sides of my family. And it is true that my ancestors worked hard; but it is also true that White settlers everywhere pushed themselves to the front of the line for everything, and all the land my maternal grandfather ever held title to was first taken from the Cherokee nation as part of the spoils of war.

<hr />

As part of my exploration of the natural beauty of the Eastern Shore that Helen Rountree's writings had drawn me to, I walked, early one morning, through the woods in Kiptopeke State Park (named after the brother of the Accomac leader, Esmy Sichan) to the bayside shore near the southern tip of the peninsula. I noted the layers of plant life from water to woods—from pepperbush and Yaupon to Virginia red cedar, American holly and loblolly pines. I listened to a symphony of cardinals, bobwhite quails, chickadees, and wrens, wishing I knew which birds were singing which part; I remembered reading that the English who arrived in Jamestown were unfamiliar with the songbirds, particularly cardinals, so abundant in this area.[15]

On the ocean side, I spent an afternoon at the Nature Conservancy's Brownsville Reserve. I had no human company as far as I could see or hear—just birds and bugs and lush plant life. My self-directed walking tour began on a high marsh habitat with salt tolerant wax myrtle and more red cedar. From the forest I heard the woodpeckers. I learned that dead trees standing in marshland, poetically, are called "snags," providing habitat for owls, flying squirrels and rat snakes. My favorite places were the salt marshes because of the abundant grasses that grow there—salt meadow cordgrass, black needle rush, and cattails, like the ones Mother would make Daddy stop by the side of the road for. A half dozen egret lounged in a wetland created from an old irrigation pond.

The landscape became a dreamscape as I imagined Thomas and Rachel walking through the woods in their heavy English clothes during the summer heat, wondering whether they found a way to lighten their attire, pretty sure their bodies were never as exposed as the Accomac bodies were. I fell even more in love with what grows in these liminal spaces between saltwater, freshwater, and solid ground, wanting to protect it from the climate catastrophe on its way. I took photographs here and everywhere else to keep all the beauty strong in my memory and to share with others what I see and how I see it.

The younger Thomas helped survey footpaths that surely became roads for carts and later for cars. Highway 13 is likely part of a route he helped survey. Most roads here are two-lane roads, and many are unpaved. Farms take up most of the space. North-south roads could not be built close to the edges of this place because so many small creeks and tributaries along the shoreline snake up into the land.

Though the peninsula does not seem big for someone driving a car, it was a whole day's walk across the width of it when the Blacklockes were here; with no horses, walking was the only means of transportation.

The last full day of my visit I found what I was most looking for—the land where two generations of Blacklockes lived. The librarian at the Accomac reading room gave me a map and helped me identify the tract the county records identified as theirs. It is on the bayside, about halfway up the peninsula near a tributary called Hunting Creek. It required some careful driving along small tortuous roads. I was not confident my GPS signal would last all the way there, but it did. The land adjacent to Hunting Creek is now residential, but there also is farmland nearby. I drove right up to the edge of the water where gorgeous grasses swayed in the soft wind. This place is remote. I felt acutely alone, but not lonely.

The land along the creek was not as pristine as I wanted to think my ancestors' homeland would be. There was litter in the grass; the asphalt road ended abruptly, swollen and cracked around the edges. Standing outside my car, I looked over the water, felt gentle breezes, and inhaled the faint saltiness coming off it.

I stood where past worlds continually transformed themselves into newer ones. I closed my eyes and saw the seventeenth century Hunting Creek of my imagination, finding Thomas Blacklocke, with a place to fish and launch boats to carry their tobacco wherever it needed to go. And then I saw back further in time, the Accomac women harvesting grasses for mats and men trapping fish. I mourned the loss that I know is coming for them. Then I went even further back in time, many millennia ago, the land and water without humans, just the deep blue with a silver shimmer of spring fish runs, tall, yellow-green grasses, maybe a turtle, a raccoon or a deer or two.

This is where I find Thomas Blacklocke, on the edge of Hunting Creek, on the bayside of Virginia's Eastern Shore, near the location of land several generations of Blacklocke ancestors held title to. I took this photograph standing near my car parked at the very edge of an asphalt road on the backside of a residential area. The "rocks" in the center of this image were actually chunks of asphalt broken off from the road. It was a late afternoon toward the end of May. Gentle breezes were blowing. There was no cell service where I was; I was very aware of my isolation from human company, and yet I also was aware of ancestors' previous presence in this space.

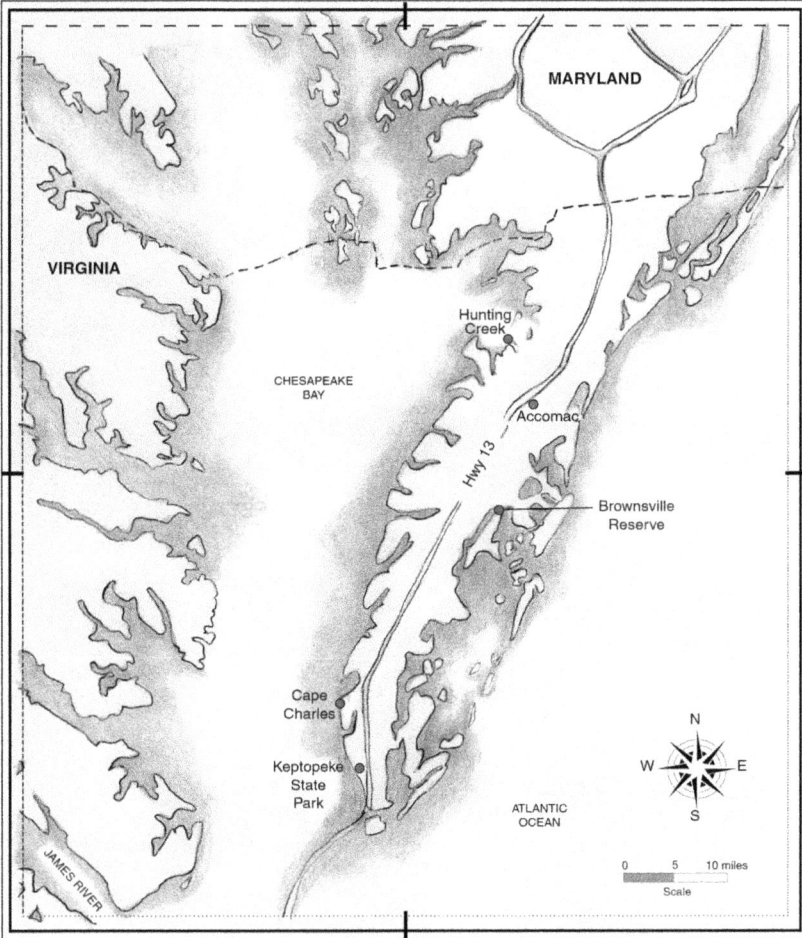

Map of Chesapeake Bay and Virginia's Eastern Shore

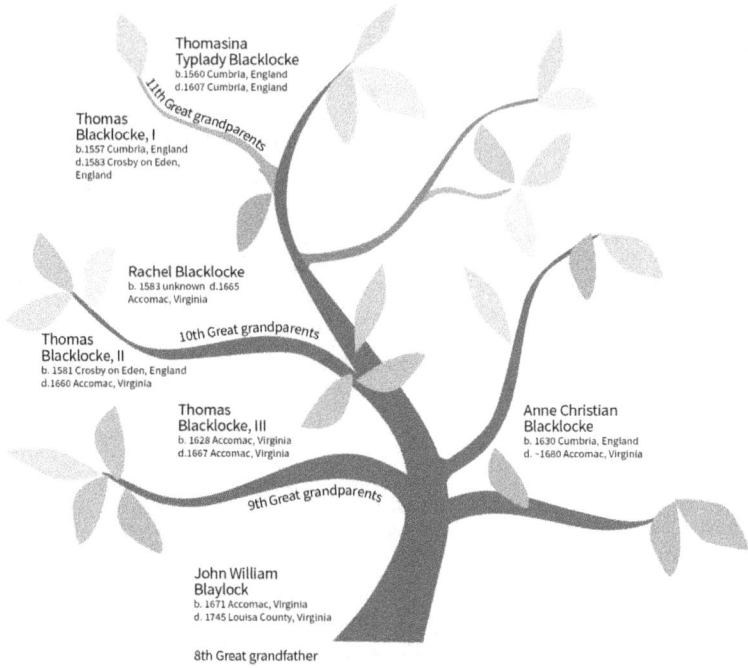

Thomasina
Typlady Blacklocke
b.1560 Cumbria, England
d.1607 Cumbria, England

11th Great grandparents

Thomas
Blacklocke, I
b.1557 Cumbria, England
d.1583 Crosby on Eden,
England

Rachel Blacklocke
b. 1583 unknown d.1665
Accomac, Virginia

Thomas
Blacklocke, II
b. 1581 Crosby on Eden, England
d.1660 Accomac, Virginia

10th Great grandparents

Thomas
Blacklocke, III
b. 1628 Accomac, Virginia
d.1667 Accomac, Virginia

Anne Christian
Blacklocke
b. 1630 Cumbria, England
d. ~1680 Accomac, Virginia

9th Great grandparents

John William
Blaylock
b. 1671 Accomac, Virginia
d. 1745 Louisa County, Virginia

8th Great grandfather

*Family tree of Thomas Blacklocke (II), linking Carlisle, England with
Eastern Shore, Virginia.*

take me to the river
(the netherlands)

THE NETHERLANDS WAS the point of departure for another maternal lineage, the Kuykendalls, my mother's mother's father's family. I planned my activities for this trip by learning as much as I could about seventeenth century Netherlands before I got on the plane, but much of my itinerary just worked itself out while I was there. I stumbled into and over information that opened more new questions and insights than I knew to ask before I set out, finding myself in the loves and losses of my ancestors Stynte and Jacob, and in the Dutch culture in which they lived.

———— ∞ ————

During the several decades I did public health research, I often found myself in Amsterdam's Schiphol Airport, sometimes for hours, waiting to connect to flights to places like Kenya, Egypt, and Zimbabwe. I shopped, looked at art exhibits, and even took abstract black and white photographs of the airport's modern architecture. Other times, it was a breathless dash from one end to another to make a short connection. Only once did I set foot outside its doors during all those years, and then, that one time, I left only for a few hours to sleep and get some fresh air in a local neighborhood.

Yes, certainly, I had been curious about this country where I knew something about my ancestral connection to it. Still, in those years, my life was so tightly bound up by my multiple roles as mother, wife, daughter, and employee that I rarely spent an extra day for personal exploration. These many years later, however, with no one depending on my presence at home, visiting the places Jacob and Stynte were born and began their adult lives was the sole purpose of my being there. I made my way out of the airport, to a train, into the city, and onward.

∽

My attention during this trip was focused on the Netherlands of the early seventeenth century—Amsterdam's Golden Age—when it was the center of the global economy and a gathering place of peoples and ideas from around the world. It was in this milieu, in 1638, that my tenth great-grandparents, Stynte Douwes and Jacob Luurson, married. Each had left homes in different but recently united provinces to bask in the glow of Amsterdam's prosperity.

Stynte and Jacob, related to me through my mother's mother's father, Joeberry Columbus Kuykendall, left Europe two years after they married to work and live in the Netherlands' colony in America. In the Netherlands, I visited their respective birthplaces of Enkhuizen and Wageningen—lands inhabited by their families for centuries, if not millennia, before their births; lands where survival depended on keeping their lowlands above water. The story of these "nether lands" was, and continues to be, water.

∽

Three of Europe's largest rivers—the Rhine, the Meuse, and the Scheldt—drain into the North Sea by passing through places now known collectively as the Netherlands. The continually shifting patterns of these rivers, caused by winds and rains, also creates shifts in land boundaries. This area was part of the Roman Empire in the seventh or eighth centuries CE, when Germanic tribes first settled. The peaty soil, rich with spongy, decayed plant materials, was fertile land for farming, but it required constant substantial effort to keep it from drowning. As river waters rose and fell,[1] the sea was a "water-wolf" in the minds of the Dutch as it relentlessly devoured their fields[2].

Keeping the water at bay necessitated that all villagers worked together for everyone's benefit. Each person's well-being depended on everyone's well-being—a core tenet of the concept of the common good—a core value of Dutch people, then and now.[3]

Over the next couple of centuries, Dutch people created dikes to wall off the water from outside and cut channels through the peat to let the bogs' excess waters drain into rivers. As peat bogs were drained, the soil sank back underwater. More dikes had to be built, and the cycle continued. Windmills—the first image I conjure when I think of Holland—generated the power that created new farmlands, called "polders." The wind turned large wooden screws that slowly pulled water from the wetlands.

———— ❧❧❧ ————

Stynte was born in 1617, in the bustling northern harbor town of Enkhuizen north of Amsterdam, within sight of the dazzling blue waters of the large shallow bay that was the Zuiderzee. These and other waters would transport her to new worlds and sustain her in them. During Stynte's lifetime, this Dutch port, second in size only to Amsterdam, teemed with hundreds of ships, their sails blowing in the wind like so much laundry hung out to dry. While in Enkhuizen, I, too, saw these bright azure waters filled with sails—sails of smaller, recreational boats, from the nearby shores of Stynte's birthplace.

Enkhuizen is in the northern province of Holland, now one of six other somewhat distinct states that united less than a century before Stynte's birth to form the nation-state of the Netherlands. The mouth of the Zuiderzee opened south from the North Sea about sixty miles inland and thirty miles across. It offered a direct route via passenger barges to many towns along its 200 miles of coastline and likely delivered Stynte to Amsterdam.[4]

I am intrigued by the transformations of the land and water here, entities I had always considered fixed in place on the map, at least during lifetimes. The Zuiderzee that Stynte knew as a child had been previously a freshwater lake, known as the Almere or Eel Lake, connected to the North Sea by the River Vile. This lake turned into a seawater bay on 14 December 1287 by St. Lucia's Flood, one of the deadliest in human history. Before the deluge, sand barges and glacier-formed boulder-sized clay barriers had separated the lake from the sea. A storm in the North Sea on St. Lucia's Day flooded the River Vile and the barriers between Almere Lake and the North Sea. Between 50,000 and 80,000 people were killed by torrents of the rising water that claimed entirely what had only moments before been homes and farmlands along the riverbanks.[5]

My heart stopped a beat as I read of the farmers and housewives and children whose lives were extinguished without warning. I thought about how everything can change in an instant, and how none of us really knows how our lives might be altered by forces beyond our control or imagination.

Enkhuizen, Stynte's birthplace three centuries later, was spared from the worst of that flood. After the previous barriers between the lake and the sea had been submerged by the flood, Enkhuizen found itself on the edge of a bay that opened directly into the North Sea. This easier access to the larger sea gave Enkhuizen greater trading prominence. The same flood provided Amsterdam, still a village in the thirteenth century, an open waterway to the North Sea and an invitation to become an ever more significant center of commerce over the next several centuries.

———∞∞∞———

Modern-day Enkhuizen reflects its abundant history and small-town charm down every cobblestone street. I took the hour-long train ride north from Amsterdam on a bright Saturday morning in June, passing by acres and acres of lush green farmland edged with drainage canals. Like me, many people on my train were on their way to visit the Zuiderzeemuseum on the outskirts of the town proper.

Enkhuizen's harbor and the lives of its residents changed dramatically in the early twentieth century when the Zuiderzee was rendered useless for international commercial trade because of the buildup of mud and sediment around its edges. Its residents continued to rely on fishing for their living, however, until 1932. To prevent new flooding and allow the dredging of new land, a human-built barrier, the Afsluitdijk, created a new lake, Lake Ijsselmeer, which extends south to Amsterdam.

The building of this dam has been controversial, in part because of its effect on commercial fishing, and because of possible influence on the ecosystem. Its economic blow to the fishing industry has been partially softened by the development of the Zuiderzeemuseum and a marina for recreational sailing.[6] Not knowing this history before my arrival, I walked through the museum with a tourist's naivety about the mixture of heartbreak and desire held in these grounds.

From the train station, the Zuiderzeemuseum complex is accessible by ferry or foot. I chose the water. The museum's open-air section is a re-creation of a village from the nearby Urk Island in the early 1900s. Though it represented life a couple of centuries after Stynte lived here, it still gave me a sense of the scale of things and the technology available to her, neither of which had changed dramatically from her lifetime until then.

I walked through small houses, saw gardens and orchards. In the water ducks and herons bobbed next to boats used for negotiating the canals. I also saw large lime kilns where seashells were turned into brick mortar. Women and men in wooden shoes demonstrated basket-weaving and sail-making. I turned the big screw next to a small windmill by hand and felt in my arm muscles the actual effort and time it takes to bring water out of swampy lands.

Outside a village house near the shore, whole fresh herring were grilled in traditional wood-burning ovens and sold to hungry tourists for lunch. I enthusiastically partook of this delicacy served on paper plates, while sitting on wooden benches, thigh-to-thigh with the other visitors. Copious amounts of herring were the North Sea's bountiful gift to Holland and the engine that drove the Netherlands' initial economic wealth. In the beginning, this herring fed only the Dutch, but new shipping and preservation technologies in the fourteenth century gave Holland the edge it needed to dominate international trade.

Enkhuizen was a key port for the herring trade, and herring was a dominant force in its residents' lives. Its coat of arms is three red herring against a blue background.[7] As I sat there, I imagined the bright blue sea shimmering with herring so abundant men could reach out and touch them. I remembered also what I had read about the abundance of fish in the rivers flowing from Virginia's Chesapeake Bay during the same time period. The good earth, so full of life, fed my ancestors of different lineages, simultaneously, in disparate places.

By the mid-1300s, the Dutch exported over 200 million herring a year to Poland, France, Germany, and Prussia. Dutch warships protected the herring trade, building their capacity for naval defense, at one time stronger than England's. The label "Holland Herring" guaranteed government-regulated product quality. Wealth from herring created capital to discover new markets through global exploration.

Dutch trading power exploded around the world as more goods to trade, including human labor, were found in new destinations[8]. Hollanders unabashedly loved making money. The sea gave them entrée, and they used it to its most financially lucrative, if morally dubious,[9] advantage.

Deeper into the museum were looms used by women to weave grasses harvested along the wetlands' edges. A grainy, three-minute black and white film from early in the twentieth century documented the harvesting and use of these grasses. The moving pictures took me, trance-like, into another place and time as I watched the communal effort of men to harvest, bundle, and then clean the grasses after being joined by women to help; the dark, heavy fabrics and design simplicity of traditional dress I imagined Stynte wearing; and the rowboats and horse-drawn carts used to transport the grasses. I loved, too, the woven mats of reed that were on display, the beauty in everyday necessities.

Telling Stynte's story, like Thomas's before this, and Jacob's, and everyone else's to follow, means weaving together natural and political histories that created the tapestry on which their lives were lived. The Germanic tribes living in this watery place were converted from their pagan religions to the Christianity of the Church of Rome around the sixth century and governed under relatively laissez-faire Roman administrative rule. In 1543, less than a century before Stynte's birth, Charles V of Spain ruled on behalf of the Holy Roman Empire. He sought to strengthen his authority over this previously-ignored swamp on the western edge of Europe. Driven by his passion for Catholicism and the threat of the Protestant Reformation, he initiated a brutal inquisition, grotesquely murdering thousands judged to be heretics.[10] When I read about this terror, I wondered, not for the first time, how anyone could justify evil in the name of Christianity. How could they misinterpret Jesus's message of non-violence so horrifically? I also wondered this as I read stories of European contact with Indigenous people in their colonies across the Atlantic Ocean.

Religious intolerance, lack of administrative autonomy, *and* increased taxes levied to pay for the slaughter of its own subjects led to the Dutch Revolt against Charles's son, King Philip II, in 1568. The revolt turned into the Eighty Years War, also known as the Dutch War for Independence, manifesting as a civil war between the opposing forces of the Roman Catholics who supported the Catholic king, Phillip II; versus Lutherans, Anabaptists, and Calvinists who supported new ideas about religious tolerance and individual freedom.[11]

The rebellion was led by Willem of Orange. Though initially appointed to govern the Dutch states for Charles V, Willem of Orange was appalled by the cruelty instigated against Protestants. He used his influence to beg for leniency, but his requests fell on deaf ears. He believed he had a moral duty to defend the rebels and lead the revolt. This protracted war is a long story of many battles, beheadings, and villages sacked and burned to the ground, with many twists and turns, including the murder of Willem himself. Enkhuizen was the site of a significant Dutch defeat of the Spanish in 1573 in the Battle of Zuiderzee.

No winning battle sustained the peace for very long, however, until May of 1578, when Protestants took control of Amsterdam. The war to unite the Netherlands' provinces was not yet won, but this was considered by historians as the beginning of the end. May 26th became known as The Alteration—a turn toward religious tolerance and freedom.[12]

After I left the indoor museum, I wandered around the town of Enkhuizen, laid out as it had been for centuries. I saw two Dutch Reform churches—Zuiderkerk and Westerkerk. Built in the fifteenth century, originally as Catholic churches, both were repurposed in 1572 for Protestant use after the Reformation made its way to Holland. The Reformation brought with it a so-called "iconoclastic fury." Images of Christ and the saints were destroyed because Protestants considered them idolatrous and also in retribution for the barbarism of the inquisition. In these two churches in Enkhuizen, as in Dutch towns everywhere, statues were destroyed and paintings covered over to remove all "graven" images found to be an affront to God. In my mind, this "fury" pales compared with the gruesome murders of the inquisition.

Stynte's father's name was Douwes Wiggersz. He was born in 1592 in Enkhuizen. He lived on Westerstraat (West Street) within sight of the Westerkerk, a Dutch Reform church that I also visited. He married Stynte's mother, Agniete Coensen, in 1608. Both were young at the time—Agniete was fourteen, and Douwes was sixteen. They had been baptized as children and then married as adolescents in the Dutch Reformed Church. No mention is made of Douwes' occupation on any document I found. Many men from his village were fishermen, but he could have been involved in other work necessary for this port city—commerce, farming, or loading and unloading ships at the dock.

Stynte's was the only birth documented for Agniete and Douwes, and her birth occurred nine years after they wed, in 1617. Her mother died in 1638, at the relatively young age of 44. Stynte was 21. The next chronological fact I know about Stynte is that 22 days after her mother's death, she and Jacob Luursen from Wageningen registered to get married in Amsterdam.

Was Stynte really an only child, or was this an artifact of insufficient documentation? Given the relatively accurate records kept through the churches at the time, I'm inclined to think it is true that she was an only child, but then I also wondered why. Most women at this time were having many babies. Perhaps her mother had trouble conceiving or carrying a pregnancy to term, or maybe there were early infant deaths, and Stynte alone survived. And it made me think that if her mother had difficulties related to childbirth, perhaps she was in poor health. And this made me wonder about Stynte's life growing up without siblings, what burdens it put on or took away from her. Questions I could not answer from the genealogical record, but which made me think of her life as a woman in these times and compare her experiences with mine.

Perhaps Stynte left Enkhuizen for Amsterdam because her family needed her to earn money to support herself, and possibly contribute to their welfare as well. Perhaps her father's business was not so good, or maybe there were extra expenses if her mother were ill. I would rather imagine a happier scenario for this ancestor of mine, however, wanting to see myself in her.

I'd like to think she went to Amsterdam for independence and adventure, wanting something more than she had in Enkhuizen. I create a story in my mind about her as a spirited young woman in Amsterdam, falling in love with Jacob as she sees him from afar, even before she meets him in person, even as he sees her and falls in love with her as well. Their mutual sense of adventure eventually propelling their journey to America.

Enkhuizen was the birthplace of Stynte Douwes. A mermaid statue is superimposed over Enkhuizen wetlands on the shore of the North Sea. Mermaids were good luck charms for sailors and it is said that they liked to play in the grasses at the edge of the sea when the tide was high, but had to beware not to get caught by a low tide. Grasses in wetlands like these were harvested for weaving mats. The reeds were cleaned by women and men and prepared for drying and weaving on a loom. Wetlands foster plant and animal diversity; grasses provide places for small fish, reptiles, and amphibians to live. It is said that mermaids would come close to shore by hiding among the grasses to get a glimpse of humans, but they would have to leave before the tide went out, so they were not stranded on dry land.

The man Stynte married in Amsterdam, Jacob Luursen, was a stonemason and bricklayer by trade. He had made his way to Amsterdam from his home in the southeast province of Gelderland. Born in 1616, a year before Stynte, Jacob was baptized in the Dutch

Reformed Church inside Wageningen's walls, just north of the Neder Rijn, the Lower Rhine River. His father was Luur Cornelius, born in 1590, his mother, was Christinje, born in 1594, both in Waginengen. They married in 1609. Jacob had an older sister, Jannetje, and a younger brother, Urbanus. Luur died in 1619 when all the children were young; Christinje died only three years afterward, in 1622[13], the same year Thomas Blacklocke was listed among the living on Virginia's Eastern Shore.

Though Jacob Luursen sired a son from whom my maternal grandmother's paternal Kuykendall family descended, Jacob was not himself called by the surname "Kuykendall," following instead the Dutch custom of being called "the son of Luur." Kuykendall was not a family name until his son had his own family in America, after the New Netherlands came under British rule as New York. Various theories about the origin of "Kuykendall" are espoused on genealogic sites. The most persuasive one *to me* was that it was an Americanization of old Dutch "kijk-in-'t-dal" that means "view over the valley."[14] In a correspondence with the town's historian, he told me he disagreed with this interpretation based on his more nuanced linguistic and cultural knowledge of this. Despite this, I came here in hopes of finding this view and this valley. I was not disappointed.

Historical society resource materials informed me that Wageningen was first inhabited by Batavian tribes who were soon ruled by the Roman Empire. The oldest written records of Wageningen were dated 838 CE. In 1263 (a couple of decades before the St. Lucia's Flood survived by Stynte's ancestors), Wageningen received civic or town rights from Rome, allowing its residents to build a wooden fence and a brick wall around the town, ringed for protection by a moat. The castle, built outside the wall, fortified the land inside and housed the bailiff and soldiers protecting the town. A bridge over the moat flanked by two towers provided access to The Castle. Its cellar was used for baking and brewing beer, beer a safer drinking option than water. A few identifiable remnants of the original castle and the wall exist. However, most of these structures were destroyed by invading and occupying enemies, including the French in 1672 and the Germans in 1945.[15]

The Lower Rhine runs along the outskirts of Wageningen. To the west of the old town is the southern edge of the Veluwe, a large, wooded area over 1,100 square kilometers in size. The Veluwe is an elevated ridge, formed over 200,000 years ago by ice sheets pushing up the hard substrata from below, a geological formation known as a glacial "push moraine." Hills one hundred meters in height now over- look wide-open flatlands south to the river.[16]

A short distance to the west, present-day Wageningen is protected from Rhine floodwaters by a set of dikes. During the winter, when the river waters rise, the lower dike is opened to allow flooding into an expansive water meadow. A second, higher dike is designed to protect against residential flooding on the water meadow's outskirts, but some flooding always occurs in houses closest to it. People who live in these places tolerate this known risk for the sake of being close to this wild, usually dry, fertile field.[17]

The town archivist informed me via email that guided tours are available through the local historical society headquartered over the castle cellar's remains. I quickly arranged one several weeks before my trip. The day of my appointment, nervous about being late, I left Amsterdam on the first train out and got there ahead of schedule. I planned to wait over a cup of coffee, but my guide, Gon, heard that I was to arrive early and hopped on her bike to meet me. She was tall, had short blonde windblown hair with bangs. She looked fit and ready for a morning of walking. I knew when I first saw her, with her wide smile and the easy, open way she moved across the bus station to meet me, that this would be a good day.

Gon is a retired professor from the nearby agricultural university for which the town is well-known. The rich, diverse soils of the Rhine floodplain made it an ideal location, in 1876, for the first Dutch college of this type.

Gon and I drank coffee at the hotel café while we planned our morning. Centuries merged for me when I found out that the Hotel De Wereld was one of two inns just outside the town gates that dated back to the time Jacob was here. The original stone cellar floor is still there, but the rest of the current structure was built in the nineteenth century.

I quite liked Gon. We were similar in age. Both of us had traveled extensively to developing countries to do research work, mine health and hers, agriculture. We both had an interest in cultures different than our own. I liked that she gave time and energy to the well-being of her community, her being with me as a volunteer tour guide on a Saturday morning just one example of how she did this.

⸎

While still in the cafe, Gon told me, "We have this place—they call it a mountain, but you know there is no place very far from sea level here. But some hills were pushed up by glaciers a very long time ago, and on one of these hills, there is a nice hotel where you can get lunch and look over the valley with a good view of the Rhine River."

Bingo! I said, "Well, that's interesting to me because it seems my family name, in old Dutch, describes a place like this." I showed her a copy of the documents I brought with me, explaining the various notions put forth about this.

She said, "Well, of course, we can't know for sure, but it is certainly possible that this is the place your grandfather wanted to remember. I will get you on the right bus at the end of our tour, and you can see it for yourself."

Perhaps she was humoring me, but I still felt the pleasure of believing puzzle pieces were falling into place.

During our several-hour walk-about, I learned quite a bit about World War II Wageningen and the signing of the peace treaty. I also learned about its small-town politics—how citizens, through planned "actions," got unwanted local policy changed or reversed—and also about the Wageningen Agricultural University's history and workings. We walked along the path that rings the upper dike between the wide water meadow and the lower dike adjacent to the Rhine. I gained an appreciation for the continually changing boundaries between water and land. I saw what was left of the wall that stood there when Jacob was alive.

Though I was interested primarily in its history up through the early seventeenth century, the town, in fact, is possibly best known historically and internationally for its role in ending World War II. Early in the war, Wageningen sustained significant damage by the German army, but it was also the scene, at the end of the war, of the unconditional surrender of the German military to the Allied Forces in the assembly hall of Wageningen University, adjacent to the still-standing Hotel De Wereld (World Hotel), where the negotiators lodged.[18]

Gon told me that even before World War II started, when it seemed inevitable that Wageningen would be a German demolition target, the townspeople brought in faculty from the Delft School of Architecture to prepare for eventual reconstruction after the war. The school's signature style was more modern and economical than the older buildings they replaced.[19] So it was not only from my father, but also from my Dutch ancestors I inherited my hard-core pragmatism, I thought. And also, it occurred to me that if the people I descended from on both sides of my family had not immigrated to America, they would have been people at war with each other. Of course, if they had

not immigrated to America, everything would have been different—
they would not have been my ancestors.

⊶∞⊷

We walked through the town inside those walls and around the brick,
cross-shaped church where Jacob's parents, Luur and Christinje, were
baptized and likely married. Named after John the Baptist (Johannes
de Doper), now called the Great Church (Grote Kerk), it is in the
same location as the single-aisle Romanesque church built in 1263.
The church passed from Roman Catholics to Protestants in 1578.
During World War II, as predicted, the city center was destroyed,
including the church. However, the church was rebuilt to look exactly
as it had before, all with the original bricks.[20] It made my heart smile
to know that people, amid the tragedy of war, continued to care about
continuity from generation to generation.

I wanted to go inside the church but was not able to because
repairs were being made to the clock tower, and some restorative work
was being done outside the church. The rest of the buildings, cafes
and hotels mostly, had been rebuilt as the townspeople had planned
before the war. While I walked around the church, a portal to deep
time opened to me. I imagined a small boy running through this
square, hair in the wind, a boy who would grow up to be a man who
took his wife and started a family across the ocean to a place he knew
little about but hoped the best for.

⊶∞⊷

I asked everyone I met in the Netherlands why people would leave the
Netherlands in the 1600s for a place so unknown. Perhaps I was
projecting onto their lives, but the physical risks were greater so
many centuries ago. The answer I got, over and over, was that people
left to escape poverty. Gon said this as well, but she also said that
travel and adventure are characteristic of the Dutch, likely true in

Jacob's time also. Dutch history of exploration and imperialism made this seem plausible. Gon had traveled around the world for her research job, as I had. Whereas Gon and I had always traveled with round-trip tickets to get us home, Jacob and Stynte moved to America with no anticipation of return. I think, with wonder, of their grit and strength.

When Jacob left Wageningen for Amsterdam, the Rhine River waters were a formidable opponent and keeping oneself fed was challenging. Wageningen's trade economy took a hit when the river changed course, moving farther south in 1421. Goods were moved across Europe on the Rhine from the earliest times of the Roman Empire just as they are today. Before and during Jacob's life, Rhine wine was the most frequently transported commodity along the river, but wood, wheat, cheese, salt, and fish were traded as well. Farmers in the area started growing another popular trade item of the seventeenth century: tobacco. This was likely after Jacob left this town but probably about the time the Blacklockes were growing it as a cash crop for export on Virginia's Eastern shore.[21]

The threat of hunger may have had more to do with Jacob's leaving Wageningen for Amsterdam than his leaving Amsterdam for New Netherlands. Knowing that his father and mother were both dead by the time he was six, my theory is that he went to Amsterdam with his older sister and younger brother soon after their mother's death to find a way to support themselves in the prosperous city. Perhaps they had relatives to take them in. Amsterdam was one of the first European cities to support orphanages, so perhaps they spent time in one of them. Jacob and his siblings stayed together for the rest of their lives—all going to New Netherlands as well. Jacob and his brother,

Urbanus, both became brick masons, an always useful trade, but especially in times of economic growth and foreign exploration.

———⟨∞⟩———

After my lovely tour of Wageningen, Gon walked with me to the small bus station where she had parked her bicycle. She gave me instructions about which bus to take, how to get to the restaurant from the bus stop, and then to get to a different train station back to Amsterdam. I was grateful for her attention to these details because it was always a little more complicated than I anticipated to navigate unknown territory. We took a selfie together, and I got on the bus. Only because she told the bus driver in Dutch where I should get off, however, did I get off at the right stop.

Once I did, I found my way to the hotel, a short walk down a path behind some woods not so readily seen from the road. Its design was modern compared with the old town feel of Wageningen; lots of people were having lunch outside. A broad field and the Rhine lay in the distance. After a salad and a Diet Coke®, I walked a few steps from the outdoor café to look over the Lower Rhine valley from the clearing there.

Several paths ran in both directions through some thick woods. Even within these woods, there were occasional openings through which I could see into the valley and river below. The trees in the woods are tall and old—some deciduous, some evergreen. The forest was cool, almost damp, a sacred quiet prevailing. I thought first of enchanted forests of fairy tales where humans might talk to animals, where witches might be plotting revenge, or a prince might appear. No less surreal, however, were my next thoughts of glaciers moving across this land, and the size and force it would take for one to push flat ground 100 meters into the air.

The trails extended farther than I took them. I did not go far in any one direction, alone as I felt in this place. These woods had a different atmosphere than those near my home: less cluttered with brush underneath. Trees towered higher, perhaps because of the elevation's abruptness compared with the meadows, or maybe because of the proximity to a large body of water that floods every spring up to its edges. I took many photographs with all three of my cameras, not knowing which one would best capture this forest's simultaneous majesty and charm.

Jacob's ghost did not step out from the trees to guide me through the woods, but I thought about him while I was there and asked myself what kind of house he would have lived in and if he would have known these woods as a boy. Perhaps his father, also my ancestor, grew up in these woods. What were the lives of Jacob's parents like here? Why did both parents die so young? At that moment in the forest, my heart hurt for Jacob, wishing he could have stayed in this beautiful place with living parents. His move to Amsterdam, however, is part of my story also. When we wish something had happened a different way, we must remind ourselves of the full consequences of such a thing, and let it be.

While I walked in the woods, looking through the trees to the river in the valley below, I believed Jacob's children eventually chose a name that their descendants believe referenced this place, and its loveliness and his happiness here were lodged so deeply in his heart that he told his children about it, children born in a world an ocean away. I felt this all the way down to the bones of my great grandmother Ethel, who was born many generations later on a real mountain in North Carolina that looked into a valley where the much smaller Dix Creek flowed.

Time travel. Jacob's descendant, Joeberry Kuykendall, my great-grandfather, sits with his dog, his image layered over one of the woods on the push moraine that overlooks the Lower Rhine River valley.

Amsterdam, where Stynte and Jacob married, and I presume, where they first met each other, was named for a dam built at the juncture of the Amstel River and the Zuiderzee. The lake that turned into a bay after the St. Lucia's Flood of 1287 allowed Amsterdam access to the North Sea. A dam, the Amsteldamme, was built to control flooding, the flooding a threat because the bay opened to the sea. Amsterdam remained a relatively small urban area for the next half-century. People who lived there made a living raising barley and rye or catching eel, pike, and carp in its marshy inlets. People lived in wooden huts with straw roofs and clay floors.[22]

A bizarre miracle in 1345 made Amsterdam a travel destination within the Holy Roman Empire for physical healing and spiritual cleansing. At a time when nearly everyone was a practicing Catholic, an old man attempting to take Holy Communion vomited up a Eucharist wafer, solid and whole. When nuns threw it on the fire to dispose of it, this host, a symbol of the body of Christ, did not burn. A church was built where the supernatural event occurred. Twice this church burned to the ground, but the wafer survived.[23]

Thousands of pilgrims made their way to Amsterdam, and many stayed; new churches were built, and at least 19 monasteries and convents were formed. Travelers and new residents brought money into the city; this influx of humans made digging the first canal rings around the town financially possible. The canals reduced the threat of flooding and made nearby waters more navigable. Coinciding with the rise of the lucrative herring trade, Amsterdam's economic strength built to the fever pitch that became its seventeenth century Golden Age.[24]

I stayed in a hotel across the street from the Jordaan, an area where working class people often lived. In contrast to other cities of the time, people of different economic statuses were interspersed among the wealthy—in part because the wealthy were more likely to be living in the heart of the city. The sizable buildings located on the canals housed residences, their businesses, and even their warehouses. Jacob and Stynte would have seen many of the houses I walked by every day around my hotel. The nearby Town Hall had been there, as had Amsterdam's Westerkerk (West Church), across the road from me, whose bells I heard multiple times daily. The tram right in front of it that I boarded from time to time, of course, was a recent addition.

I visited a special Rembrandt exhibit at the Dutch national Rijksmuseum. Rembrandt was living and painting in Amsterdam while Stynte and Jacob were there; presumably, they walked the same canal rings, saw the same people and buildings, possibly passing each other from time to time. Though most of what domi-nated the exhibit were Rembrandt's depictions of Bible stories and portraits of wealthy merchants or groups of businessmen, I paid more attention to the many quick sketches he made of landscapes in and around Amsterdam and portraits of people who were not rich. Rembrandt's renderings felt authentic—neither idealized nor pitiable, neither unusually beautiful, nor in rags, neither leisurely lounging, nor begging on the street. In all of them I looked for the faces of Stynte and Jacob, wanting to see how their lives were going, what was happening to them, whether they were okay or not.

I found more clues to Stynte and Jacob's lives at the National Maritime Museum. A restored ship that sits on the waters' edge is similar to one they would have sailed in to go to America. Onboard, I walked the space for the shared living quarters with stacked sleeping hammocks. With special virtual reality equipment, I flew like a bird over the harbor during the city's Golden Age, able to view sailors, seaman, and soldiers saying goodbye to loved ones as they embark on a ship at the quay. Inside the museum, more than fifty paintings glorified Amsterdam's Golden Age sea prowess.

An interactive exhibit focused on the dark side of Amsterdam's power: colonial domination, violence, and slavery, illustrated by the stories of an enslaved young woman, a peasant boy whose family's fishing livelihood was threatened by the creation of new land for development (a story that never ends), and a barge ride down the coast of the Zuiderzee toward Amsterdam. I pictured Jacob as the small boy and Stynte as the young woman riding in the barge.

———— ∞ ————

Before I left Amsterdam, I spent a day writing, walking, and taking photographs, transitioning from being in one place to being in another, something that happens so much more quickly in our modern world than it did for Jacob and Stynte. As I wrote, I imagined them as young adult residents of Amsterdam. I speculated about Stynte's life as a woman in those times and in this place. I wondered whether she worked as a domestic servant or in the market, even after she married Jacob.

From my reading of the genealogical records, I believe that Stynte and Jacob went to the New Netherlands before they had children, around 1640. And I still cannot get out of my mind questions about how they decided to do such an audacious thing. What of those they left behind? What an unpredictable way to begin a family. They were taking part in momentous times. They knew there were people who had been living in the land they were going to occupy. Had they thought at all about how their lives in New Netherlands affected the lives of people there before the Dutch?

I have continually second-guessed the fallout of my own leaving decisions, particularly the emotional upheaval in the lives of my children when I left my first marriage. I wonder how it continues to affect their lives and my relationships with them. The heartbreak is that leaving a marriage (but never in my mind, leaving my children) felt at the time like the only action I could take, but it still hurt people I love. I continue to struggle with the unknowable answer to the question of whether it would have hurt them less than if I had stayed, which I assumed at the time. I wonder to what extent Stynte and the other ancestors who left the Netherlands second-guessed their decisions to go to the New Netherlands once they settled into their lives here.

———— ❧ ————

The Dutch were more interested in using America as a trading post rather than settling it as a colony, though some settlers were still necessary. Wealthy Dutch residents could obtain large tracts of land in the New Netherlands as part of their "uppatroon" system if they brought over enough people to farm their lands productively. Kiliaen van Rensselaer was perhaps the most successful patroon, obtaining thousands of acres of land in and around where Albany, New York, now stands.[25] Van Rensselaer was from Gelderland, the same province as Jacob and his brother, Urbanus, and likely he personally recruited them to settle his land in America. Jacob and Stynte got on a ship and set sail, with Urbanus and his wife, to live on Rensselaer's land.

In the Netherlands, I attempted to coalesce Stynte and Jacob's lives and stories around mine. I identified in myself and my parents' families the deep pragmatism of people who would plan repair in anticipation of destruction, an acceptance of the hard work necessary to farm lands close to the sea, and enough confidence and sense of adventure to cross the ocean. Our lives began lining up across time and space. It is in the vortex of this place, these conditions, these people, in relationship to others, that my own story was emerging.

Amersterdam through my window. More than traces of Stynte and Jacob's Golden Age Amsterdam remain today. The city, built around canal rings, is almost structurally identical to its seventeenth century layout. Existing buildings from this period are well-preserved and identifiable. Artists living in these times rendered abundant images of the city and its inhabitants. With a little mental removal of vehicles and stop lights from the urban landscape, I could visualize what Stynte and Jacob saw in their day to day lives there. I imagine them passing Rembrandt, making sketches of the city they shared for a time.

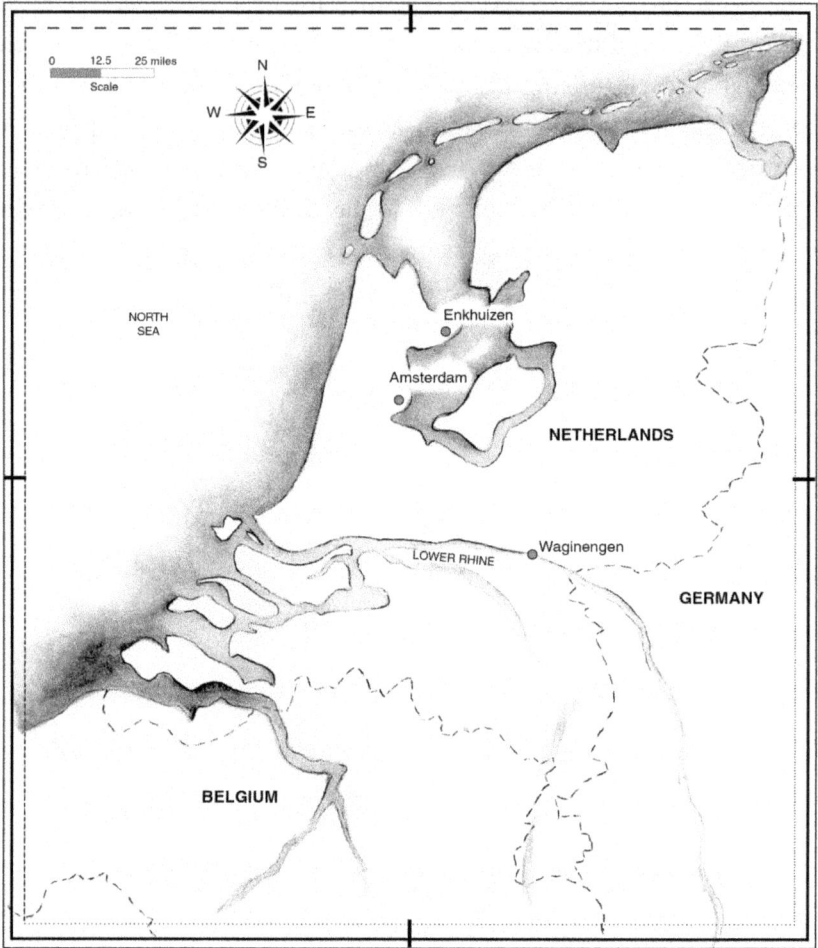

Map of The Netherlands and the North Sea

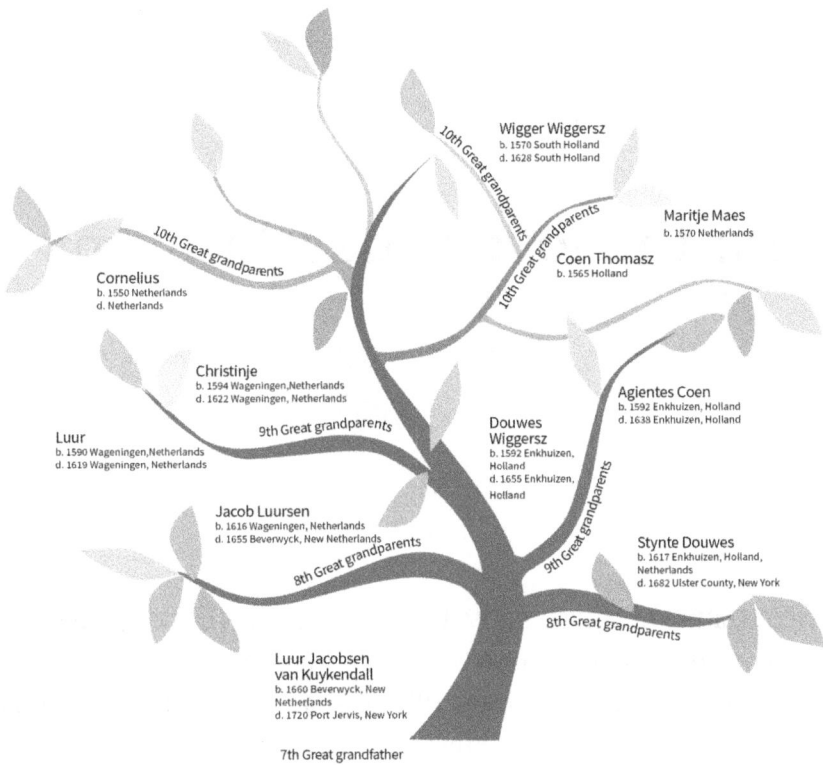

Wigger Wiggersz
b. 1570 South Holland
d. 1628 South Holland

Maritje Maes
b. 1570 Netherlands

10th Great grandparents

Coen Thomasz
b. 1565 Holland

10th Great grandparents

Cornelius
b. 1550 Netherlands
d. Netherlands

Christinje
b. 1594 Wageningen,Netherlands
d. 1622 Wageningen, Netherlands

Agientes Coen
b. 1592 Enkhuizen, Holland
d. 1638 Enkhuizen, Holland

Douwes
Wiggersz
b. 1592 Enkhuizen,
Holland
d. 1655 Enkhuizen,
Holland

9th Great grandparents

Luur
b. 1590 Wageningen,Netherlands
d. 1619 Wageningen, Netherlands

Jacob Luursen
b. 1616 Wageningen, Netherlands
d. 1655 Beverwyck, New Netherlands

Stynte Douwes
b. 1617 Enkhuizen, Holland,
Netherlands
d. 1682 Ulster County, New York

9th Great grandparents

8th Great grandparents

8th Great grandparents

Luur Jacobsen
van Kuykendall
b. 1660 Beverwyck, New
Netherlands
d. 1720 Port Jervis, New York

7th Great grandfather

Family tree of Jacob and Stynte and Luur's Dutch ancestors.

for the love of delphiniums

"MOTHER'S FAVORITE FLOWERS WERE DELPHINIUMS," my own mother told me one summer's day—my thoughts full of my grandmother Ethel's long-ago Kuykendall ancestors. Before Mother's revelation, I would have thought Ethel's favorite flowers were the blazing red and yellow tulips that, every spring, lined the stone path leading to her front porch—Dutch flowers for her paternal Dutch ancestors. Delphiniums, too, it seems, grow in the Netherlands, and all over the Northern Hemisphere.

When I mentioned the delphiniums to my cousin Erika, she confirmed what Mother told me. Erika had heard the same thing from her father, Mother's younger brother, Lamar. This was a moment of grace for me, when a tidbit of surprising information from Mother's childhood bubbled up into the middle of a conversation, my conversations with her otherwise fraught by dementia's grip on her mind and memory.

"Your grandmother grew the most beautiful flowers in Haywood County, and the most beautiful were her delphiniums," Mother continued. "People on vacation in Waynesville for the cool mountain summer would drive out to the country to buy Mother's delphiniums because they heard hers were the best. Everyone knew. She was smart, and she knew how to grow the most beautiful flowers."

My grandmother and granddaddy grew up poor in the Appalachian Mountains of North Carolina; before the Great Depression, my grandfather had been able to support his family by selling and repairing Singer Sewing Machines, but he lost this means of livelihood when the bottom fell out. During the worst of it, he dug up stumps and sold them for firewood at ten cents a truckload. Eventually the family was able to make enough money to survive as truck farmers, and even after the Depression they continued to support themselves by raising bedding plants for other farmers. Mother was the second of four sisters in her family—with two brothers, one at either end of the birth order. She and her siblings grew up knowing long days in the fields and hunger at night. The fear of not having enough stayed with Mother all her life, as it did for many from her generation.

By the time I was born in 1955, my grandparents had managed to see all their children in college and almost all of them married. Granddaddy was able set up a new shop in town where he got back to selling sewing machines, now Pfaff machines. They still grew food for themselves. They always had a garden, a big one, that provided food in season and for canning and freezing for the winter months.

From my rich store of memories of my grandmother, I could imagine her, though usually shy around strangers, talking with enthusiasm about these flowers she had grown and loved. She didn't suffer fools—or foolish grandchildren—but she was kind. And of course, being the Southerner that she was, she always was polite. There was a softness around her; she put people at ease.

I can see her coming in from the field or out the back door from the kitchen of the white, wood-framed farmhouse when she heard a car come up the gravel driveway. She'd be wearing a faded shirtwaist dress with an apron over it and low-heeled pumps caked with red clay from the garden. She'd take time to make sure the people who drove out for her flowers got to pick out the ones they wanted. She would cradle the flowers she cut for them in the crook of her arm. These 'not from around here people' would maybe get a glass of sweet tea while she tied the flowers in a bouquet.

Delphiniums, also called larkspur, are grand, regal flowers, each tall stalk with ladders of five-petaled lush, almost lavender blue blossoms that can be lighter or darker depending on the variety. I found photographs of them online after Mother's surprising disclosure. I thought they'd be lovely in the sunny area on the side of my new house. Their color would dazzle against the neutral gray siding. I began a plan to grow some myself, thinking through what I would need to do. More than just an aesthetic addition to the landscape, I wanted to grow them to honor this ancestor, my grandmother, now more than four decades after her passing—a grandmother whose connection to my life I lately had been learning more about, through photographs and old letters, was stronger than I had known it as a child.

I ordered delphinium seeds from an online seed store. I had hoped they grew from bulbs—that seemed easier to me—but they grow from small, dark, shiny seeds. I planted them in small containers with starter soil, keeping them in the garage so they'd be in the cooler darkness they needed for germination.

I thought, also, that growing my own delphiniums might please my mother. Pleasing my mother was no easy task ever. . . a lifelong, crazy-making struggle, in fact, and now complicated by her dementia. Every morning while I was growing up, Mother would be at the table already, having slept poorly. She had a list of my indictments from the day before. These might have included not washing the dishes immediately after supper, wearing a dress that was too short, getting home a half hour late after a church group meeting—signs of my lack of love for her. Even after I was an adult, she continued to make me feel that I didn't visit enough, call enough, ask after her well-being enough. Her familiar refrain was, "What have I done to deserve being treated like this?" I loved her, but not the way she wanted me to. I resented the deep well of emptiness that she wanted me to fill, but I believed it was my responsibility to take care of her. To me, this was the ultimate demonstration of my love, even if her dementia kept her from understanding it.

Mother's suffering was intense, and it hurt my soul to think about it. She was embarrassed when she could not remember things; she also was scared and paranoid and lonely. She kept forgetting that my father died a decade ago and believed he was not around because he left her for her a long-ago church friend. Mother felt fresh grief every time she realized Daddy had died, which seemed like fifty times a day. Painful memories her conscious mind locked down for good reason surfaced as obsessive thoughts of anger and shame. Yes, there also were moments of *light,* like when she thought about her mother's bright blue flowers, but they were too few to balance the rest of the horror show. There is nothing good about dementia. I am glad for people who have a gift for working with people with this condition. I am not one of them. I have learned lessons from it, but lessons not worth the pain of it.

But still I strove to do something, anything, to make it better. It is common for children of people with dementia to ask their parents questions about a happy event in their past that they cannot answer because they cannot remember. Instead of these memories bringing the joy we hope to see in loved ones faces, these attempts bring frustration, a bit more suffering. It was a difficult lesson to learn myself, easier to see the irony of it when others were asking their parents what they had for breakfast or who had come to visit them. Some pleasant memories did, however, rise up, unbidden, through the incomprehensible workings of a dementia-diseased brain. Mother had remembered my Grandmother's delphiniums.

More than once, I walked into her room as she was still awake inside a dream of a childhood Christmas at her mother's house. Each time she asked me if I'd seen who was downstairs, if the guests were still there, and why I was not dressed up for Christmas dinner. This dream made her as happy as I ever saw her in those days, but it was ephemeral—and I finally understood that I had nothing to do with this happiness—except to *not* tell her it is a delusion. Why would I? I was open to her reality being her reality. She was communing with people I couldn't see. If it made her happy, I didn't really care whether the thin veil between this world and some other one was a metaphysical experience or a metaphorical way of understanding what was happening in her brain. She believed it; it was true.

Growing delphiniums to elicit mother's pleasant memories of her mother was most likely more about trying to make myself feel better. But inspiration comes from where it comes from; it seems almost impossible for any of us to make it happen, try as we might. For anyone who has attempted, in some rational, linear way to create something or make something happen, most of the time you can get just so far, and then it feels like there is a brick wall in your path.

Until . . . until all of a sudden, I saw the first delphinium seedling come up through the dirt and eureka! I heard my grandmother whispering in my ear! She asked, *"You want some relief from your mother's gut-wrenching, soul-sucking dementia? Want to know more about me than you could understand while you were a child?"* She said, *"Get your hands in the dirt and enjoy growing and nurturing these beautiful flowers! Find the joy of sharing them with others. Take some to your mother when they bloom. Maybe they will make her happy and maybe they won't, but their beauty will make you happy and others who see them. And while I'm giving you advice (young lady!)—get yourself to the mountains and see the kin you have left there—and bring some of those beautiful blue flowers to the Greenhill Cemetery for your granddaddy and me."*

And several days later, more seedlings shot up through the soil. I felt my grandmother smile in my heart.

Wedding day. My mother and my grandmother on Mother's wedding day, August 21, 1954, at my grandmother's house in Waynesville, North Carolina. My grandmother's delphiniums sit on the fireplace mantel to the left of my mother.

muhheakantuck

The River that Flows Both Ways (New York)

I FIND symbolic power in the rivers that flowed through each of my immigrant ancestors' stories, sources of life-sustaining water and energy and conduits for moving people and moving goods. My ancestors Stynte and Jacob left Amsterdam to settle in the Dutch colony of New Netherlands near "the river that flows both ways," so named by its original inhabitants because the ocean tides move seawater in and out of its lower reaches twice each day. As salty ocean waters flow north, they dissipate into fresher ones. Ecosystems vary gradually as the river extends farther from the ocean, reflecting decreasing levels of salinity.

The arrival of Dutch colonists, however, was more like a sudden, abrupt gush of salt into fresh waters. With little time for adaptation, human and other-than-human relationships co-existing for millennia were quickly unsettled by their arrival. After visiting the Netherlands, I went on the road again to see the place where Stynte and Jacob's stories continued as they settled and started a family near the river that flows both ways.

⟵⟶

During the Golden Age of Amsterdam, Stynte and Jacob lived at a global crossroads where they encountered and co-existed with people from outside the Netherlands, people from places where the Dutch traded—people who had darker skin, who wore different clothes, and who had different ideas about the world than they did.[1] The Indonesians, Jamaicans, and Brazilians they may have seen in Amsterdam were foreigners in *their* homeland. In New Netherlands, however, Stynte and Jacob became the strangers in a strange land—a feeling I have frequently experienced myself, and part of what pulls me into their story.

The Mohican, Lenape, and Mohawk nations inhabited land in and around the river that flowed both ways for a dozen millennia before the first Europeans arrived, and all three nations identified themselves, each in their own language, as "people of the river." It was the Algonquin-speaking Mohican people with whom Stynte and Jacob had the closest contact in their colonial home. Their next-generation descendants who moved south along the river lived among the Esopus Munsee, part of the Northern Lenape "hoop" or "circle" of several confederated Indigenous nations. The Lenape, like Mohicans, spoke an Algonquin language and shared similar beliefs and lifeways.[2]

The Munsee were the first Indigenous people seen by Englishman Henry Hudson and the crew of the *Half Moon Bay* during his 1609 voyage on the river the Munsees called the Muhheakantuck. The Dutch financed Hudson's search for the elusive northwest passage to Asia that led him to this river, and they decided to start a new colony nearby according to his reports of a potential lucrative beaver fur trade. They called the river that Hudson traveled the North River. Years later, the English renamed it the Hudson River for their countryman, after they took the surrounding territory from the Dutch.[3]

A second band of Munsee, the Upper Delaware Munsee or

Minisink, were indigenous to the lands settled by Jacob and Stynte's grandchildren and great-grandchildren, farther south and slightly west of the Hudson River Valley. The third Munsee band, the Southern Munsee lived closer to the Manhattan and New Amsterdam area. They are not relevant to my ancestor story except that encounters between settlers and Indigenous nations anywhere in the Dutch colony had repercussions for everyone within the land it claimed.

North and west of Munsee country lived members of the Mohawk nation, one of the Five Nations Confederacy. They spoke a language as different from Munsee and Mohican as English is different from Japanese.[4] They were long-time allies of the French, and often at war with Mohicans and Munsee. As part of the Five Nations (and later, the Six Nations) Confederacy, they are still commonly referred to as Iroquois, but this is thought to be a French misuse of the Mohican language name for them, likely not a flattering one. Their own name for themselves is *Haudenosaunee* ("People of the Longhouse").[5]

◄═══►

Stynte and Jacob's first home in the Dutch colony was on a wheat plantation known as Rensselaerswyck, owned by pearl and diamond merchant Kiliaen van Rensselaer, from the province of Gelderland. Van Rensselaer sponsored Stynte and Jacob's passage in return for a term of service. In 1629, Van Rensselaer bought vast acreages lying east, west, and, north of the Hudson River, surrounding the Fort Orange trading post built five years earlier. Thirty-seven people arrived in 1636 to begin work on the land. By 1642, 100 people were working there, likely Stynte and Jacob among them.[6]

◄═══►

At the root of Dutch and Indigenous discord were divergent beliefs about land ownership and rights. No doubt a desire to own land was at least part of Stynte and Jacob's motivation to move to New Netherlands, a desire that was fulfilled, as it turned out. To make it possible for colonists to own land, the Dutch West Indies Company had made claims for specific territories explored by Hudson, in what is now called New York. The Company's directors also understood it must formally transfer specific lands for its use from the Indigenous people who were living there.

The concepts of private versus communal land ownership were neither cross-culturally incomprehensible, nor mutually exclusive for either the Dutch or Indigenous people.[7] Some communal sharing of land was expected from both sides. Both cared about territorial integrity and property rights and boundaries. Each took care to grant rights to particular places and to particular people for specified time periods. Both accepted the notion that land could be militarily conquered or peaceably transferred. Both had formal procedures to acknowledge the transfer of land use rights. The differences between the two groups were subtler than commonly believed and ripe for creative ambiguity, misinterpretation, or perhaps, manipulation. A recipe for trouble.

Indigenous people did not believe land was free for use by anyone, but it could be used by particular individuals or families when their chiefs, known as sachem (sāCHəm), gave them the rights to it. Sachems only gave land rights to people who were willing to respect local customs and concerns. Small groups or villages communally owned the land that they were given rights to until they moved to a new location, at which point the sachem could allot it to another group. It was not free to strangers but could only be obtained as a gift or by outright seizure. Importantly, rights to a designated piece of land were not granted forever. These ideas about land use rights were more fluid than Europeans' ideas about private property ownership, in which exchange of land for gifts or money was considered final.

The first transfers of land rights between the Dutch and the river people followed Indigenous ceremonial traditions marked by gift-giving and payment of wampum. Wampum took the form of shell beads strung in intricate patterns—longer strings indicated greater value. I can see how the notion that Native people sold Manhattan for a handful of beads and trinkets somehow evolved, but as a gross misrepresentation of the meaning of "wampum." Wampum was considered currency, but it was more than that. Some wampum communicated a story about the transaction in the pattern of its beads. For Indigenous people, wampum was imbued with symbolic meaning about relationships and connections created within the negotiations.

Dutch colonists augmented Indigenous ceremonial negotiations with their own cultural practice, the signing of written contracts. Templates for deeds were among the first forms printed on colonial presses. Once completed with the relevant transaction information, they were read aloud to both parties *in Dutch*. It was the intent of the deed to secure sovereignty of the land from sachems, similar to making a treaty, though it is not clear that it was the intent of the sachems to make the transfer forever binding.

⬅⟹

Why would sachems, for any reason, agree to transfer the use of their people's land to colonists? Initially, it seemed, good will was an important motivation. For sure, there were material goods from Europe that Indigenous people desired, things that had practical value and made their lives easier, and things they believed were charged with mysterious spiritual power, such as anything made from copper. Historian Robert Grumet believes that sachems may have also used land transfer as a way of creating an unspoken debt of reciprocity, believing if they gave a little extra, the other side would feel obligated to meet them more than halfway on the next negotiation.[8] This makes sense to me. We all do that, don't we?

⟵⟶

Fort Orange, built near the headwaters of the Hudson River, was essentially a trading post for beaver furs, managed by the Dutch West Indies Company.[9] It was strategically located at the nexus of several ancient Indigenous trade routes that had existed before the French or Dutch arrived. Beaver skins were bought from trappers there and sent to Manhattan in late spring, summer, and early fall months until the river froze over during the winter.

Fort Orange was technically on van Rensselaer's land, and this fact became the source of some tension over the question of who had authority over the people living on Rensselaerswyck. Peter Stuyvesant, a newly appointed director general of the New Netherlands, requested this question be settled by the Dutch government. In 1648 they officially gave New Netherlands rights to van Rensselaer's land within a 3,000-foot radius of Fort Orange (estimated to be the distance of a cannon-shot) to create the town of Beverwyck—essentially taking this land back from van Rensselaer.

In 1652 and 1653, Stuyvesant offered plots of land for houses and gardens to people who had worked off their terms of service to van Rensselaer, Stynte and Jacob among them. By this time, he and Stynte had two daughters, Agniet and Jacomyntie, and one son, my ninth great-grandfather, Luur (named for *his* grandfather it seems). Luur was only two years old when they moved to their house in Beverwyck.

With the influx of former Rensselaerswyck residents, Beverwyck grew quickly from forty dwellings to 120, with a church and poor house in the center. It was a meeting place for Indigenous trappers and Dutch, French, and English traders. Its residents catered to the needs of the growing beaver trade. Besides traders, there were bakers, brewers, tavern keepers, and blacksmiths. Jacob was a stone mason by training and likely helped build houses for the rapidly growing numbers of people moving into the village. Dutch goods were easily obtained for colonists and Indigenous people. A constant flow of ships moved down the Hudson River to New Amsterdam, carrying tens of thousands of beaver skins out, and bringing back material goods from the Netherlands desired by the colonists.

With no separation of church and state, the Dutch Reform Church was a part of life in the colony. Attendance at Sunday worship service was required for everyone. The church took charge of the well-being of the community, believing risk of misfortune was a human condition that should not be judged. The quicker one recovered from it, the faster that person could contribute to the greater good. I wish this was a guiding principle in how Americans care for each other now.

As I read details about life in Beverwyck, I can picture Stynte tending her family garden full of many of the same items they grew in Dutch gardens and that we now grow in ours: lettuces, spinach, beets, radishes, asparagus, and herbs such as rosemary, lavender, thyme, sage, dill, and parsley. She might have had an apple or cherry tree in her yard. She may also have learned to grow food Mohicans grew, such as pumpkins, cucumbers, and squash.[10]

$\longleftrightarrow$

Though relationships between Beverwyck residents and Indigenous trappers had been mostly peaceful, conflicts involving Indigenous people anywhere in the New Netherlands—with other Indigenous people or with settlers—heightened colonial security concerns everywhere. People moved in closer to the fort for protection, and physical boundaries between colonists and Indigenous people became less porous. Palisades, fences of wooden stakes fixed in the ground for the purpose of defense, were built around Beverwyck to ease settler anxieties. Traders were restricted to meeting with Mohican trappers outside the walls rather than in local bars or private houses. This created more division between those inside the wall and those outside.

Court records paint a picture of Jacob as being somewhat quarrelsome with many people, including former bosses from Rensselaerswyck.[11] Nothing in those records makes me believe that Jacob and Stynte had more or less engagement with Native people in and around Beverwyck than others or that they felt more or less in need of the palisades around the village to protect them. What I do know, though, is that Jacob and Stynte owned land that once had been Mohican territory, and their presence among the other settlers was changing the world around them.

⟷

Jacob lived on his land for only a few years before his death in 1655 at the young age of 38, three hundred years before I was born. His son Luur was only five years old. No cause of death was given in the numerous mentions in court documents about matters of his estate.

Financial help was given to Stynte by the church's social welfare committee, including some temporary care for the children while she sorted out his estate. She sold the land and paid debts brought against the earnings. Court records show that she remarried and that her new husband, Claes Teunissen, represented her in the estate proceedings.[12]

Given the times, it is unlikely she could have survived there as a single mother.

The beaver trade peaked a couple of years after Jacob's death, and the economic boom quickly went bust when the over-harvesting of beavers caused a glut of wampum currency and inflation.[13] Stynte, with Claes and her children, soon moved south along the river valley to a new Dutch frontier of Indigenous land. Perhaps Claes was looking for more land to farm. Perhaps Stynte was looking for a place where she could think about the future and ease her young widow's grief.

⟵⟶

The site where Beverwyck once stood was built over multiple times as it became the English and then the American city of Albany. In the 1970s, archeologists excavated several Beverwyck houses before a major highway was to be constructed there. My husband and I traveled to Albany to find Jacob and Stynte's home on this side of the Atlantic. On our first afternoon in town, we made our way to the western edge of the Hudson River, under a web of concrete flyovers, at the site of their Beverwyck house and garden.

Trying to erase in my mind what centuries of ruin and reconstruction had left behind, I lowered my view to the path along the river to imagine wooden buildings with simplified Dutch lines, possibly with animals roaming around muddy roads. The fort had been the center of town where most official business was conducted, including Jacob's frequent court appearances. Religious services were conducted in a block house nearby, until a church was built. There are scant renderings from that time of what it looked like. Referencing maps and blueprints, the artist Len Tantillo painted a few images of what Beverwyck might have looked like when Stynte and Jacob were there.[14] In my imagination, I inserted them into the landscape along the harbor.

The next day, a chilly, rainy Monday, I made my way to the New York State Museum, adjacent to Empire State Plaza. As if it has been curated just for my research, one of the new exhibits featured the nearby Beverwyck excavation site. I saw encased in protective glass artifacts such as yellow brick, cooking utensils, pottery shards, men's hats, including a beaver hat, women's linen head coverings, children's shoes, and fermentation vats—much of which had been uncovered by archeologists decades before. Objects from pre-contact Indigenous lifeways and the geological history of the Hudson River Valley were here in ongoing museum displays as well.

Russell Shorto's book *Island at the Center of the World,*[15] about the Dutch colony here, first drew me into wanting to know more of the story of my Kuykendall ancestors. For much of Shorto's research, he relied on resources from the New Netherlands Research Institute reading room in the New York State Library, located on the fourth floor of the museum building. To use this reading room myself while I was in Albany, I only had to sign up and get a pass at the reception desk. One person was allowed in the small reading room at a time. For a whole day, I was that person.

I found court records and birth and death records naming Jacob and Stynte but also ancestors from maternal lineages marrying into Jacob's patrilineage—Aert Tack and Jannjente and Jurian Abels Westfall and Johannes Westfall and Luur and Cornelius. I had read some of this information on genealogy sites, but to hold these books in my hands and find the names of people I had begun to know as family right here printed in these books! Yes, here they were on these pages at my fingertips, and they were real people. I smiled each time I found a familiar name.

Sometimes I also sighed hard, sometimes I felt a catch in my throat as I recognized their complicated family connections to one another, the burden of responsibility, and the mix of wonder and strain of being in this new place. I often found myself talking to them in my head. "Jacob, what demons were you wrestling with that you kept clashing with bosses and neighbors?" And, "Stynte, I can't even imagine the heartbreak of Jacob's death and possible terror at finding yourself in debt and alone."

I savored the feeling of knowing I had been on the right track in my ancestor investigation.

After I had accomplished what I needed in the library, my husband and I walked around the state government plaza where the only building whose architecture seemed photo-worthy was the curvilinear structure known as the Egg—fascinating to look at and difficult to photograph close-up. The moist drizzle from the wind and rain fogged up the lens of my camera. All my photographs came out surreal and out of focus; perhaps I was hung-over from a day of backward time-traveling.

◄═══►

After Jacob's death, Stynte and Luur moved with Claes somewhere south along the Hudson River Valley, but I was not able to pin down exactly when or where. The small village of Rochester is mentioned in some of the genealogy sites. More often their new home is identified as Kingston or Wiltwyck, but it was called Esopus when they moved there, named after the Munsee peoples who first lived there. In and around Esopus, my family tree branches out to include the multiple Dutch and German lineages of the women that Jacob's son Luur and grandson Cornelius eventually married. I followed the river and the land southward, in the steps of my ancestors, and I was to discover with some dismay, where my ancestors found themselves part of the Esopus Wars.

◀═══▶

In 1653, Dutch colonists from Beverwyck began buying farmland near a trading post south of Fort Orange, located where the river diverts into the Rondout River and Esopus Creek.[16] Among the first group of settlers were my ancestors Jurian Abels Westfall and his young, pregnant wife Marretje. Fur traders preceded the farmer settlers in staking out a commercial site at this location, anchored at the confluence of several ancient Indigenous trading routes, including the Minisink Trail, and close to several bodies of water.

Everyone knew the land here was extremely fertile; indigenous Esopus farmers produced two crops of corn a year on more than 200 acres. Esopus sachems negotiated the sale of some of their land to the new arrivals—most likely to ensure their ability to trade for European goods, assuming there would always be enough land for everyone. But more settlers kept coming, and they always wanted more land.

◀═══▶

While European settlers were encroaching on Esopus territory west of the Hudson, violence broke out often between Dutch colonists and Indigenous people in places now known as Manhattan and Long Island. In the beginning, these were small skirmishes resulting in a few deaths on either side, but they often erupted into full-scale battles of gruesome proportions.

Hostilities begun by the first West Indies Company director general, William Kieft, were so horrendous that colonists begged him to stop. They also sent representatives across the Atlantic to the Netherlands to ask government officials at The Hague to relieve him of his duties. Even with Kieft's eventual removal, however, conflicts continued. The Mohawk, Mohicans, and Lenape all suffered loss of lives and livelihoods and struck back fiercely to defend their people and land.[17]

Settlers on Esopus land undoubtedly knew the physical risks of pushing their way into this new edge of Indigenous territory. The colonial community was small. Each settler had to have known someone who had killed an Indigenous person or been killed by one. All Dutch settlers must have felt some dread in their bellies when they settled a new frontier. Yet they continued to move outward.

◄═══►

Where Stynte had resettled with her children and her new husband, Dutch farmland soon pushed up against Indigenous corn fields. Hogs and horses and chickens destroyed indigenous Esopus crops. Esopus farmers got even by slaughtering the offending livestock. Dutch farmers raised tensions by paying Indigenous workers in brandy, even when leaders of both sides begged them to stop. And not only farmers: Dutch traders who sailed in and out of the Esopus River used alcohol to cheat Native people when doing business. The familiar plot line in all colonization stories, in America and elsewhere, goes like this: colonizers bully the people whose land they invade and steal; those people retaliate, often pushed to brutality to match that of the colonizers. The retaliators are labelled "savages," these days, as "terrorists." This story was no different. A vicious cycle of outrage and heartbreak.

◄═══►

And here I begin a story that is hard to tell and hard to hear. Please take a deep breath, say a prayer, and open yourself to compassion for the suffering of all involved, and those reading it.

In the spring of 1658, for reasons undocumented, a young Esopus man killed a Dutch trader and burned a farm to the ground. In response, Director General Peter Stuyvesant traveled to the new settlement with sixty-one soldiers to secure the peace and arrange protection for the colonists. Local sachems warned Stuyvesant that they might not be able to control young warriors spoiling for a fight if colonists continued to ply them with alcohol. Interpreting this as a threat, Stuyvesant offered to put up Dutch soldiers to fight Esopus warriors. When his offer was refused, he then "suggested" that the sachems sell him a tract of land near the mouth of Rondout Creek.

Stuyvesant demanded that the colonists make themselves less vulnerable to attack by concentrating their settlement into a smaller area that could be more easily defended. He and his soldiers helped them build a fort near the mouth of Rondout Creek where he had just obtained land. He left a small squad of soldiers there after he returned to New Amsterdam in June. He incorporated the area around the fort and named it Wiltwyck or "savage district." Aptly named. But who were the savages?

I found frequent mentions of Jurian Abels Westphal in Wiltwyck court records, often regarding land transactions and tax payments. In fact, some of the farmland he rented was owned by Peter Stuyvesant himself. Jurian had emigrated from Germany to work on Rensselaerswyck and was a contemporary of Jacob and Stynte, though Jurian lived much longer than Jacob. Once freed from his obligations to van Rensselaer, Jurian moved to Beverwyck where he met and married a seventeen-year-old barmaid, Marretj van Noordstrandt.

Marretj had come to New Netherlands as a baby with her parents and two older siblings after they lost everything in the Burchadi Flood[18] that devastated their home on Noordstrandt Island, in what is now Germany. In New Amsterdam, her family farmed an area now known as Brooklyn. Her mother died soon after arrival, and her father remarried and had seven more children. With so many mouths to feed, Marretj was bonded out to a tavern owner in Beverwyck. There she met Jurian. After they married, she and Jurian moved to the Esopus Wiltwyck settlement where they lived for the rest of their lives. They had six children. Their third child, Johannes, was the father of the woman who was to marry Stynte and Jacob's grandson, Luur's son, Cornelius.

←⟹→

Even after Stuyvesant's visit, settlers continued to sow the seeds of discord with the Munsee—seemingly trying to pick a fight. They stole corn from them, regularly harassed them in public, and continued to pay for labor with brandy, knowing the harm it would cause and the trouble it could stir up. Reports of further provocation brought Stuyvesant back to Wiltwyck in October. To the astonishment of the sachems who came to talk to him, he blamed the Esopus people for the settlers' fears, demanded reparations at the high price of 100 strings of wampum and many acres of the most fertile farmlands to pay for the costs of the fort. Adding insult to injury, he requested they leave the area altogether.

The sachems, stunned by his audacity, asked Stuyvesant to reconsider his demands, but he would not. To delay making these concessions, the sachems offered to meet him again the next spring to hand over the land Stuyvesant was demanding. By next August 1659, the Esopus still had not surrendered any land; neither had Stuyvesant returned with gifts he had promised. Several sachems visited the fort on September 4 with a partial payment of the wampum, asking the villagers to ask Stuyvesant to consider a fairer settlement. In the meantime, 500 Esopus warriors were mobilizing in nearby villages.

⟵⟶

Settlers made the opening move in the First Esopus War, unable to maintain their cool in light of what they perceived as a threat from the sachems early that September. On September 20, only 18 days after the sachems' diplomatic overture, a group of Dutch colonists attacked several young Esopus men who were sleeping off a night of drinking too much brandy in nearby woods. The Dutch killed one man, wounded another, and the rest got away. The next day, Esopus warriors returned to attack a group of settlers, killing some and taking the rest hostage. The remaining colonists retreated to their fort, now surrounded by the 500 warriors waiting for this moment.

The fort commandant, Ensign Dirck Smith, angry and disgusted by the colonists who attacked the Esopus, grudgingly dispatched a message to Stuyvesant in New Amsterdam. Esopus warriors, however, captured the courier and his bodyguards and then lay siege to the fort. Open warfare had begun.

When Stuyvesant finally got the news, he called up volunteers among Dutch and English colonists and allies from among other Indigenous nations on Long Island. He arrived in October, just after a twenty-three-day battle had ended without a clear resolution. He left reinforcements at the fort and returned to New Amsterdam. Diplomatic attempts reduced tensions in the short term.

Stuyvesant, more politician than peacemaker, wanted a show of force against the Esopus to make colonists feel secure and unafraid. He ordered Ensign Smith to go on the offensive in the spring of 1660, knowing their warriors would be hungry and vulnerable after their winter food stores were depleted.

As Stuyvesant had hoped, a series of attacks in March, April, and May weakened the Esopus defense. Dutch soldiers captured a dozen Esopus hostages early in March and sent them to Fort Amsterdam. After continued losses, Esopus sachems sent reports to the Dutch that they wanted to make peace but were afraid to come in person. Stuyvesant cruelly rebuffed these requests, waiting to further weaken their nation before he negotiated.

Late in May, Smith led a raiding party with an Esopus prisoner as their guide. Across the Rondout River, they spied several Native people planting crops and fishing. Among them was the oldest and most revered sachem, Preuwamakan, fishing from a canoe. The creek was too high for the party to cross, so they withdrew. When they returned to the stockade, a young woman informed them they could reach the place they wanted to attack by crossing a ford that was a three-hours march away and then descending along the opposite bank. It was chilling for me when I read an account of this battle to see my eighth great-grandmother, twenty-seven-year-old Marretje Westphal, named as the informant. When I look at the dates and do the math, I realize she was likely pregnant with my seventh great-grandfather, Johannes Westphal.[19]

When the militia found the place they were looking for based on Marretj's directions, it had been deserted, except for the old sachem.

"What are you doing here? *You dogs!*" he shouted. He aimed his gun at them.

They took away his gun, six knives, and a hatchet. They killed him with a "whack of his own hatchet" rather than bother bringing him as a prisoner. Their guide and prisoner, Dissquartas, was the sachem's son.

The sachem's death was the final blow to the Esopus resistance Stuyvesant was looking for; he was ready to accept surrender. The

Esopus knew they had no choice but to do so, but this gratuitous murder intensified Indigenous people's hatred of the settlers.

This animosity became a festering wound, even beyond the peace treaty on July 15, 1660. The Esopus gave up lands around the fort, returned prisoners, made payments of corn, and promised peace. The Dutch returned three prisoners but sent the rest of them to Curaçao as slaves—hostages to elicit good behavior.

The Esopus remained defiant in their fury over the prisoners held in Curaçao. Two prisoners were returned in 1662, but this did not appease them. The settlers continued to expand their holdings, building Nieuwdorp (New Village), now known as Hurley, west of the Wiltwyck fort, on upland overlooking broad fertile flats along Esopus Creek. Settlers sensed the tension this created among their Esopus neighbors. In April 1663, they asked Stuyvesant to send gifts and troops, but he did not, at least not in time. Were Marretj and Jurian among those who requested help? How had their lives been affected by the continuing violence? Had they had any change of heart? Did they ever see the Esopus as humans like themselves? This last question I ask myself about people even now when I hear of cruel treatment of other human beings, some of them their own fellow citizens.

On June 7, Esopus warriors destroyed Nieuwdorp and burned Wiltwyck nearly to ground. Amid flames and smoke, they killed 20 settlers, captured 45, leaving 69 survivors behind. Skirmishes continued but did not rise again to the level of a full siege. Dutch diplomatic overtures resulted in the release of a few Dutch prisoners who provided Stuyvesant's appointed commander Marten Crieger with intelligence used to find and attack an Esopus fortress.

Crieger's men found the fortress abandoned and burned it down.

The rest of the summer and fall, the militia searched for the remaining hostages. When at last they found a new stronghold, they made a surprise attack. They recovered hostages, and destroyed structures and food supplies, breaking the back of the resistance. The Esopus, reeling from their losses, and under pressure from Indigenous Dutch allies, began looking for a way to end the war. The Dutch demanded a return of all hostages. Held in widely scattered camps, their return took many winter months to complete.

In May 1664, three Esopus sachems arrived in New Amsterdam to cede most of their remaining territory. The men still in Curaçao were never brought back to their families. Can you imagine the heartbreak felt by their families? How you would feel if a family member was sent so far away, never to return? The Esopus population, having been 10,000 before 1600, numbered fewer than 3,000 in 1664, having suffered as many as 1,000 deaths in the first half of the 1660s to smallpox and war.

$$\longleftrightarrow$$

I was fully conscious of these historical details as I visited the town of Kingston, south along the Hudson. I went first to the Old Dutch Church on Wall Street, where several ancestors were baptized, married, and eventually buried. The markings on the old gravesites have been worn away—for centuries, I imagined—so I could not pinpoint the whereabouts of particular people's bones. I walked around the whole cemetery, three-fourths of the churchyard, to ensure that I had been in proximity to my ancestors, their bones under my feet. They were my kin even if I was troubled by their settler legacy. Even as I knew I needed to be troubled by that legacy and not look away.

I thought about the events and consequences of the Esopus Wars and my own relatives' involvement as I walked out the gates beyond the churchyard. On the way to a bar and bookstore called "The Rough Draft," we passed a parking lot with a sign identifying it as the place where the stockade was built by Stuyvesant to protect the colonists on land that had been Esopus territory before the wars.

Right *here*, my brain reminded me, 500 Esopus warriors laid siege against colonists after young Esopus men were attacked and murdered. I thought about what the physical experience of being surrounded by 500 warriors would be like. Right *here* Stuyvesant met with the Esopus sachems multiple times before and after this siege. I was unsettled and disturbed that a place with so much weight of violent history about it was now an unremarkable parking lot where people go about their everyday lives. As if there weren't Esopus and Dutch ghosts here. Just another tourist town in New York along the Hudson River, close to the Catskills. No mention anywhere of Indigenous genocide. Pretending nothing happened.

⟵⟶

I did not want the grief of past events to blot out my desire to honor the beauty of land that was here. To transform that grief into a desire for repair, I spent as much time as possible away from the built world, exploring the riverine forests and wetlands along the Hudson and its tributaries on the way to and from and around Kingston, Rondout River and Esopus Creek. The first stop was Shodack Island, the place where Henry Hudson first encountered Munsee people. It is now a state park, with a silty, muddy path through the shoreline vegetation. Signs along the path, identified stands of grasses on the waters' edge as invasive species inadvertently brought from the Netherlands from seeds stuck to canvas bags of grain.

We also spent some sweet moments in the Nature Conservancy's

Swyer Nature Preserve, a tidal swamp off the estuarial tributary Miller Creek. Large-leaved mud plantains fanned across expanses of low ground. It felt tropical, if not otherwise. Dense patches of ferns spread out elsewhere. Our boots clacked against the half-mile wooden path that kept us out of the muck on the way to the observation tower. Miller Creek flowed into the Hudson on the other side of the tower, and trains sped by in close proximity. White-flowering bushes, dragonflies and ladybugs were present in abundance. Salt-laced humidity hung in the air.

Perhaps my favorite trail walk was along the Esopus Bend Preserve where we moved through vine-entangled forests to open meadows and lily-pond wetlands. A little farther away we followed a sandy trail to the yellow, two-story, wooden Esopus lighthouse built to lead boats safely on and off the Hudson.

◄═══►

Stynte and Jacob's son, Luur, and his wife Grietz had over a dozen children; birth records indicate they lived in Kingston and the nearby villages of Hurley and Marbletown when their first children were born. Children born to them in 1698 or afterward were born in the area known as Minisink, the original homeland of the Southern Lenape nation of Minisink. This trail of the same name, thought safe enough for settler travel after the English takeover in 1664, was known to colonists as the Queen's and then later, the King's Highway. Luur and Grietz and their children settled at the end of the Minisink Trail, where there is now a city called Port Jervis, near the Delaware River, close to the intersecting boundaries of the current states of New York, New Jersey, and Pennsylvania.

Jurian Westfall and Marretj's son Johannes Westfall, who was in the same generation as Luur, moved his family to Port Jervis around the same time that Luur moved his there. About half of Luur and Grietz's dozen children married Johannes's offspring. Luur's son Cornelius, from whom I am descended, married Johannes' daughter, Marretje. (Yes, another Marretje.) It is in Minisink that Cornelius and Marretje wed and started their own family. One of their sons, Abraham, found his way to Buncombe County, North Carolina, many years later.

⟵⟶

It was during this trip to New York, that I may have cleared up the mystery of the lineal surname Kuykendall, at least for myself. It was after Luur's family moved to Minisink that he began giving his children the surname of van Kuykendall. Previously, sons in his family had followed the tradition of identifying themselves as the son of someone. Jacob used Luurson (spelling varies because of variations in transliteration); and Luur used Jacobson. Though Cornelius, Jacob's grandson, was not named van Kuykendall in his baptismal records, he eventually was given this name during his childhood, now following the English naming custom as an English subject. As noted in the previous essay, American Kuykendall descendants have speculated that it was derived from words in old Dutch meaning "view over the valley," in reference to the forested rise overlooking the lower Rhine River outside Wageningen. The archivist from Wageningen disputed this translation, but I had wanted it to be true.

Now that I thought about Jacob's story from both sides of the Atlantic, I have changed my mind a bit. Jacob's parents died when he was a small child, and he moved to Amsterdam. Did he have enduring memories of his boyhood home? *He* did not give that name to his family. His son gave the name to his family after New Netherland became the English colony, New York, and its citizens were required to have surnames as the English did. Would Jacob's sentimental stories of Wageningen have been passed on to Luur? Maybe, but I don't think so because Luur was only five years old when Jacob died. And, Luur waited until he was the father of six children to give this name to his family.

Now in this place, I wondered, could "van Kuykendall" have referred to the view over the Hudson River Valley, known worldwide for its vast beauty? And though I saw both the Lower Rhine and the Hudson 300 years after Jacob did, I would argue the Hudson is the more beautiful of the two. I love the original story, but I think my new version might be the correct one. The translation issue is still a concern, but maybe it was a mistranslation a generation out. It is still a mystery of course, but it is a surname recognizable in the hills and valleys of the mountains of North Carolina.

◄═══►

I wanted to see the old Minisink Trail, now New York Route 209, where Luur and Johannes brought their families farther into Lenape land. The Lenape Ridge Trail is purportedly part of the original trail, so we stopped at a state park in Port Jervis to walk a part of it that also connects farther on to the more well-known Appalachian Trail.

While we hiked this lush forest path, I thought that being in those woods was about as close as I could get to experiencing something of the worlds of my ancestors or the Munsee people. There have been changes in this natural landscape since they were here—at a minimum, newer trees and a warmer climate. It was still the Little Ice Age when they arrived, but no longer, and the planet continues to warm.

I also thought that however close I could get to seeing the natural landscapes they saw, I could never imagine what it would be like to live inside the landscapes of their experience that formed what they knew and believed about the world. I think about how different their lives were. They had never used an electrical appliance, talked on a telephone, seen a photograph, or used a flush toilet. They did not know what lands lay west of their home, what a germ was, that humans would be able to fly one day, even land on the moon. They knew birth and they knew death. They knew pregnancy and childbirth were potentially lethal events for both mother and child. They knew nothing about evolution, the separation of church and state, or the equality of women and men.

And if I could not truly imagine the way they understood the world, was this not also the same for the Indigenous and European people entangled in each other's lives at that time? Their lived experiences were so different from each other that I wondered how they were able to find as much common humanity as they did. I wanted to think that what is similar between me and my ancestors and what was similar between the Indigenous people they lived among and their descendants, was a belief in love—for family, for friends. I found this to be true in my research work in Africa and Asia. I could find common ground with my colleagues from vastly different cultures when we began talking about our children and our parents. The tragedy though is that what might have brought settlers and Native people together was not enough to hold back the social and political tidal forces of what made them different and that tore them apart.

⟵⟶

I can imagine that Marretje had every good intention when she helped the militia find the old sachem; she may not have thought he would be murdered like that. She was protecting her children and her neighbors and herself. She was not aware of the geopolitical forces of racialized imperialism at work in her life. I can only speculate what her life as a teenage barmaid had been like, or ask whether she loved Jurian more than she was grateful to him for relieving her of that work, or even that he gave her a better life as his wife—I am hoping that he did. It is unlikely she had much to say in the decision to move to Esopus. Clashes between settlers and Indigenous nations were the only reality she knew.

Of course, she was afraid for herself and her children. Of course, she saw the Esopus as "the other." Of course, she wanted to be respected in her community. Of course, of course, of course. Actions taken that day may have saved her life and allowed for the chain of events that led to my birth. Marretje and Stynte's families were entwined over the next decades, and the union of their grandchildren became new branches on my family tree.

And yet. And yet, it caused harm. The whole of it was wrong. Even if individual actions made sense, all of it together was an evil force of human hatred in the world, all told, continues to create pain and suffering for all involved—and needs repair.

What is my responsibility as her descendant to right an old wrong?

$$\longleftrightarrow$$

The Esopus and other people of the river continued to look for ways to accommodate the presence of Europeans even after New Netherlands became New York and the colonists broke away from England and declared themselves to be a new country. The Esopus moved farther and farther west and joined with other Mohican people. The few remaining Esopus descendants now live on a reservation in Stockbridge, Wisconsin, the Mohican Band Stockbridge-Munsee Community.[20]

⬅⟹

After the removal of most of the Indigenous people around it, the river that flowed both ways became famous the world over as renowned White male artists captured its lush beauty and breathtaking light. Captains of industry, at the same time, built factories on its shores that polluted its waters so badly that eventually life in the river died. Folk singers led campaigns in the 1960s advocating for its clean up and industrial regulation, and now, once again, life thrives in the waters moved in and out by the Atlantic tides.[21]

But for how long?

⬅⟹

The river that flows both ways
Muhheakantuck
Muhheakantuck
Muhheakantuck

Esopus Bend Nature Preserve. Esopus Creek is a tributary of the Hudson River near Kingston. We walked a path alongside the creek through a mixed hemlock forest and onto a path. This preserve is on land used by Dutch and English colonists developed for agriculture. The Esopus Creek Conservancy that manages this preserve aims to promote biodiversity by protecting the natural habitats of its flora and fauna.

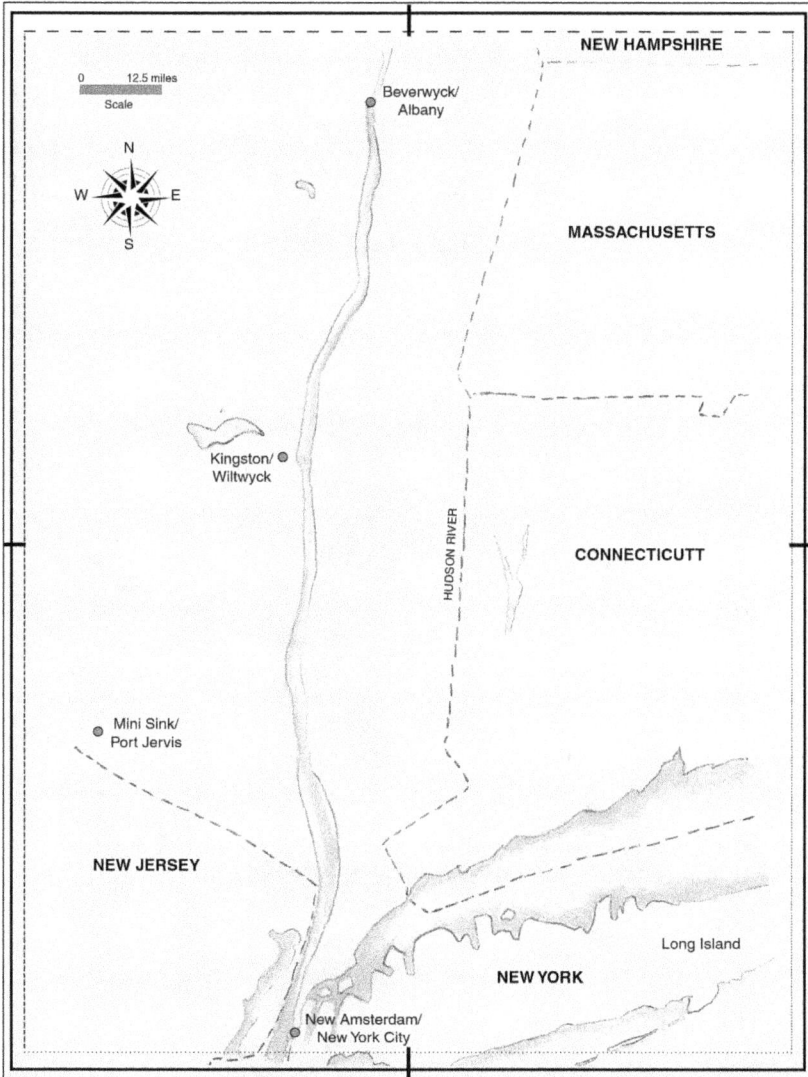

Map of New Netherlands/New York.

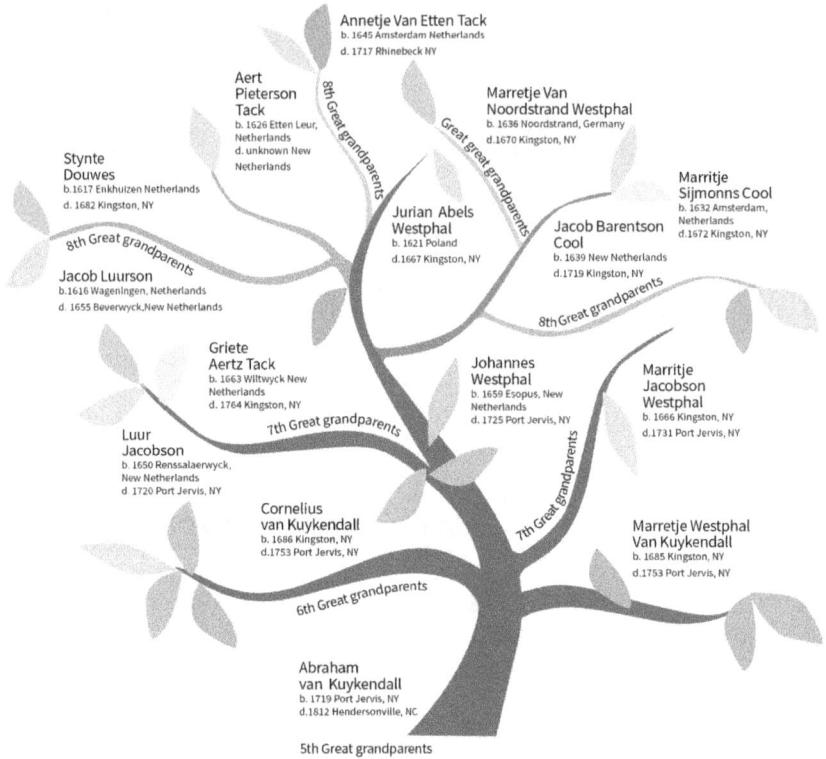

Family tree of Abraham Kuykendall, with Dutch ancestors who migrated from The Netherlands, including Jacob and Stynte.

concealed, revealed

I HAD A SURPRISING, heart-opening experience during a short winter trip to Florida, in the presence of Syd Solomon's paintings in the *Concealed, Revealed* exhibit at the John and Mable Ringling Museum of Art in Sarasota, Florida. Sarasota and this museum were landscapes familiar to me from childhood. Solomon's work held me in thrall but also sent me back in time. I felt as if this show had been curated specifically for me, to reveal influences in my life previously concealed from my consciousness—an experience now becoming familiar to me as I continued my ancestor investigations. Though not intended to be part of that journey, I found myself navigating between old emotions and the need for gratitude and grace.

———— ✻ ————

Just as Syd Solomon was moving from commercial design to painting, he was called into military service during World War II. Missing out on the early recognition of his talents as an abstract expressionist like his more famous peers[1] such as Rothko, DeKooning, and Pollack, who for one reason or the other did not serve in the war, Solomon's talents were put to work as a member of the Army's camouflage design unit, whose mission was to conceal whole environments from the view of Axis powers from land and sea, including areas in California and in Europe. While in Europe, Solomon was caught in Belgium's Battle of the Bulge. He suffered frostbite there, making it painful for him, even years after the war, to live in New York in the winter. He thus settled in Sarasota Florida's warmer climate. There, he and his wife lived in a house on the water and raised a family. Their summers spent in the Hamptons on Long Island, however, kept them in touch with the New York artist community.

The John and Mable Ringling Museum of Art, an ornate museum curiously situated in an otherwise sleepy beach town, was the center of Sarasota's local art scene. Solomon was friends with its director, Chick Austin. Throughout Solomon's life in Sarasota, he taught at the museum's art school. He often brought out-of-town artists and writers to his house, built on the tip of Siesta Key across the bay, creating a salon of sorts that kept him and the museum in conversation with the larger art world.

Solomon's work evolved from loosely figurative paintings to more geometric abstracts, then to greater emotional expressions of color and gesture. The sand, water, and sky, shaped his art. Natural elements were intensely evoked, even in abstraction. In 1961, Solomon painted *Silent World*, a five-foot-tall, vertically-oriented, acrylic on gesso panel with rich hues of blues, greens, reds, and yellows. Underwater explorer Jacques Cousteau gave the work its name (similar to his 1953 book title, *The Silent World*) when he saw it in Solomon's studio. The painting conjures the feeling sky light breaking through the ocean into the deep waters below. *Silent World* was acquired by the Ringling Museum of Art in 1962 as its first piece of abstract expressionism and the first piece from a living artist.

The year the Ringling Museum purchased *Silent World,* I was seven years old and living with my family in Sarasota on Morrill Street. The next summer, between second and third grade, I took a two-week art class at the Ringling Museum. This was no doubt my mother's good idea. Somewhere in her life as a housewife, she had an artistic yearning that she was willing to sublimate through me. I happily acquiesced. Though only seven, I was aware of her call to beauty in our everyday lives. Even in the modest houses we rented as we moved from place to place, she created an intentional aesthetic of clean, simple lines, reflecting the bare-bones simplicity of her life in Depression-era Appalachia. I absorbed from her the idea that you should always create the most beauty you are able to from whatever you have around you.

I loved those art classes at the museum. I was where I wanted to be. This was every bit of who I wanted to be. Learning about art. Making art. I remember the sprawling grounds of the museum. My class of a dozen seven- and eight-year-old boys and girls sat under an expansive banyan tree dripping with Spanish moss while we learned color theory. We also roamed the museum's ten galleries that each opened up to the long, pink-walled, and many-columned walkways surrounding the Italian-style courtyard and sculpture garden. I was a princess in a palace.

I remember two pieces of art I made during those weeks. The first was an exercise in color mixing: gluing tissue paper of different colors on one large sheet to create new colors. This translucent layering of color like this still shows up in my photographic and collage work.

The other piece was a tempera painting, an abstract of loosely-shaped pink, gray, and white contiguous rectangles. It was displayed on parent's night at the museum on an outdoor wall facing the court-yard. I beamed as my teacher said lovely things about my painting to my parents. My very down-to-earth, Midwestern, working-class father, though, was quick to let me know it didn't make sense to him. He asked aloud what I had been learning these past two weeks, if not how to render an image that looked like something real.

I loved my father hard; he was the steady presence of my child-hood, and I knew he loved me unconditionally. Somewhere in my child's heart, however, I knew that I had learned something during these art classes that he did not know. I didn't feel the need to argue with him, but this was mine, not his. My pride in what I had created was not diminished because he did not appreciate what I had painted, nor did it deter me from wanting to create more art like it. I wished he had liked my work, but I was awakened to the fact that my parents' sensibilities were not wholly aligned with those of other adults I had come to find some authority in, like this art teacher.

A couple of decades ago, when Mother and I were remembering these art lessons, she bemoaned that she had sent me off to class every day in the cutest summer outfits, and I would come home with paint on my clothes. At the time of this conversation, I was in the middle of a mid-life crisis and in therapy for the first time. Her remark triggered a thought that something about her concern for my clothes must have kept me from being the great artist I should have been. This, of course, was crazy, but I went ballistic.

"What did you think would happen to my clothes in art class, if not get paint on them?" I asked. What had she said to me when she saw me in my childhood state of euphoric messiness, something that I imagined no doubt had left psychic scars?

Glumly, she said, "I'm sure I said the wrong thing. I always do." I just let her answer hang in the air. I wince to remember this childish-ness now.

A couple of decades after that conversation—and three months before a global pandemic that would make this trip my last travel for a while —here I was on a winter vacation, staying only minutes away from the Ringling Brothers Art Museum. I was surprised at how much detail I remembered about my life there even though I had not returned to Sarasota since childhood. I found the short street where we used to live and approximate location of our house, the gleaming white down-town church where we went every Sunday, and the two-story, white-washed elementary school, now partially hidden between trees grown wide and tall. The number one item on my "to do" list while we were there, however, was to visit the museum.

———— ✺ ————

When we first arrived, we wandered the grounds, saw the banyan trees. I imagined my young self, wearing the cute shorts and top Mother dressed me in that morning, sitting under the hanging tree limbs, hanging onto the teacher's every word. My whole body smiled at the memory of it. We entered the museum proper through an outside doorway to the temporary exhibits. We first walked into a squares-within-squares atrium space--designed with a skylight, black-green vines covering the walls behind columns defining an inner square, further outlined by wooden benches, two on each side with openings to the wall behind. Skylights opened up, lifting me into a bright blue sky with bright white clouds.

Then we walked down a hallway into the Solomon exhibit, the first room displaying biographical photographs and documents. I read he was connected to Sarasota, he came here after the war to paint, he was friends with the museum director. Some of his older work was on the walls, a portrait of his wife. And then I saw some early paintings on paper. And I recognized something. Just a fleeting thought, but it reminded me of what I had painted as part of my art class. And then I got to the next room where the real paintings were, the oils and acrylics on canvas and panels.

When I first saw these paintings, my body buzzed and a flower bloomed open inside my heart. Something that felt substantive and real to me in these abstracts drew me in. I could not leave them. My husband, Ron, was in the first room still reading about Solomon.

I couldn't let go of one image in particular, *Silent World*. When I finally got Ron in the room to help me contain my adrenaline rush, we read the text under the painting together. He asked, "What year did you take art lessons here?"

We deduced that I had to have seen it when I was there as a child. If I made an abstract painting in my class, it was because it was part of the curriculum. The teacher would have shown us this painting, newly acquired by the museum, as an example. And maybe its creator Syd Solomon made a guest appearance.

⚬⚬⚬

During intermittent periods of my artistic adult life, squeezed in and around my "real" work, I sometimes made abstract paintings. My pieces often took on the rectangular shapes of the early painting I did in my art camp. I never felt I was "getting" it, though. I thought that my abstracts were missing something—solidity, expression—and questioned if they were even art (My God! What is art anyway? A question I never stop asking myself.) I didn't know what the problem was or how to fix it, so I abandoned it.

But now, in Syd Solomon's work, I could see what his paintings had that mine lacked. I felt the presence of a connective tissue that evoked all the intensity of the land and sea around him. He used color and texture, and form to cut straight to the viewer's heart. He captured that essence of whatever we know and love about the ocean and the sky and put it onto a canvas. And yet, I cannot explain technically how he did this, just that this is what I felt when I stood in front of his work.

I wondered what I needed to do to bring this to my own work. Perhaps I needed to commit to a deeper motive than my eight-year-old joy of putting paint on paper (and perhaps also my clothes). I am not disparaging this motive for art, and it is no small thing for making art to bring joy to the artist.

To make a painting that reaches out and stirs something in the soul, however, I saw required a commitment to reaching down inside oneself. Plumbing the depths of emotion and meaning in one's life is what I think separates a visual image from art. Sometimes it is about beauty, but sometimes it is not. What comes up could be revelatory or even transformational. Some artists visit and revisit the same themes over a lifetime, working its mystery.

Perhaps abstract expressionism gave Solomon a way to make sense of his WWII experiences, even as it was a way to convey his experience of the ever-changing sea.

While I was still at the museum that afternoon, I got a call from my mother's hospice care nurse saying that my mother's health had made a sudden, sharp decline. Mother had been physically healthy most of the past decade, even with dementia, but this had changed. The nurse suggested we return to North Carolina sooner than we had planned. She might have as little as a week left. This was a shock; we changed our plans to get home as soon as we could.

After the call, I sat for a moment on the steps leading down to the courtyard, where I could see the dusty pink wall on which my own awkward gray, pink, and white rectangles had hung decades ago. I thought back to that parents' night at the end of art camp. I tried to remember what *Mother* said about my artwork. I couldn't remember, so I surmised she said nothing. Daddy's comments likely made her feel guilty about spending money on this class. But I knew she was not sorry I had the experience—even if she had extra laundry to do because of the paint on my clothes.

My decades-earlier, forty-something mid-life-crisis-self had focused on the wrong part of the story. I knew as I sat on those steps, with a grace I did not have during that conversation with her, that the real story was her love for me that got me to those art lessons, that emboldened her to ask Daddy for the money to pay for them. This was

the gift she gave me. Her love was the connective tissue in my life—
the substrate of art and beauty.

Portrait of an artist as a young girl. Me, in Sarasota, Florida, in the
second grade, before the summer I took art lessons at the Ringling
Brothers Museum of Art, where I made my first abstract paintings,
layered over a recent photograph of a banyan tree on the museum
grounds.

part three
fatherlands

daddy's girl

I GREW up believing I was temperamentally and physically more like my father than my mother; most of my family members reinforced this notion. Through reflections generated in the writing of this book, I also recognized a link between Daddy's storytelling proclivities and my own.

———— ✦ ————

As proof that I was "Daddy's girl," my maternal grandmother Ethel and my mother Norma both told the story (over and over) about how Ethel's attempt to take care of me one weekend when I was almost two years old was cut short the first night by my ceaseless cries of "I want my Daddy!"

My father got out of bed to answer Ethel's telephone call and then got in the car and drove two hours to come get me. When he got to her doorway, I was delivered straight across the threshold from my grandmother's arms to his. A high point in the telling of this story for both Ethel and Norma was their imitation of my wailing mispronunciation of "daddy" as "daa-ee." In my teens, I found this story tiresome, but I also knew it was a happy family story about the goodness of my father and how much I loved him. And Mother's wise choice of a husband.

It was all true. Rudy was the calm, strong, easygoing, logical counterpoint to (in my mind) my anxious, overprotective, emotionally-needy mother, who was the more looming presence in my day-to-day life. And it wasn't just my less-complicated love for him that made me Daddy's girl, it was also that we were alike in many ways, appearance being one of them: I had his blue eyes, and his fair complexion.

⸺⚬⚬⚬⸺

My father had a severely logical, rational outlook on life. Everything was to be done methodically and systematically, with efficiency as the goal, even if efficiency was unnecessary. For example, when our family traveled, he insisted that we were on the road as early in the morning as possible so that with less traffic we could get where we were going in the least amount of time, regardless of when we actually needed to get wherever we were going.

And when Daddy was around, every domestic task assigned to me was turned into a time-motion study. If he wandered into the kitchen while I was doing dishes after supper, he would lecture me on drying the plates in a stack top-to-bottom to save time instead of taking them out of the rack and drying them one at a time. I absorbed this belief in efficiency as a virtue and am always a little surprised—and frustrated—when those around me are not judging their efforts this same way.

Being the daughter of this logical, systematic, and efficient man likely led me down the career path of social science, the *social* part in response to his constant wondering about why human beings act as illogically as they sometimes do. His answer was that it was an unsolved mystery called "the human factor." My challenge, then, was to solve it.[1]

⸺⚬⚬⚬⸺

I often explained my father's hyper-rationality in terms of a genetic inheritance from German parents and growing up in a town heavily influenced by German sensibilities and culture. A stereotype maybe, but one that feels true. Which aspects of one's character and personality are biological and inherited, and which are learned through socialization? An interesting question that generations of psychologists and sociologists have studied and debated, but I (as one of them) have come to believe it is not all that important to answer precisely. Daddy was born wired for logic and reason (and possibly, like me, for introversion and shyness) in a place inhabited by many others similarly wired, and these sensibilities were culturally reinforced.

In the mixture of seriousness and light-heartedness that defined my father, the serious part predominated. My father's most poignant childhood story was this one: at age seven, Rudy had a paper route and contributed part of his earnings to the family's finances, as was expected of him and all his siblings. Rudy had eight dollars in his savings account in 1929 when the stock market crashed. He lost it all. He never recovered from that loss of innocence, nor trusted anyone when it came to money. Eventually he saved money in banks again, but he kept his finances very secret and spread his resources among different accounts. It took some emotional strong-arming to finally persuade him to show me his financial records when he was in his 80s, when it was evident he needed me to help manage his money.

The cataclysmic effects of The Great Depression on both my parents' families robbed them of any sense of control over their well-being. Having lived through similar family deprivations, even in very dissimilar places, contributed to their common worldview. They knew what it was like to go hungry sometimes. They both saw their parents make sacrifices for the survival of their families, and they made some as children. Everybody's energy was focused on money and working.

I also associated Daddy's silent emotional hardening against misfortune with the German culture he grew up around. The Great Depression was the perfect opportunity for Daddy (and his family) to flex this muscle. This stoicism dovetails nicely with logic and rationality. Emotions throw a monkey wrench into getting things done quickly. Even the happy feelings are messy, but the sad ones slow us down and make us especially vulnerable.

As a parent, Rudy was not a big fan of crying children. He grew up believing that emotional outbursts were unnecessary, perhaps even dangerous. "What good does it do to show others your pain and suffering? It makes you seem weak, and it makes it harder to get on the other side of it. We all have pain and suffering. Why should yours be more important than mine?" Or vice versa. Daddy would say, "Your crying is *making everybody else miserable*. So just stop it." So, we did.

Anger was forbidden also. I remember only two times when Daddy's anger at me manifested physically. (If he ever got mad at my younger brother Greg, I don't remember it.) The first time was when, at about age three or four, I refused to take some kind of bad-tasting syrupy medicine. After a few minutes of me crying and pushing the spoon away as it came toward me, he suddenly picked me up from my seat at the kitchen table. He held me facing him in his outstretched arms as he moved at a near-run with me to the bathroom and set me down in the empty bathtub. In shock, I stopped crying, opened my mouth, and took my medicine. No yelling. No more crying.

I don't even remember why he was angry with me years later when I was in my teens—something about what I was or was not eating, I think. He picked up an extraneous and non-breakable object off the supper table and threw it across the room, hitting and bouncing off our refrigerator. Stunned and hurt, I broke all the rules about not crying and left the table. No one followed me. Interestingly, my brother remembers this incident as my father being mad at my mother, and that she left the table in tears. In any event, somebody left the table crying.

I remember these events because they were rare. Daddy hated to lose control, and we were afraid he might break apart or explode if he got mad at us. And what he mostly got mad about was *our* tears, shouting, arm-flailing, kicking the door, pounding the table, so we kept inside ourselves as much of the undesirable feelings as possible. My brother, being a boy, got away with more overt anger than I did, though he may not agree when he reads this, but then I would ask him to explain the boot through the window.

Mother would rarely admit to anger, though she did cry a lot, especially when I was a teenager. She was always hurt rather than angry, and I always assumed it was because of something I'd done, even if I wasn't sure what that might have been. Which begs the question of why I didn't just ask her.

And as I got older, I also understood that some of this ability to keep emotions at bay, or at least under control, is biological. Gift or curse? I'm not sure. Daddy's brain and body just reacted more slowly to provocation or pain than other people's did—certainly more slowly than my mother's. He processed the world around him differently. And stayed calmer. And presumably made better decisions faster because there wasn't a red flare going off in his brain.

And I am like him in that way. Being slow to anger was, in part, a learned behavior, but it also is partly physical. I do not experience blind outrage or paralyzing terror very often. Nor am I quick to cry, or even feel the sadness. I do feel things deeply, but they rise up in me more slowly and are not as visible to others. It made it easier to pretend I didn't feel angry, sad, or regretful. People often assume I am okay when I am not, which could be good or bad, depending on the circumstance. Tamping down my anger had its drawbacks on my psyche over the long-term, but certainly it's a dysfunctional coping mechanism in long-term relationships. Having control over it, however, made my outward relationships with teachers and bosses and other people in authority less fraught. I took away their power to

see me hurt, even if it kept me from getting what I might want
or need.

⸙

My father's seriousness made him a responsible family man, a good
employee, and a good provider. His lighter side also was a gift to us.
Though shy in some ways, he loved to tell stories to his family and in
small, familiar groups, especially funny stories—and jokes. He kept a
small, dark green metal file box filled with jokes he had typed on
white index cards. Many of these rely on cultural references specific to
the '40s and '50s, so they were not so funny to my brother and me,
born after that. For example: "How did the robber escape the police?
He put a dime in the scale and got a weigh (away)."

Puns were his specialty. He scoffed when people remarked that
puns are the lowest form of humor. One of the first books he bought
for me when I learned to read was the *1001 Riddles* by George
Carlson[2]. I read them all. I still remember this one: "When is a door
not a door? When it is ajar." I still think it is hilarious and repeat it
sometimes when getting in and out of the car, much to the despair of
others riding with me.

Daddy, too, would tell his jokes over and over, prefacing them
with, "I might have told you this joke before." He would continue
even after Greg and I would say, "Yes you have, so please stop." But he
never did stop. The main problem with my father's sense of humor,
however, if you asked me and my brother, was that it was bereft of
irony. Much humor of the second part of the twentieth century left
him clueless. He never understood what was funny about television
shows like "Laugh-In" in the 1960s, or much later, "Saturday Night
Live," and certainly not "The Office."

⸙

Though he told many stories about childhood buddies he hung out with on the Mississippi River, as an adult, he had few friends. Mother, Greg, and I always worried that he felt bad about that. Greg and I had school friends. Mother's friendships happened at church, and to the extent that she and Daddy had a social life with non-family adults, it was with Mother's friends and their husbands.

Now I think Mother may have been projecting her own anxiety onto him. Daddy was at work with a crew of maybe a dozen men every day. He was an introvert, as I am. He may have been as happy to come home and relax as to go out with other men. He didn't drink alcohol and so was not interested in bars. From reading his letters to my mother, I know Daddy was lonely when moving from place to place before he and Mother got married, but we never heard him complain about not having friends outside the family. He spent most of his time with my brother and me when he was home, for which we were always grateful.

※

School occupied a place in my father's childhood about halfway between serious business and joy. He took going to school seriously. He had a perfect attendance record—a habit that would follow him into his adult work life. My father was a math whiz, but this did not make him a good student. Perhaps it all moved too slowly for him, was not interesting enough to sustain his attention. He thought books were important, but he was not a big reader. He mostly read the newspaper. He graduated from high school, but his only other formal schooling was midshipmen school when he was a merchant marine. No one in his family went to college. He thought college was important for his children, however, and began saving for my education even before I was born.

※

After Daddy graduated from high school in 1941, he traveled 200 miles east to the big city of Chicago. He got a job as a bus ticket agent. Before too many months had passed, America entered World War II. Daddy left Chicago to join the Merchant Marines. He spent the war on ships delivering much needed goods to US allies. He sailed the seas and visited many big cities around the world (including Amsterdam— a set of postcards he bought there now sits on my bookshelf). Even during war, he loved his life on the ship, fodder for lifelong story-telling to his family and friends.

When the war was over, he returned to Chicago and got a job working as an installer for Automatic Electric, a company now part of Verizon. Many years later, men who had served as Merchant Marines during the war were given veteran's status, but this was too late for my father to have availed himself of GI Bill money to go to college. I regret this missed opportunity for him and have imagined what his mathematical mind could have done with a college degree.

Knowing how much he loved life on the water, I always wondered why he left it. I never asked, though, because I didn't want him to think I was questioning his love for me. My existence, after all, had depended on his coming back to dry land. Instead of traveling the oceans of the world, he traveled the country in a car. It was a job that required him, and then his family, to always be moving. Towns that we would eventually be leaving for other towns. I had no idea that I, like him—albeit in very different circumstances—would have travel stories to tell.

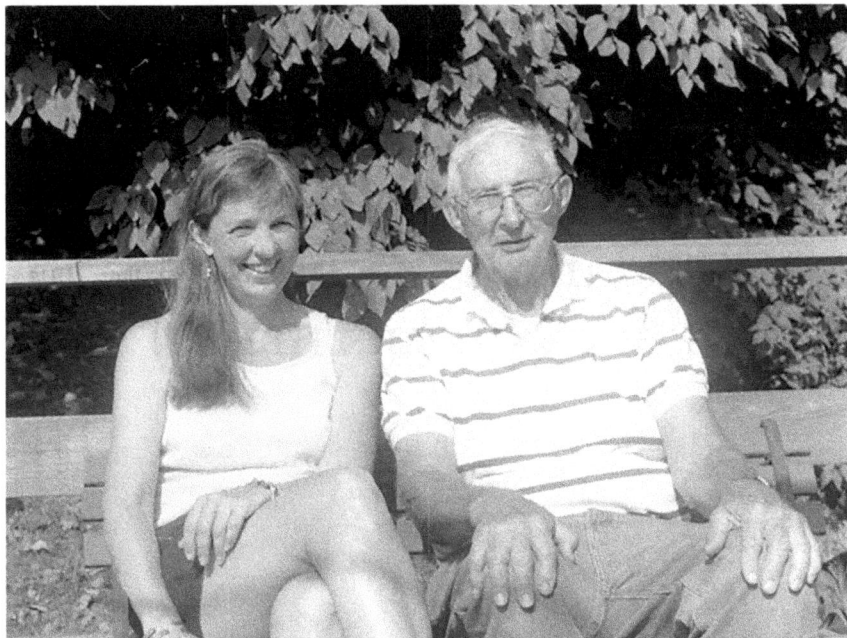

Daddy's girl. Summer 1997. I am sitting next to Rudy on my parent's back deck at their house in Waynesville, North Carolina, where they moved after he retired in 1987. I took this double portrait on black and white film on my 35mm Pentax K1000, pressing a button under my foot, attached to a cable hooked to my camera's shutter release. Daddy had been our family photographer when I was growing up. While he was in the Merchant Marines, he often processed his own film. Later, he used a lot of slide film, and I have notebooks full of his photographs.

the land that could not keep you (germany)

I KNEW my grandfather as William Henry, his Americanized name, but he was born Wilhelm Heinrich Stock in 1891 in the village of Bannesdorf. Bannesdorf is located on Fehmarn, an island off the coast of Germany in the Baltic Sea. He was the fifth of Wilhelmine Witt and Heinrich Arendt Stock's thirteen children. His mother's family, the Witts, had lived on the island for centuries. Wilhelm's father, Heinrich moved to Fehmarn from Heiligenhafen on the northern mainland coast, just about thirty miles across the water from Fehmarn. Wilhelm's paternal lineage can be traced there for generations. I went to Fehmarn to learn about my grandfather's life before America.

⬯⬯⬯

I chose to fly into Hamburg, Germany because its international airport is the closest one to Fehmarn. I did not know, however, when I made those plans, that Hamburg was where my grandfather actually left Germany for the United States. I knew I could get to Fehmarn from Hamburg by train, traveling north through Lübeck, and over the bridge across a short length of the Baltic Sea. I found my grandfather's village of Bannesdorf on the map, not too far from the larger Fehmarn Burg where I would be lodging. Fehmarn is directly south of Denmark.

I had an afternoon free in Hamburg to look around before I left for Fehmarn the next morning. By chance I learned about the nearby Ballinstadt Emigration Museum. When I got there, I found the story of my grandfather's journey to Iowa grounded at the museum site—its buildings having been the old emigration halls and his point of departure from Germany. His name appeared on a passenger list of a ship that left from there, and I saw photographs of that ship that took him across the ocean. I walked the ground he walked; it was my first glimpse into a much more complicated story than I could have imagined as a child.

I read on the passenger list that my grandfather left Germany via Hamburg in October 1907, at age fifteen—fifteen! He likely arrived in Hamburg some days before by train. Though there was no bridge from Fehmarn to the mainland, trains crossed the sea by ferry. His train came through Lübeck to Hamburg, the same route I'd be taking in reverse the next day. In Hamburg, he joined thousands of other Germans and Eastern Europeans bound for the United States of America. From what I learned at the museum about the emigration process, I visualized my young grandfather's days before leaving his homeland.

Once he got to Hamburg, young Wilhelm made his way to the Emigration Halls on Vedel, an island in the middle of the Elbe River. There, he began the official process of leaving. He paid for his ticket and registered his personal details in return for a control card. This card admitted him to the sleeping hall where he stayed until his emigration papers were approved and a ship was available. The control card was his meal ticket as well. He was examined by a doctor, maybe for the first time ever, to make sure he was fit for travel. After his medical exam, he took a bath; his clothing and scant luggage were disinfected while he cleaned up. He had to wait some days for a ship; no doubt he spent his extra time wandering around turn-of-the-century Hamburg, seeing the famous City Hall and St Peter's Church.

He left the day his paperwork cleared. His name was called, and he exchanged his control card for a passenger ticket on the aptly named *S.S. Amerika*. One more medical check-up ensured he would not be turned back in New York. Once on board, he left Hamburg down the Elbe River on to the North Sea. His ship turned south through the English Channel, then headed out across the Atlantic Ocean. He arrived in New York City after eleven days at sea, on November 10, thirty-four days shy of his sixteenth birthday. From there, he bought a train ticket and made his way across the US to join a large German immigrant community in Scott County, Iowa. There he was met by his older brother Theodor, who had taken the same journey from Hamburg four years earlier. Some years later, his younger brother Georg Karl would follow.

Wilhelm, Theodor, and Georg Karl were part of the massive migration from northern and eastern Europe during the nineteenth and twentieth centuries. Over five million people departed from the port of Hamburg for the US during that time—143,000 left the year before my grandfather left.[1] An estimated 2,500 people emigrated from Fehmarn itself.[2] Scott County, Iowa, was the destination for many emigrants from northern Germany. The land they settled was previously occupied by Meskwaki and Sauk people who were violently removed by the US military to make way for White settlers. My grandfather arrived over half a century afterward. How much did my grandfather know of that history? I'm guessing very little.

———✿———

Walking on the grounds of the old emigration hall, I could not stop thinking about what hit me hardest when I saw the passenger list—Wilhelm was only *fifteen years old* when he left his family and his homeland. I thought about myself and my children at that age and imagined roles reversed with me as the grandmother to my teenage grandfather, wanting to protect him from fear and sadness and dislocation that I was afraid his journey would bring him. I was reassured to some extent at the thought that he traveled with people he knew from Fehmarn, people who spoke the same Low German dialect he spoke who would help him get to Scott County. At age fifteen, leaving home and going to America had some appeal as an adventure—the possibility of freedom and opportunity he would not have had otherwise in a home full of many siblings.

What would it be like to be out in a wide-open world after a whole life in a small village? Did his young age make his travel harder, with less experience and maturity to help him out? But perhaps it made his move easier as well; maybe he was more open to new things, more agile and flexible, and more willing to take risks. Having moved so often in my young life, however, my heart was still tender for the homesickness and outsider-ness I projected onto his new life.

Only months before Wilhelm left Fehmarn, his mother Wilhelmine gave birth to her twelfth child, Rudolph. My grandparents gave this name to my own father, perhaps as a loving gesture to the memory of Wilhelm's family.

I also identified with Wilhelm's mother when I thought of his trip, having seen my own children off as they crossed the country or an ocean—the anxiety I might have felt for his safety, and the gladness at knowing he and his brother would reunite. What might I have tucked away in his trunk to make his trip a bit more comfortable? Maybe something to eat, like a cured sausage or cake, or something to make him think of home, like a quilt or photograph?

The morning after my museum visit, I traveled by rail to Fehmarn, riding with people making day trips to beaches along the coast. With the pace and vantage point of train travel, I saw the lush landscape passing by. Train travel also made clear my language difficulties. My preparatory German lessons were not adequate even for figuring out how to buy a ticket or where to sit. I continually had to admit my inability to read German and ask for help from strangers.

Every time I got on a train, I made some sort of mistake—getting on cars that did not let passengers out where I needed to get out or sitting in a seat reserved for specific segments of the ride. I felt at constant risk of humiliation trying to get from one place to another, the rules seemingly different for each train trip I made. More often than I would have liked, I had to step outside my comfort zone to beg people to help me figure things out.

I was quite unsettled by all this, considering I was a fairly seasoned traveler. This was the first time I felt so off-balance. I traveled extensively for many years, mostly in Africa and Asia, but because it was for my job, I always had a lot of support from people who could translate language and culture. Without that safety net here, I inhabited some strange personal space that seemed to be a separate reality from that of others—feeling physically safe, but after my unexpected wrangling with translation issues, worried about how I would handle losing a passport or twisting my ankle while traveling solo. I found myself more cautious and exhausted than usual, limiting the amount of time spent out in public places as a conspicuous outsider. Disengaging felt easier than risking exposure as a foreigner.

I began to understand, however, my grandfather's reticence that I experienced as a child. He likely felt uncomfortable speaking with people he did not know well, including my mother and me, family by marriage, people he saw infrequently. What kind of break with reality did my grandfather's trip to America—and his life once he got there— feel like to him? I had never considered the outsider-ness he may have felt, possibly compounded with shyness that seems to be a family trait, even in his own home, even many years later, but I began to relate.

⸺ ⟡ ⸺

On a satellite map, the island of Fehmarn is an uncut emerald sitting on the blue silk scarf of the Baltic. A bridge connects Fehmarn and the German mainland across the narrowest point between the two—about a third of a mile. The bridge opened in 1963, more than five decades after my grandfather left. The flat seventy-six square miles of mostly industrialized farmland has fifty miles of coastline. Fourteen thousand people live there, with 6,000 in Fehmarn Burg and the rest in forty-two villages around the island. Seaside activities and a large nature preserve attract tourists, most of them German. The island is a haven for sustainable energy capture; the wind blows across it nine days out of ten, and the sun shines more than 2,000 hours a year.[3]

Fehmarn was first inhabited by a Slavic tribe during the early Middle Ages. It came under Danish rule in the early tenth century. In 1848 Denmark was defeated by Prussia, a German state before Germany's unification.[4] This history of Danish rule explains why my "23andMe" profile listed nine percent of my DNA as Danish, even though none of my genealogic research showed ancestors from Denmark. This short summary belies this region's complicated historical entanglements with Denmark and German states, marked as they were by much political and military conflict.

———— ✦ ————

On Fehmarn, I stayed in the cobblestoned "old town" section of Fehmarn Burg at the Wisser's Hotel, established well before my grandfather was born. The building was the site of a famous battle in the 1848 Prussian defeat of the Danish.[5] On my first day there, I wandered into the visitor's bureau close by. The woman behind the desk there rolled her eyes when I told her I had ancestors from the island, letting me know she'd heard this often. Still, she phoned someone to confirm her suspicion that I am related to Peter Stock (pronounced in German as "schtock"), who lived just a quarter of a mile from where we were sitting.

"Here's the address. It's just up the road. He's retired. He'll be at home. Just knock on his door and introduce yourself," she said. A nightmare scenario for my shy self. She also gave me the email address of the island's archivist, Heinz Voderberg. Before I went to bed that first night, I emailed Voderberg all the information I had about my grandfather's family, including photographs.

I got up early the next morning and walked around the Burg. I used my phone GPS to see how close Peter Stock's house was to my hotel. When I walked the couple of blocks to this lovely German-style brick house, it was still too early to knock on a stranger's door. My first priority had been and was still to get to my grandfather's village, Bannesdorf. Chastened by my language difficulties and seeing little English signage in a town filled mainly with German tourists, I pushed my hand-written Google-translated travel request through the open window to the driver of the first unoccupied taxi I found.

The driver spoke English; even better, he lived in Bannesdorf so he knew where I wanted to go. We headed to the church, St. Johannis, where my great-grandparents were married in 1884 and buried in 1911 (Heinrich) and 1939 (Wilhelmine). The taxi driver was about my age. He was too young to have known my grandfather or great-grand-parents, but he knew other Stocks and Witts. His grandfather had been friends with one of my grandfather's brothers.

And he also told me about my cousin Peter Stock. And that I should knock on his door and introduce myself. We got to the small hotel and restaurant (the Gasthof) adjacent to the churchyard, and the driver stopped to let me out. I paid him and he graciously agreed to come back in a reasonable amount of time to get me.

I walked through the gate. The church was surrounded by several rings of gravestones, with white gravel pathways between them. Each headstone in this cemetery sits in front of a small, well-tended garden. I knew Heinrich and Wilhelmine were buried here based on my great grandmother's obituary in the Fehmarn Burg newspaper (photocopied and passed down through my parents and translated to English by my German neighbor in North Carolina)—and a photograph of my great-grandparents' gravestone. I also knew not to expect to see their headstone here still. I was told that in Germany, markers remain for fifteen to thirty years but eventually are removed and replaced by those of more recently dead people buried on top of the previous grave.

Wilhelmine's obituary recounted a story of her house burning down some years before her death, catching fire from flames that began at the church and carried by strong winds across the churchyard. She could save nothing from the house except herself. I asked the taxi driver about the church fire as he dropped me off that morning. He said, yes, the wooden church tower burned at one point and had to be rebuilt. I asked him if there were houses close enough to have burned as well, and he said, yes, that was true.

The obituary paid tribute to my great-grandmother's resilience in the face of a difficult life, especially after my great-grandfather Heinrich passed away in 1911, at age fifty-two, four years after his son Wilhelm emigrated. This story situated the lives of my great-grandparents and my grandfather in the physical place where I stood. Before embarking on this ancestor journey, I searched for something I could bring from America to leave for these ancestors. I carried shells from the Atlantic Ocean, the ocean that brought their son to America to become my grandfather. I placed one of them near the church gate, a symbolic entrance to their lives.

⁂

My great-grandmother lived most of her life within steps of this church yard while three of her sons crossed an ocean for a faraway place called Iowa. What different lives they lived. Being there, time, but not space separated me from great-grandparents I wished I had known.

A dense landscape of houses bordered the churchyard on three sides. The fourth side opened onto never-ending acres of farmland that once grew oats, rye, and beets for local farmers. It now grows wheat, rapeseed, barley, and corn for agricultural corporations. I left the churchyard to walk down Kirchenstieg ("stairs to the church") road, occupied on both sides by the Gasthof, and beyond that lined with mostly brick one-story houses with low German-style roofs, flattened at each end of the center peak. Similar to American ranch-style houses, but more like a square than a rectangle. Middle-class houses. Doors opened directly onto the brick road; cars, and motorcycles parked in front on the street.

One street over, the homes are similar but newer. It was a quiet weekday morning except for the buzz of a saw in someone's garage. A few people were around and saw me. I felt conspicuous—a stranger walking around their neighborhood. We waved, but I couldn't find my voice to say anything aloud.

Directly behind these newer houses were the farm fields; I stepped onto their edges as far as I thought I could go without trespassing. Acres and acres and acres of flat ground were made green by small shoots of grain. So much blue sky filling up the horizon. And against all of this were massive white metal towers with blades spinning slowly in the everlasting wind, looming so tall against the backdrop, as if they were aliens descended from outer space. They moved in a slow, graceful dance, slightly out of sync with one another. When later I found them on a satellite map of the island, I was amazed at how far away they were from me, how tall they really were.

The taxi driver returned later than we agreed he would. Still, the wait gave me a chance to sit at a picnic table on the hotel grounds and write in my orange journal, listen to the quiet, interrupted intermittently by bird song or the breezy voices of maids from the upstairs windows. The sun shined brighter and hotter than I expected in early June.

When the driver got back, he was unfazed by my concern about his late arrival, but he was resolute about my need to visit Peter Stock. I told him I planned to see Peter after lunch. Peter's house was on the road back into town. Rather than driving by the house as I had suggested, the taxi driver pulled into the driveway and told me he will *let me* get out there and I could make my way back to the hotel on foot when I finished. This didn't exactly seem like a favor, but I was not able to talk him out of this idea. Providentially, another car pulled into Peter's driveway at the same time. I reluctantly stepped out of the taxi to take advantage of the moment.

The man who got out of the car was dressed in white. He was curious about why the driver left me there. I asked in broken German if he was Peter Stock.

In English, he said, "No, I rent a room in Peter's house."

I also had prepared a Google-translated statement in German for Peter, explaining who I was and why I was contacting him. The nice man who was Peter's tenant turned out to be an E.R. doctor just getting off his shift. I showed him the note. He knocked on Peter's door from an inside hallway, but there was no answer.

My face flushed red, mortified in the face of all this effort extended in behalf of someone who had shown up so impolitely, so out of the blue. He called two more numbers before he got to him. Peter was out of the country on holiday. He said he'd be happy to see me when he got back the next week. Unfortunately, that would have been after I left. *So close.* I chatted with the E.R. doctor for a bit. He explained to me how to get to the nearby beach and wished me well with the rest of my visit.

After I got back to my hotel, now very hungry, I saw an email response from Voderberg, the archivist. He confirmed the information I sent him and added to it a detailed family tree. Peter Stock's paternal grandfather, Peter Jürgen Stock, was indeed my grandfather's older brother, the oldest son who stayed and didn't go to America. I did not come looking for cousins, but it was nice to know about them. The archivist later gave me Peter's email address. I exchanged several emails with him after I returned home. Mine were in English and Googled translated to German. His were in German, and I Google translated them into English. He was a gracious correspondent.

After I returned to the US, Voderberg sent me a photograph of Peter Jürgen's (Cousin Peter's grandfather) house in Bannesdorf, which was recently demolished to make way for the Gasthof now there. After seeing it, I knew that while I was sitting at the picnic table near the church, I was sitting right in front of the location where my great-grandparents' house had been, the house my grandfather grew up in, and that Peter Jürgen inherited as the oldest son. The headstone I saw in the church cemetery for Peter Jürgen Stock and his son Paul's family (Cousin Peter's father) is where my great-grandparents had been laid to rest. This cemetery space also was passed down to the oldest son. More puzzle pieces fitting together in my family story.

❧❧❦❧

Voderberg wrote to me in an email that at the turn of the century, there were said to be four occupations in Fehmarn: farmer, farmhand, fisherman, and emigrant. Lodgings were too small for most families to keep all their children at home once some of them got older. After finishing school, many older children had to leave their family's houses to live elsewhere—if possible, with an employer who could hire them as farmhands or domestic workers. Fewer and fewer farmhands were needed as farming became more mechanized, making the occupation of "emigrant" more of a necessity. Voderberg also wrote, "Of course, private matters also played a role." I considered what this might mean, the kinds of tension and conflict that might have existed in a patriarchal family of a dozen children.

My grandfather identified himself as a farmer or farmhand, having written the German translation, "Landmann," on the passenger list of the *S.S. Amerika*. In Bannesdorf, I stood on the field edge of his village, where my grandfather worked with his father and brothers on other farmers' fields. Here, his family also grew vegetables and raised chickens and cattle for their own consumption on what little land they had access to. Wilhelm was not in line to inherit any land of his own. Whatever his family earned from farming was not enough to feed all their children. Wilhelm left for a place that promised enough farmable land to provide for himself and whatever family he would come to have.

⤨⤨⤨

After my trip to Bannesdorf, I spent the next couple of days wandering around Fehmarn Burg and then down to the sea to the south. I did not want to get distracted from my ancestors' lives on this island and thought that sticking to a walking distance radius would focus me in this way. I woke the next morning to the very early summer sunrise. In tandem with the very late sunsets, the early sun made sleep difficult at this northern latitude of fifty-four degrees. Late summer light always feels like a gift, but where I lived farther south than this in America, there were still more than ten hours of darkness at night, compared with only five or six here. These long summer days were part of the rhythm of my grandfather's life here, along with the extended periods of darkness in the winter—an aspect of his life I did not consider before being here.

After getting coffee, I meandered through town in an easterly direction and found myself next to an open meadow softly laced with poppies along the edges. The meadow used to be a clover-covered pasture when cattle were bred on this island, before my grandfather left. Stands of hardwood trees were now in the distance in one direction and a silhouette of the old town buildings in the other. My heart opened wide in these lovely, open spaces. I took many photographs; I did not want to miss any of this big, vital beauty. And even so, I felt anxious, thinking I might not capture the whole of it or would not be able to convey to others the warmth of the sun on my skin, the breeze through my hair, the sounds around me. How could I communicate that my grandfather's history here also made my relationship with this island personal? It was now my history as well.

After returning to the Burg for lunch, I left again on a southerly route toward the shore, seeing again open blue skies and meadows.

These flowered meadows were lusher than those seen in the morning. The farther I walked, the more thickly the poppies were woven into the green wheat, along with other wildflowers, notably cornflowers—a heart-rush of beauty. Breathless, I gasped for more air, grasping to hold it in my mind at the same time. I was drowning in it, but I was not dying. No need to hurry. This landscape would not go anywhere, but it came on so suddenly in my awareness; its intensity was so unexpected. I became undone by this sweet, generous world. These poppy fields felt no less enchanted than the ones encountered by Dorothy in the Wizard of Oz. Unlike Dorothy and her companions, I did not lie down to sleep.

Immersed in poignant beauty, I kept walking. This vast field transitioned into wetlands where the water formed an inlet, and tall grasses created a border between sea and shore.

Farther on, I arrived on the sandy beach full of canvas-covered cabanas where tourists sat and watched, hypnotized, as the waves rolled in and out. I took off my walking shoes and socks, rolled up my jeans around my knees, and stepped into the Baltic Sea where the frigid water met the silky sand, washing over my bare feet. In the liquid distance, aqua blue met sky blue, reaching out to eternity. This was the first body of water my grandfather crossed to leave this island for America. An ending and a beginning.

I put one of my Atlantic Ocean shells into the water and picked up six stones from the wet ground to bring back with me for my father's and my grandfather's graves.

I am here, I am here, I am here.

He *was here*. I wanted to know what he was thinking and feeling as he left this place. When I was a child, I knew my grandfather loved me, but we were not close. He certainly never spoke to me about his German home, young as I was, as silent as he was. He would have been shocked to learn I had made this trip—that I would be curious about his life here or his journey to Iowa. I wonder what he could have told me about what his life was like while he was growing up here, what it was like to travel so far away from home, why he did. If my father had been able to make this trip with me, would being here have ignited his memories of stories he heard from his father and uncles about this place, about their mother and father and siblings and their lives here, their decisions to leave, their journeys? What might he have learned about his father, about himself?

After being on this island, in the churchyard in Bannesdorf, and on this beach, I knew more than I had known before. I didn't hear a voice or feel vibrations emanating from below, but being *here*, standing on this ground, I felt contentment and a full heart.

✺

In America, Wilhelm became William. He arrived in the promised but contested land of Iowa, a participant in America's Manifest Destiny. William met and married my grandmother Augusta, a daughter of Prussian immigrants. They multiplied and prospered, and their own children became recipients of the American dream. And I was to learn another story of that place that happened before William's: the story of people who had been forced off land he was soon to occupy.

St. Johannis Church in Bannesdorf. The main body of this church was brick and rather ordinary in most ways. What made the church so beautiful to me was the wooden tower in the front with its peaked bronzed cap roof, now an oxidized turquoise, contrasting with the surrounding natural green landscape and man-made gray hardscape. Obsessed by its charm, I walked several times around this building over the ground where my ancestor's bones are buried, near where my grandfather and my great-grandparents had lived and worked.

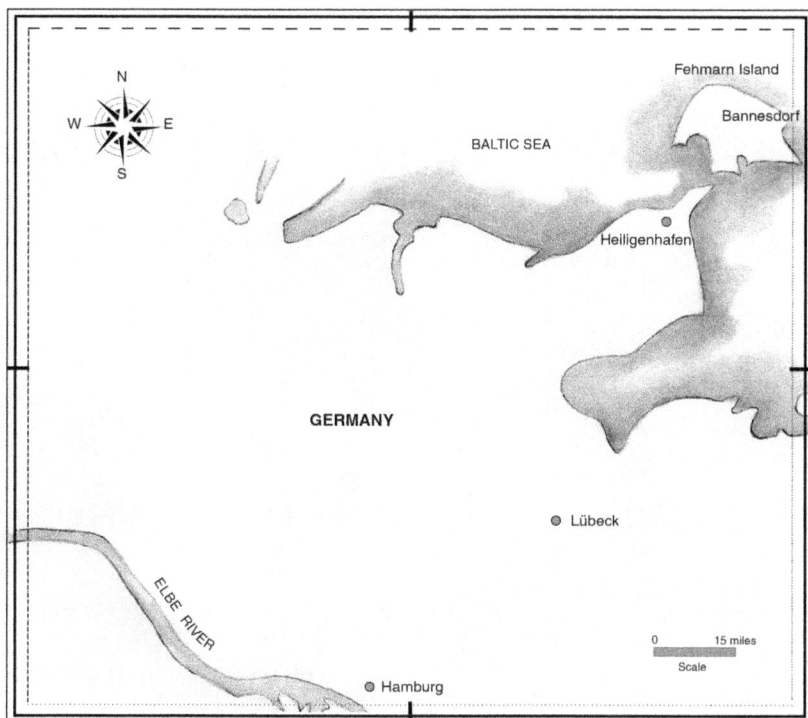

Map of northern Germany, including Fehmarn Island

fertile soil (iowa)

EMERALD OCEANS of corn and soybean fields meet the deep blue sky rising forever above them. Walcott, Iowa's landscape is more gorgeous than I had expected, but also, more troubling. These vast acres given over to factory farms are so harmful to the health of our planet, our culture, and our bodies. How do I make sense of my German family's connection to ecocidal industrialized farming practiced on the land where my father's German families settled?

⠢⠢⠢

My great-grandfather William Daniel Lindemann from Mecklenburg, Germany was the first of my paternal German ancestors to settle here in the 1880s. Next came his future wife, my great-grandmother, Bertha Muhs, in 1889 at age twenty-three, from Barsbek, Germany, in the same Schleswig-Holstein region of northern Germany as Fehmarn. William Daniel and Bertha married less than a year after she arrived, on the first of February 1890. Her aging parents, Peter Muhs and Catrina Stoltenberg Muhs, arrived three years later in 1893. My paternal grandmother Augusta Victoria Lindemann was born to Bertha and William Daniel in 1898—their fourth child and the first American citizen by birth in my father's lineage.

The Lindemanns, circa 1911. This portrait of the Lindemann family was taken in a photographer's studio with an animal skin rug on the floor and decorative curtains in the background. Bertha and William Daniel are seated, surrounded by their older daughters, Alma, Amelia, Augusta, and their son, William Johannes. The youngest daughter, Edna, sits between them. We see neither smiles on their faces, nor signs of unhappiness or hunger. Bertha is about forty-five years old when this was taken, her long, dark, high-collared dress, matronly in contrast to her daughters' white-laced attire. My great-grandmother appears robust and healthy, and I see a familiar softness around her face.

In the above photograph, my grandmother Augusta stands directly behind her little sister and slightly behind her father, her hand draped on his shoulder, most likely as directed by the photographer. Her hair is pulled back off her face to tame her curls, with a big white bow showing from around her ears and neck. My aunt Delores (Daddy's sister) wrote on the back of the photograph that Augusta was fourteen years old in this photograph.

My grandfather William Henry Stock arrived from Fehmarn, just north and across a small strip of the Baltic Sea away from Barsbek, Bertha's birthplace. William Henry and Augusta were married December 6, 1916, nine years after his arrival, only a few months after the death of Augusta's father. She was eighteen years old. William was twenty-five. The wedding photograph was made at the Lenz Studio in Davenport, where they were married. They said their vows in Plattdeutsch, the Low German dialect of Schelswig-Holstein. A wedding meal for family and friends at her mother's home followed the ceremony. The *Davenport Demokrat*, one of the many German-language newspapers in Davenport at the time, published their wedding announcement.

In the wedding photograph, I read her expression as one of serenity, like she believes this marriage is a good thing, like she is happy.

Augusta would have been about nine years old when Wilhelm arrived in Walcott. How soon after my grandfather arrived did he meet Augusta? Did he watch her grow up as he was working as a farm hand? Did their families know each other in Germany? Did the death of her father hasten their wedding plans? I wish I knew more about them as a couple, wanting their story to have been a romantic one, wanting my grandfather's homesickness to have been cured by my grandmother's love and affection. Wanting my father to be born in love, wanting their love to cascade down into my life.

William and Augusta were married for fifty years. William was always quiet in my presence. Augusta was the one I knew better. Augusta's letters to our family spoke of William affectionately, referring to him as "Dad." And judging by the upright character of my own father, William and Augusta were decent people and good parents. I believe that their love did flow to me through the love of their son.

Before German settlement, this place where my ancestors found their new home was grassland prairie that had never been cultivated. The Indigenous Meskwaki and Sauk people hunted there in the winter but never planted crops on the prairie. Before their removal by the US government in the 1830s, the Meskwaki and Sauk grew corn, squash, beans, and a small bit of tobacco, but only in the forest clearings near the riverways. Rather than plow, they used sticks to dig holes in which they planted corn, squash, and beans together—the three sisters of Native cultivation.[1]

Even the first White settlers did not grow crops on empty prairie land when they initially arrived, believing that if no trees grew in a place, it was not fit for farming.[2] Had they tried, the thick sod underneath the prairie grasses would have been impossible for animal-driven plows to till. They used the prairie for pasture and lived closer to the river. To grow food, they cleared wooded landscapes more familiar to them—the same kinds of lands lightly cultivated by the Indigenous people who lived across the river.

Prairieland was turned into farmland when, in 1847, John Deere invented a mechanical plow that could bite into the tough prairie sod, tear up its dense, tangled roots, and turn it over. The ground became tillable a year or two after first plowed by Deere's machine, once the uprooted grasses had sufficiently rotted and become compost or mulch. When farmers could dig past the former barrier of thick roots, they had access to nearly 40 inches of extremely rich soil built up over millennia of cyclical grassland growth and decay. New technology created fresh possibilities for what were considered empty spaces—working around barriers nature created.[3] Of course, they were not empty.

If only we could rewind this movie and change the script a bit.

Walcott became the town center for the nearby corn and wheat farms on the once-unplowable grassland only a dozen miles west of Davenport. Walcott is home to the American Schleswig-Holstein Historical Society, which I joined before my trip to Iowa. Many of its members are third- and higher-generation Schleswig-Holsteiners; most live in Walcott, where their families have lived and farmed since they migrated here a century or more ago. Karen is the society's genealogist. As a benefit of my membership, I was offered three hours of Karen's time for genealogical research. During my trip to Iowa, Karen and I met at the Society's library and talked—socially-distanced from each other—across a big wooden table.

A mutual interest in family history was our common ground. I wanted to know where my grandparents had lived in Walcott. Their Walcott address was not so easy to pinpoint. Neither my paternal grandfather nor his in-laws owned land; there were no deeds to identify their residences. My grandfather had likely worked as a farmhand initially and then rented land later for his own farm.

Karen had plat diagrams from the early 1900s with the names of the families who owned the various farms where he might have rented land. My grandparents' addresses on census documents are just rural route numbers, but they are clustered by residence. Karen believed that I could find where they lived by identifying the landowners whose names were closest to my grandparents' on the census list.

"Stoltenberg" was the landholder's name closest to my grandparents' names on the list. Yes! I recognized this as my great-great-grandmother Muhs' maiden name. Karen verified this. These Iowa Stoltenbergs were not in my direct lineage, but they had to have been kin to me in some way. It made sense that my grandparents lived on their land as renters, and possible that the Muhs family's path to Iowa had been facilitated by Bertha's mother Catrina's family. It was a close enough connection for me. I mapped the route to the Stoltenbergs' farm.

Karen is the keeper of many archival photographs taken in Walcott; she compiles them into books on local history. She had a photocopied image of a Walcott picnic reunion of dozens of people from Fehmarn. The names of my grandfather's brother Ted and his wife Alvina were among the few written beside faces in the image. Karen had been trying to identify as many of the other people as possible, and she asked if I saw my grandfather among the group. I was disappointed not to find him in the picture, but I had never seen a photo of Ted before, so that was a welcome surprise. He was tall and gangly in comparison to my shorter grandfather. The photograph was taken in 1938, sixteen years after my grandparents moved from Walcott to Davenport.

⸎

With maps in hand, I set out with my husband, Ron, to find the place that could have been my grandparents' home. I felt satisfaction in connecting the dots in the story of my grandparents' lives, solving a mystery of sorts. More than that, however, it strengthened my personal connection to them by understanding something about their lives that I did not know as a child—that they had been farmers, as my other grandparents had been.

Long driveways to the farms came off dirt roads and were laid out in much the same way since my grandfather farmed here, though the land probably was a denser patchwork of smaller fields then. The roads were numbered as if they were extended directly from Davenport. The old Stoltenberg farm bordered 80th avenue. It is crossed at one point by Highway 130 or New Liberty Road.

Looking at the old plat map, I couldn't tell how far north off Highway 130 the farm had been, because nothing was numbered. We drove up and down the road several times, stopping from time to time for me to take photographs of the fields and the barns. These verdant masses were more photogenically interesting to me as I got closer to their rolling hills and intermittent farm buildings, and I saw them in the constantly-changing light emerging through shape-shifting clouds.

I identified Hickory Grove Creek on the plat map as a landmark near the Stoltenberg farm, but I saw no signs for it on the road. Then, in our last planned drive south down 80th Avenue, I noticed a line of trees on both sides of the road. It occurred to me (finally) that these trees were growing near water. As we got closer, we found the camouflaged bridge over what I then realized is Hickory Grove Creek. The creek was not so small—maybe forty feet across at the bridge—with mud-brown water flowing southeastward toward the Mississippi River. Under a hot, sharp sun, I photographed it from both sides of the bridge, while I listened to birdsong coming from the trees.

I couldn't be sure exactly where my grandparents lived in relationship to the creek, but I was confident that they had been on this road and knew this waterway; it had been part of their lives. I looked out at land where they had likely farmed. I wished I had been around them more and known them better when they were alive, but looking out over the fields from the edge of this creek I could imagine them as a young farm couple with small children in tow.

⧖

Being in this place made me want to know more about how lush prairie land had been turned into green fields of livestock feed. Through extensive reading, I was able to weave this story through my family's history there, and thus I could understand how it influenced my life as well.

Many decades before my ancestors got to Walcott, but only a few decades after its Indigenous inhabitants had been driven off the land, settlers were able to buy land cheaply, for as little as seventy-five cents an acre. The land in Walcott was used to grow cash crops on the newly-tillable land—initially wheat and corn, and for a time, also potatoes. The Walcott economy grew around its agricultural purpose; places to store the harvest were built, and Walcott became a railroad stop. Steam-powered farm machinery increased the productivity of the land, as diesel-powered machines continued to do later, making it possible for fewer people to work the same-sized fields, setting in motion a way of thinking about farms as food factories.[4]

World War I greatly increased the demand for wheat and corn production here and all over the Midwest. The increased supply created to meet this demand turned quickly into too much capacity, however, once the war ended, abruptly, in 1918. Farmers were left with more supply than demand; crop prices plummeted, and farmers were unable to recoup investments. This scenario, along with the need for fewer people to work the fields, left many farmers and farmhands without a way to make a living. Government price supports kept some farmers afloat until 1920, but a steady exodus from rural to urban areas began. The number of farms in the US contracted by nearly half a million in 1922, the year my father's family left Walcott. As farm life was becoming no longer sustainable for my grandparents, the American farm crisis of the early 1920s dragged the national economy into an eventual stock market crash at the end of the decade.[5]

※

I knew my father as a city boy and, mostly because he had never talked about it at all, I had not realized that my paternal grandparents had grown up as children of farmers or started their young married lives as farmers. It was only my mother's family I thought of as farmers, and it was the summers of my childhood spent at my maternal grandparents' family's farm in the Appalachian Mountains that seeded my idea of what a farm was supposed to be. The food we ate there had been grown in fields or orchards—or in those of their neighbors. Strawberries, green beans, tomatoes, corn (eaten fresh on the cob), apples, milk, and butter—all from the farm, fresh or preserved. My mother had grown up eating what the land would bear, and when we visited her parents, she made sure my city girl hands dug far enough into the soil to know where good food came from.

Over the years, I have read and been influenced by writers like Wendell Berry, Barbara Kingsolver, Michael Pollan, and Robin Wall

Kimmerer to believe that how our food is grown and distributed matters,[6] without toxins in the ground or on the plants, with the goal of regeneration rather than extraction. Since my paternal grandparents left farming in Walcott, however, most farmland there has been taken over by industrialized farming that produces food for animal feed, or unnecessary additives for processed foods, and focuses on yield per acre rather the health of the soil or the nutritional quality of what was grown.

The short-term efficiencies of toxic chemical fertilizers and pesticides used in factory farming, formulated to increase yields of genetically modified seeds, causes long-term damage to our environment. These toxins kill off beneficial microbes that would otherwise contribute to fertility of the soil and the eco-system within which the farm exists. The massive number of acres of heavily-tilled, mono-crop factory farms contribute to rising temperatures on the planet by releasing large quantities of carbon into an atmosphere already overloaded by greenhouse gases—carbon that is much more useful in the ground.[7]

⸺ ✧ ⸺

The farming crisis that expelled my paternal grandparents from the corn and wheat fields of Walcott never really ended, morphing into one long continuous ecological calamity. Soil erosion created the Dust Bowl of the 1930s. Tilled crops left bare ground in furrows between rows; heavy rains washed away organic matter in the uncovered soil; as organic matter was lost, the soil's capacity to absorb water was reduced, causing further soil run-off. According to a 1936 government report, an estimated 30 billion tons of soil had been lost in Iowa alone since its vegetative cover was destroyed through cultivation during the previous hundred years.[8] The authors of the report suggested that the fields of native prairie should have been left as pasture or perhaps, harvested for winter animal feed or mulch only. I wish that had been so, but then what would my father's family's story have been?

If only their words had been heeded! Farming practices that more closely followed the natural order of things were suggested by the report: keeping as much land as possible for non-tilled crops and pasture; planting cover crops such as clover that add nitrogen to the ground; adding organic matter from farm manure to increase nutrients and water solubility. Using manufactured fertilizers for soils deficient in essential plant nutrients was recommended only as a last resort, but it was that practice that became the status quo as farms got bigger and the number of farmers got smaller.

Ammonium nitrate manufactured for explosives for World War II by both the Allies and Axis countries was repurposed after the war as a chemical fertilizer. Its use, in tandem with evolving genetic technologies, created crop yields previously thought impossible. To absorb these high yields, corn and soybean harvests became filler materials—such as high fructose corn syrup, hydrogenated oils and many other starch and oil-based chemicals—in many processed foods. Corn was fed to cows and chickens taken off pasture lands to live in Concentrated Animal Feeding Operations (CAFOs), reducing the amount of land needed for livestock.[9]

—————ം⊗⊗ം—————

What I saw in Walcott was in such contrast to the Farm at Penny Lane in Chatham County, North Carolina, where a couple of years before visiting Iowa, I began spending two hours a week volunteering to help tend its one-acre organic garden. That work brought me into a community of people vulnerable and food-insecure, for whom the farm is a source of nourishment and healing. Solar, wind, and human energy are used instead of fossil fuels or chemicals. Diverse crops are rotated among different beds, land is allowed to go fallow, and cover crops are grown. Chickens and bees contribute to an interdependent eco-system with plants and animals.[10] Working there, even two hours a week, heightens my awareness of the natural world and the local community, and my interactions with others nourish me emotionally.

I also buy as much local and organic food from farmer's markets as I can, and shop for the rest of it at a food co-op, grateful that I live in a place where this was possible. I often worry that I should be doing more but have felt helpless in the midst of the unlimited resources and political influence of corporate agriculture. My time driving up and down the farm roads in Walcott, heightened my concerns.

In Walcott, I found myself in the middle of what Indigenous activist and water protector Winona LaDuke calls "a war on the land."[11] There was no way for me to ignore it, and yet it felt to me like everyone else ignores it in a conspiracy of silence. Is it possible industrial farmers do not know they are desecrating the earth, or is it impossible for them to contemplate an alternative to their present agricultural practice?

⚬⚬⚬

In each field we drove by in Walcott, I saw white signs with a red stripe in the middle. The word "Pioneer" appears in large letters across the top. Pioneer manufactures the genetically modified P1197AM seed growing in the cornfield where I photographed the sign.

Pioneer Seeds, originally Pioneer Hi-Bred Seeds, is now owned by CorTeva, the agricultural arm of the global chemical company conglomerate, DowDuPont.[12] In 1926, Pioneer Hi-Bred began selling seeds for a brand of corn developed by the company's founder (and later, vice president under FDR), Henry Wallace, who applied his interest in genetics into developing a high yield corn for an overproductive market. The other logos on the Pioneer signs were for pesticide and fertilizers brands sold by CorTeva. Madden Ag services was also listed on the sign. They are a third-party sales agency for Pioneer. All the fields in Walcott were growing either genetically modified soybeans or genetically modified corn, each field rotated yearly, from one to the other.

The beauty that I ascribed to these farmlands came from what also was problematic about them for me. These expanses of monoculture sameness create the spare form and blocks of color of minimalism (not unlike abstract paintings that I love) that bring relief in a world that wearies us with its overcomplexity. I took my best photographs of this farmland with the widest-angle lenses—these gave me the big picture but lost the human-sized details.

Likewise, the standardization inherent in factory farms such as these incorporates these farms into a global economic system of production and exchange that displaces what is local and unique about the land on which they exist and the people who farm them. These are elements that would be beautifully captured by a more narrowly focused lens from a closer vantage point, similar to everything lush and lovely at The Farm at Penny Lane, where I most often capture its beauty at close range.

<hr />

There still were people living around Walcott who are distant kin to me. The names in my family tree that branches back into northern Germany were all over this place. I wanted to find some ties of relationship, and yet, I could not feel a whole-hearted affection for this place, because I knew the beauty of it comes from this landscape of bright greens unnatural to the original eco-system. I might have been one of these farmers if my ancestors had had a different experience and stayed on the land. My grandfather's break from farming, however, made me an outsider here now.

<hr />

I went to a Saturday morning farmer's market near the Riverfront in Davenport, glad it was open, but concerned about the lack of mask-wearing during a pandemic. I was looking to find out where food was being grown for human consumption, preferably organic. I had seen no vegetable gardens while driving around. I knew that corn and soybeans were the main crops, but why nothing else? Few stands at the market sold vegetables, and those that did sold produce grown across the river, in Illinois.

"So where is all the organic produce?" I asked the twenty-something young man at the only organic stand I could find.

"There isn't much," he said. He told me that he and his twin brother are fifth-generation farmers in Illinois. Their father gave them twenty-five acres on which to experiment with restorative farming practices—like using only organic fertilizers and pesticides, diversifying crops, and reducing tillage to maintain soil health and keep carbon in the ground. His father's conventional farming methods were becoming unsustainable. More and more land under cultivation was needed to make the same amount of money because per-acre margins are getting smaller and smaller—3,000 acres is the bare minimum needed to make any kind of profit. I heard the anxiety behind this story, but also the excitement and energy of a new generation who loves farming but knows something must change.

⸘

One farm in Iowa that does produce food for people to eat is the Red Earth Gardens, a regenerative, organic farm located on the Meskwaki Sak and Fox Nation settlement in Tama, Iowa.[13] Begun in 2013 to address concerns about food sovereignty, it aims to maximize ecological benefits of Indigenous land use ethics (such as no-till farming) and grow high quality, nutritious produce. In addition to providing healthy food to the people living on the settlement, it provides work and education for tribal members who want to farm, offering opportunities to the next generation that might not be possible outside the settlement. Though I was not able to visit Red Earth Gardens in person during my Iowa visit because of the strict Covid-19 quarantine in place, I have seen the beauty of it online and follow its activities on Facebook. It reminds me of all the goodness I feel at The Farm at

Penny Lane, and the many ways farming can create human connection across generations.

⸭

I pursued my vegetable garden question with genealogist Karen in an email. I later worried that even asking it might have appeared to be a critique of the farming practices of members of the genealogy society, though she didn't hear it this way. She told me no one grows vegetables much. The land is too valuable to grow anything but cash crops. These words echoed those written by Wendell Berry that industrial farming makes it "uneconomic" for a family to produce its own food.[14]

When I mentioned to Karen how beautiful these fields are and how amazing it is that there are so many people here who had worked this land for so many generations, she agreed. She said, "I don't think a lot of younger farmers appreciate how lucky they are that their ancestors found this fertile land that sustained them and their families for so long."

They are lucky in some kind of way I thought, but what about soil depletion and other environmental costs? Doesn't anyone know about that?

I liked Karen a lot, and I wanted her to like me. We have a common heritage. At that moment I saw no reason to create a schism between us by asking her further questions. I chose to focus on our similarities, but wondered to myself, where I should step in and voice my concerns, and where I should stay back? How much difference will it make anyway?

At that moment, I chose a human connection rather than risk conflict, but I'm not sure now if I chose correctly. Can we have authentic relationships if we don't speak our truths? I suppose it comes down to how much we can agree to disagree versus which differences of opinion might end a relationship. I rarely test these boundaries, afraid of what I do not want to know, because what would I do if I did? Not asking is pretending that the conflict doesn't exist.

⚉

When I returned home from Iowa, I wanted to find out more about restorative farming, also called regenerative farming. I start listening to *Field Work*, a podcast hosted by two young Midwestern farmers, Mitchell Hora and Zach Johnson, both in love with the farm life they grew up in but also deeply worried about Mother Earth.[15] Their mission is to promote and report on step-wise farming solutions for keeping carbon in the ground—such as reducing oil consumption, using ground cover, and growing something other than corn and soybeans on part of their land.

They face a wall of resistance from conventional farmers. It is hard to change when farming has looked the same for many years. Especially when it looks like it is the most cost-effective way to farm. There are, however, cracks in the veneer of that resistance. Feeling like being on "a treadmill that I couldn't get off" is the frequently-used phrase to explain what drives their podcast guests to finally try something new. They see no other way to slow the exhausting, constant press to work harder to cultivate more land to earn the same amount of money. Guests testify in defense of restorative practices they have field-tested—not for some spiritual connection to the Earth and each other that seem good enough reasons to me—but because they make sense economically.

I am struck by the care with which the young men suggest new practices to their elders who are guests on their show. They prepare their conversations as if what they are saying might be considered heresy, but they want their listeners to know it is grounded in data and economic good sense. They are careful to protect their relationships with their farming communities. I admire this but also worry that change is happening too slowly to avert the worsening climate catastrophe.

After my trip to Iowa, I continued to think about the question I posed at the beginning of this chapter: how do I make sense of my connection to this place? Its dire beauty troubled me enough to do more reading and listening, to make sure I had a real understanding of what I might be critiquing. Through this time spent thinking about this, I felt, not for the first time, a strong passion for doing something to help change things.

I am glad I trod lightly with the people I met in Walcott while I was there, but I also wanted to develop a relationship through which I can explore what motivates them, keeps them farming in this uneconomic and environmentally destructive manner, and creates resistance to change. Perhaps this is the way to test the boundaries of our connection. I also want to share stories about a different way of growing food —like at The Farm at Penny Lane. I want to be part of new things. If I had not let myself feel those nagging feelings while I was in Walcott, as I might have done at a different time in my life, I might not have continued to think so hard about a way forward to help heal and repair. The story of this land came to me as the gift of my ancestors' call. This story and whatever follows are gifts I hope to pass on to my descendants.

William and Augusta in Walcott, Iowa. An archival portrait taken on my paternal grandparents' wedding day in December 1916, superimposed over a photograph I took on 80th Avenue in Walcott, close to where I believe they rented a farm. They said their Plattdeutsch vows in a photography studio in Davenport, Iowa. My grandfather is wearing an edelweiss corsage in his lapel.

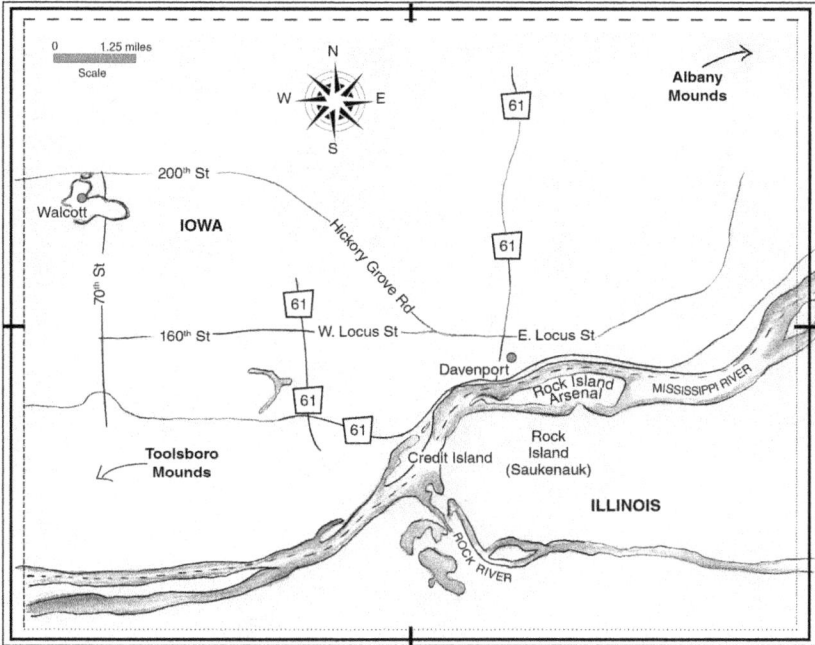

Map of eastern Iowa and western Illinois

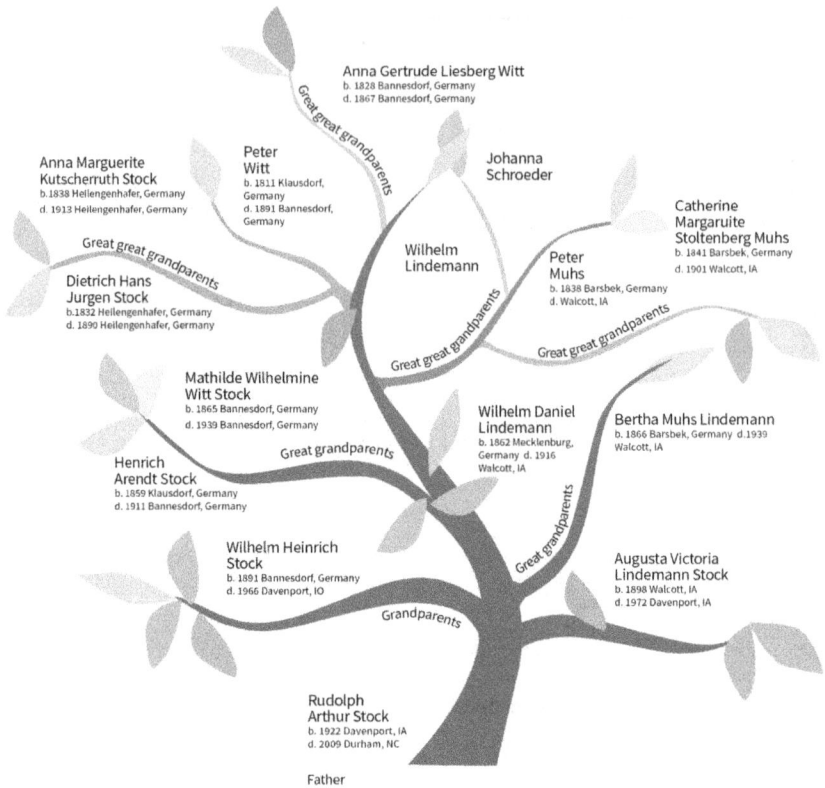

Anna Gertrude Liesberg Witt
b. 1828 Bannesdorf, Germany
d. 1867 Bannesdorf, Germany

Anna Marguerite Kutscherruth Stock
b.1838 Heilengenhafer, Germany
d. 1913 Heilengenhafer, Germany

Peter Witt
b. 1811 Klausdorf, Germany
d. 1891 Bannesdorf, Germany

Johanna Schroeder

Catherine Margaruite Stoltenberg Muhs
b. 1841 Barsbek, Germany
d. 1901 Walcott, IA

Great great grandparents

Dietrich Hans Jurgen Stock
b.1832 Heilengenhafer, Germany
d. 1890 Heilengenhafer, Germany

Wilhelm Lindemann

Peter Muhs
b. 1838 Barsbek, Germany
d. Walcott, IA

Great great grandparents

Mathilde Wilhelmine Witt Stock
b. 1865 Bannesdorf, Germany
d. 1939 Bannesdorf, Germany

Wilhelm Daniel Lindemann
b. 1862 Mecklenburg, Germany d. 1916 Walcott, IA

Bertha Muhs Lindemann
b. 1866 Barsbek, Germany d.1939 Walcott, IA

Great grandparents

Henrich Arendt Stock
b. 1859 Klausdorf, Germany
d. 1911 Bannesdorf, Germany

Wilhelm Heinrich Stock
b. 1891 Bannesdorf, Germany
d. 1966 Davenport, IO

Augusta Victoria Lindemann Stock
b. 1898 Walcott, IA
d. 1972 Davenport, IA

Great grandparents

Grandparents

Rudolph Arthur Stock
b. 1922 Davenport, IA
d. 2009 Durham, NC

Father

Family tree of my father, Rudolph Stock, with paternal and maternal ancestors, all born in Germany except for my grandmother, Augusta Lindemann Stock.

home/town (iowa)

I HAVE MISSED my father since his death in 2009 and wished he could have been with me in Germany to visit his ancestral homeland. I went to Davenport after my trip to Fehmarn to honor his memory and his German heritage. My visit to his hometown more than a decade after his death made me see more clearly how his life *there* influenced mine and still does.

Even before going there, I often used the story of being Daddy's girl to explain some things about myself. It was comforting to find places in Davenport where I connected some new dots about his life that felt interesting and satisfying to me as a way of understanding myself. Unexpectedly, I also found in Davenport a shift in my perception about who I am because of the ways in which I also am *different* from him and this place—and more *like* my mother.

Rudy was born in the town of Davenport in 1922, the same year his parents moved there from rural Walcott. Daddy was the first of his siblings to live all his life in town. Town, not the farm, was imprinted on his psyche. It defined the rhythms of his life—the comings and goings of so many people on street cars and bicycles and trains. Men worked in factories instead of wheat fields. A deep loud whistle initiated the day rather than a crowing rooster. Big families lived in small houses crowded together along paved, tree-lined streets. Neighborhoods were divided into rich and poor, German and Irish. Train tracks bisected the town into commercial and living quarters.

The town's physical space reflected German logic and order—beginning as a six-block by six-block matrix of streets and avenues, laid out as if on a blank slate and continuing to grow in this systematic way with the arrival of new settlers. Until he graduated from high school, Daddy lived mostly within this grid where he could easily count the blocks he would have to travel to his usual destinations, most within a two-mile radius of the house he grew up in on Dixwell Street.

This house still stands; people still live there. When I saw it, I had a hard time imagining five boys, two girls, and two adults living in that small structure. I was not surprised, though, to see where it is in relationship to all the other places Daddy spent his time. Daddy's family would not have had a car. He would have walked or ridden a bicycle everywhere he needed to go: school, the Friendly House, his paper route, and the river. My grandfather's work was also nearby—just blocks away at his first job at an aluminum company, and then later when he worked across the bridge at the Rock Island Arsenal, maybe a bus ride away.

In the early twentieth century, Daddy's Davenport was an ideal location for industry—on the Mississippi River and on a railroad line. Manufacturing brought people like my grandparents off the farm because farming was no longer able to sustain the same number of families. Several large employers—Ralston Purina, Oscar Meyer, the Rock Island Arsenal—in Davenport and Rock Island brought in people for labor. Labor unions rose up (though not without conflict) to ensure employees were fairly treated.

Growing up in this town, my father found himself elbow-to-elbow with men who labored hard every day to reach a semblance of middle-class life, who organized labor unions, and who went on strike when it was necessary to defend their means of support—and still do.[1] Daddy eventually became one of these men, not in Davenport, but in many other towns where his company sent him to install telephone equipment. He belonged to a union. He sometimes, reluctantly, went on strike. He was better able to care for his family because of the concessions the union negotiated with his employer. His pension and supplemental health insurance helped take care of my mother for years after his death, exempting me and my brother from ever having to pay for her care.

Though unions that provide these protections largely have been dismantled, what my father learned growing up close to the industrial center of this town, I also grew up believing. That is, a social safety net should be a basic right. I also grew up believing that working to support my family was a responsibility I could not shirk, even as it was more complicated for me as a woman to embody this belief.

⚬⚬⚬

The Davenport stories my father most liked to tell were about his otherwise carefree urban childhood—carefree in comparison to my mother's more restricted, protected, rural one in the North Carolina mountains. As a city boy he had access to the freedom and the wildness of the Mississippi River—something he would not have had if his family had stayed in Walcott. He hung out along the water with his buddies, became the excellent swimmer he always was (and wished his children had been), and smoked cigarettes that he rolled himself, starting when he was eight years old and stopping when he was eleven. His nickname among these friends was "Roots," for reasons he never explained.[2]

When I was young and we visited Davenport as a family, we'd drive by the river and sometimes visit the locks near the Rock Island Arsenal where my grandfather worked most of his adult life. It was only during my recent trip there that I found Daddy's hangout on the river, Credit Island, now a park. During a rambling walk along the water, I was happy to be in the place my father so loved, and I saw why he did. I imagined him here, giving himself to the pleasure of the river—an antidote to the graver matters of work and family. I think it was here on this river, watching ships come in and out, that he began to feel wanderlust for the bigger, wider world—a wanderlust that he acquiesced to and passed along to his children.

∞∞∞

Daddy also told stories about his time at the Friendly House—the Davenport equivalent of the Boys Club. He played basketball and pool and swam there in the winter. He often mentioned that Jock Mahoney, who eventually played Tarzan in several movies, also hung out at the Friendly House. In my parents' boxes of memories, I found a newspaper clipping with a photograph of Daddy with several other boys when he was about fifteen years old, at the Friendly House. He is standing slightly bent over a pool table, a familiar arm akimbo, holding a cue stick in the other hand. He looks as untroubled as any other teenage boy. I recognize a bit of my grandfather's posture in that hand-on-hip gesture.

The Friendly House still serves the same local community in Davenport, now housed in a newer building. I found the original, however—a school-like, two-story brick building. Concrete stairs that my dad would have scooted up to get in a game of hoops or pool before going home for dinner lead to the front doors. These doors now open to a homeless shelter. The words, "The Friendly House" are chiseled into stone above the arched opening. I stood in front of those doors and looked outward into what has turned into a sea of empty concrete nothingness. In decades past, these streets surrounding the Friendly House would have been crowded with men working in nearby factories.

The morning after I visited the old Friendly House building, I woke up early thinking about the ghost town that had once been the industrial center of Davenport, that had sustained my father's family throughout my grandparents' lifetimes. Two decades after my grandfather passed away, the factories that kept Davenport's industrial economy vibrant, began to shutter. This became a common but gut-wrenching sight in urban spaces as America stopped making the goods it consumes, outsourcing these jobs to other countries. People who were given entrée into a middle-class life as factory workers had it taken away. An ugly landscape of emptiness and broken everything—desire turned heartbreak.

I returned the next day to this barren field of desolation to take another look at what was there rather than what was not. I had a few jumbled memories of the industrial side of Davenport from my long-ago visits, among them the red checkerboard Purina logo on the side of a white silo and my baby brother holding his nose to stifle the smell of the Oscar-Meyer slaughterhouse. The Purina logo was still visible a mile or so down the road in a space now owned by a conglomerate corporation.

In the vaster, emptier space a few miles away, the only real activity was at the defunct Kraft plant, where a dust storm obscured its front façade as a wrecking ball loudly and repeatedly bashed into its brick walls. Stillness was everywhere else. Mangled wire fences surrounded bare parking lots, weeds grew through cracked cement surfaces, and piles of wood and half-finished structures of uncovered steel-beams dotted this landscape of loss. Whatever it had been, now crumbled into pieces of something else, possibilities never realized.

The economic destruction of people's lives to feed the beast of continuous economic growth continued to reveal itself in a collapsing empire and loss of natural resources. This was so evident to me in this deserted space as a natural progression from the original sin of the genocide and theft of land from the Indigenous people who had been there first. An ongoing (w)reckoning. My intolerance for injustice, I realize, is inherited from both my parents. From my father's side it comes from a sense of responsibility and a rational, logical understanding of right and wrong. From my mother's side, it is emotional outrage at the suffering of others. I somehow find my path in the world as the abstracted observer, the reporter of the big-picture stories, while I seek to mitigate suffering within personal, caring one-on-one relationships. I often worry that that is not enough, but I try to give myself the grace of knowing it is perhaps the only possibility.

⌘

During our family trips to Davenport, we must have frequently driven past Daddy's high school *alma mater,* Davenport High School, but I have no memory of it. I went to look for it this visit and was amazed to find such a beautiful building. I learned that it was designed by locally-renowned architect Fredrick Claussen in the Renaissance Revival style he was known for. The four-story building is an exquisite traditional European design adapted for Iowa geography and geology. It was built from locally sourced Marquette raindrop sandstone, its exterior streaked brown and tan, evocative of nearby prairie farmland. A red tile roof, terrazzo mosaic and hardwood maple flooring, plate French glass doors and picture windows[3] all add beauty and charm unusual for a public high school.

The beauty of this building was not something my father would have thought about *ever* when he was attending classes here, but I can barely get enough of looking at it and photographing its commanding presence. It takes a wide-angle lens and a bit of distance to get the whole of it in a single shot. It is the exterior details I am crazy about. A dozen columns flank its entryways and decorative stonecast faces of Roman gods are set above windows and doors, providing a subtle contrast to the right-angled stones of varying sizes and patterns.

⌘

And then my undoing. Daddy's life brought me here, but I realize everything that makes me love this building is because of my mother's gifts to me. I sometimes find myself setting Daddy and Mother up in an "easy/difficult" dichotomy, but in reality, it is always somewhere down the middle of their separate influences that I live my life. They were "both/and" for me. It was part of her sometimes-difficult emotional side that also valued the creation of beauty even when it was not a rational, logical thing to do. I found myself wishing I could ask her if she had seen this beautiful building when she visited Davenport with Daddy. Gut-punched with love and appreciation for my recently deceased mother. Missing my mother in Daddy's hometown.

I found in Davenport much of what I knew of my father—his love of the river, his working-class expectations of life, his steadfast work ethic, his engagement in a community where he felt comfortable. He found his workaday world in this eco-system of human interactions with each other and with nature. I saw his beautiful river and all the lush life around it. I recognized an inheritance of German stoicism and rationality, but perhaps, also a wistfulness for someplace else.

What was revelatory was that in trying to find myself in my father here, I also found myself in my mother. Maybe Rudy chose Norma to balance his rationality with her love of beauty, his coolness with her warmth. It is somewhat of a relief to appreciate the whole of what I have from my parents as complementarity rather than conflicted—to appreciate my dual inheritances from them as I understand my authentic self to be, at its best, a calm presence filled with deep caring about the beautiful, fraught world.

Davenport High School. My father's graduation portrait from 1939 layered over a photograph taken by me in 2020 of the building where he attended high school. It is an exquisite adaptation of traditional European design consonant with relevant aspects of natural realities of Iowa geography. I blink back tears as I think of this boy who became my father.

river crossing (iowa)

MY FATHER RUDY'S wistful accounts of his Huckleberry Finn days growing up in Davenport, Iowa, close to the Mississippi River, intertwine in my memory with his fascination with the Sauk warrior, Black Hawk, who, nearly a century before my father was born, fought for and lost the homeland he loved. Rudy and Black Hawk were born just across the water from one another. My father hung out with his buddies, leaving his cares behind as he swam in the river on a small island on the edge of Davenport called Credit Island. He walked on the same ground on this island where Black Hawk fought as an ally of the British in a battle against the Americans in the War of 1812.[1] Daddy frequently mentioned Black Hawk during our visits to his hometown when I was a child. Though I never saw him reading it, his fraying, turquoise copy of *Black Hawk's Autobiography* stayed visible on our family bookcase throughout the years.

This book made its way into my own home after my father's death, and a few years after that, I read *Black Hawk's Autobiography* for the first time. In an uncomfortable "a-ha!" moment—or more accurately, an "oh no!" moment—I first began to understand the personal implications of *my* White settler heritage as it related to the theft of Indigenous people's lands. Reading Black Hawk's story made me curious about the specific details of how it dovetailed with my paternal ancestral legacy. This became part of my quest as I traveled the summer of 2020 to Davenport.

Once there, I saw that Black Hawk seemed to be everywhere in the collective consciousness of those who lived nearby. It would have been impossible for my dad to grow up in Davenport in the early twentieth century without the mystique of this Sauk warrior infiltrating his imagination. Black Hawk's name was on banks, hotels, car dealerships, and all manner of non-Native establishments, often with his iconic silhouette with feathered headdress in the logo.

I was confused to find his persona used in this way when I knew he had resisted America's army as an act of war to stop the genocide of his people. Did the White people who lived here and saw his name everywhere know anything about him or how they had benefited from his defeat and humiliation by their settler ancestors? I had to wonder how many generations of settlers had had to pretend that nothing had happened to the Sauks and Meskwakis before most residents would truly not know of the genocide that occurred.

⚬∞⚬

My father was a child during the Great Depression and grew up in a family that struggled with money. They had felt anti-German backlash during the two world wars. I doubt Daddy or his immigrant ancestors considered that *they* benefited from the dispossession of Black Hawk's homeland. They came here to earn money, to raise a family, to make a better life for their descendants. Native dispossession occurred through no action of their own, and because of that, I'm sure they felt no responsibility for the violence of that history. They benefited from it, however, and thus, so did I.

My father's copy of *Black Hawk's Autobiography* was a bread crumb dropped for me to follow toward this destination. He never told me why he was so intrigued by Black Hawk. I assumed it was a boyhood fascination with Indians, or perhaps he knew the history of Black Hawk on Credit Island in the War of 1812. At about the time other ancestor stories began whispering in my ear, I took Black Hawk's autobiography off the shelf and read it, twice. The translation from Sauk to English by Antoine LeClair was difficult prose to follow, but its contents were as much of a reason as any other that I felt the weight of my ancestors' presence in Native dispossession. It is a story that connects me through them to the Indigenous people now living on the Meskwaki settlement in Tama, Iowa. It is yet another story of sorrow and wounding. Before you read it, take a deep breath, and let it out.

The warrior Black Hawk was born in 1767,[2] more than a hundred years before my first paternal ancestor made his way to Walcott. Black Hawk was a lineal descendent of the first Sauk chief of the Thunder Clan. He was born in the village of Saukenauk on the eastern side of the Mississippi River, at its confluence with the Rock River, now part of Rock Island, Illinois. He began his training as a warrior at age fifteen after distinguishing himself in battle against Osage warriors. Over his lifetime he was recognized for his bravery and his leadership in combat, often fighting in alliance with other Indigenous nations and even with the British.

Saukenauk was an idyllic summer village set in a beautiful riverine forest.[3] This was home to Black Hawk's clan, one of twelve that resided there in the warm weather. A watch tower on the highest bluff along the Rock River gave Saukenauk residents a view of many miles in each direction. Meskwaki allies lived in a village across the Mississippi River from Saukenauk. Eight hundred acres of corn were cultivated along two miles next to the Rock River. Horses fed on bluegrass pasture surrounding the village. Springs gave them drinking water, and river rapids brought with them more than enough fish for their needs. Cold winter months were spent on the western side of the river in smaller family groups, closer to the places the men would hunt before they all returned to Saukenauk in the spring. I can picture Black Hawk as a teenager in these places, strong and handsome, loving the carefree beauty of his summer village and learning to take on the responsibilities of an adult hunter and warrior with his elders.

The Sauk and the Meskwaki, like nearly all North American Indigenous people at the time, cared deeply about the preservation of the earth, letting fields lay fallow between harvests, never overgrazing, giving something back to the land and its inhabitants to replace whatever was taken. Though the concept of territory was meaningful to them, property ownership was not. This was a fundamental difference between them and the American settlers and the source of past, present, and future misunderstandings and heartbreak.[4]

∞

While I was in Davenport, I crossed to the eastern side of the Mississippi River (now the boundary line separating Iowa on its west side and Illinois on its east side) to visit the Black Hawk Historic Site that was once Saukenauk, verifying Black Hawk's description of its beauty. The land Black Hawk loved is crisscrossed by several hiking trails that showcase the beauty of the river and the forest. Virginia creepers, wild grape, and even poison ivy, wind themselves around large oak, catalpa, and hackberry trees. Close to the ground are young may apples, stinging nettles, jack-in-the-pulpit, and burdock.

On the edge of the woods is a prairie restoration garden, full of grasses and wildflowers that served the needs of the Sauk who lived there: rosinweed was made into tea, goldenrod was chewed to help a sore throat, and dried lead plants' leaves were made into powder to stanch bleeding. Nearby, there is a bird sanctuary, aptly named after

Black Hawk's wife, Singing Bird. Red-winged blackbirds, black-capped chickadees, robins, nuthatches, goldfinches, cardinals, mourning doves, chimney swifts, blue jays, orioles, crows, red-tailed hawks, and seven kinds of woodpeckers all sing their songs in this place.

My husband, Ron, and I spent a morning and part of the afternoon walking these grounds. We followed trails on the Rock River until we got to where they had been washed out by flooding. Exposed layers of limestone along the riverbank tell how this land had been deep under-water over 400 million years ago, its layers of sediment created from eons worth of seashells pressed under the weight of time, containing fossilized imprints of ancient marine creatures.

The feathery crown of the belted kingfisher, another bird that lives nearby, reminded me of the headdress seen in portraits of Sauk warriors. This bird dives straight into the water with its pointed beak to catch fish. Belted kingfishers drill six-to-eight-inch holes into the riverbank to lay and protect their eggs.

We backtracked over the first trail to find a place for a quiet lunch as we watched the river flow by. The largest toad I have ever seen, almost completely camouflaged in the bright green grass, kept us company. On the other side of the river, we saw a quarry. We weren't too far from civilization, but it was mostly quiet; possibly there were fewer people than usual because of the pandemic. We felt safe in the open air here. A long tree snag had fallen into the middle of the water but was stuck on something, rocking forward as if it were about to loosen itself in the current and move on, but it never did.

Moving away from the river we followed trails deeper into tall-treed forest, shaded by its lacy overstory, soft and lush inside this sanctuary. The path led to a lightly illuminated meadow with hard-woods filtering sunlight like stained-glass windows on a bright day. The trail wound back into what felt like a deep forest even though residential property lies close to its edges. It was easy to understand why the Sauk and Meskwaki chose this land as their summer home, and why they would not have left it except under duress.

⸺oᴓᴓꝋ⸺

They were, however, forced to leave it. And that is what made it possible for my paternal grandparents to come to America.[5]

⸺oᴓᴓꝋ⸺

In 1804, General William Henry Harrison negotiated a treaty with representatives of the larger Sauk and Meskwaki nations that ceded to the nascent United States of America all their lands east of the Mississippi River, including Saukenauk. No translators were present, and the Sauk and Meskwaki men who were there did not speak English. Sauk and Meskwaki people protested that the treaty was null and void because the signers obviously did not understand what they were signing, and in fact, were not legal representatives of their nations.

These protests went unheeded by the Americans. Indigenous leaders continued to argue their case, but because the treaty allowed the Sauk and Meskwaki to stay on so-called ceded lands until the government was ready to sell them, the day-to-day lives of the Saukenauk residents remained relatively unchanged—until 1828.

Life in Saukenauk was upended that year when lands ceded through duplicity were surveyed by the US government to prepare for sale to White settlers. The Indian agent assigned to the area informed the Sauk leaders that their people must now leave Saukenauk and all other villages east of the Mississippi River. Internal conflict about how to respond to this directive coalesced around two prominent Sauk warriors, Black Hawk and Keokuk.

Black Hawk believed the Sauks should resist. His political rival, Keokuk, did not. Keokuk agreed with Black Hawk that the treaty was illegitimate, but he did not want to fight. He had visited several big American cities on the east coast, and Black Hawk had not. Keokuk was certain they would never be able to win against the American army.

Isn't this a conflict we all find within ourselves all the time? Take the path of least resistance and live less happily with the outcome, but, we tell ourselves, with a surer guarantee of something better than if we fight and lose? In this case, it was a well-known White trader in the area, Colonel George Davenport, who urged Black Hawk to see Keokuk's side of things. As Black Hawk was later to find out, Davenport had positioned himself to be first in line to purchase Saukenauk land.

Keokuk quickly moved his followers to the western side of the river, to what is now known as Iowa, to build a new summer village where the land was not yet under US treaty. Black Hawk and *his* followers, however, did not join them. They kept returning each spring to Saukenauk, crossing from west to east back across the river after the winter hunt. Each spring they found more White squatters in the village. Black Hawk wrote in his autobiography,

" . . . *the white people appear to never be satisfied* [italics added] . . . [they] had already entered our village, burned our lodges, destroyed our fences, ploughed up our corn and beat our people. They had brought whisky into our country, made our people drunk and taken from them their horses, guns and traps, and I had borne all this injury, without suffering any of my braves to raise a hand against the whites." (pp. 78–79)[6]

This became too much for Black Hawk, and he resigned himself to the loss of what he believed was his rightful place in the world and moved his people to the western side of the Mississippi River to make a new summer village. *But then he changed his mind.* Feeling duty-bound to defend his homeland and the principle of right and wrong, in the spring of 1832, Black Hawk led his followers—warriors, women, children, and old men—back across the river into the contested eastern lands. He did not feel safe in Saukenauk, so he moved them to a different village farther north on the river, a village he thought was protected from American intrusion.

The presence of women, children, and old men in his entourage indicates to some historians (and to me) to be a sign that he did not begin his actions with the intent of war, though the possibility of it had to have been on his mind. Receiving faulty intelligence from trusted friends, he believed that he had enough Native allies to defeat the Americans. Skirmishes and small clashes forced him into combat against a state militia raised to defend settlers. Federal troops joined the militia; by all accounts Black Hawk and his warriors fought valiantly as they were chased over what is now Illinois and Wisconsin, but they were vastly outnumbered.

When he knew he could not win, Black Hawk tried to surrender, but his attempts were unseen or misunderstood—or ignored. In early August, when they got to where Wisconsin's Bad Axe River flows into the Mississippi, he sent non-combatants back to the western side of the river with a few warriors as protection, while he and most of his warriors stayed to fight. As these people tried to cross over, however, they were attacked by the Americans. At least 250 Native people died in that aggressive, unnecessarily violent assault, probably 100 of them drowning in cold, fast waters attempting to dodge gunfire. Black Hawk wrote of this Battle at Bad Axe,

---

"Early in the morning a party of whites, being in advance of the army, came upon our people who were attempting to cross the Mississippi. They tried to give themselves up; the whites paid no attention to their entreaties, but commenced slaughtering them. In a little while, the whole army arrived. Our braves, but few in number, finding that the enemy paid no regard to age or sex, and seeing that they were murdering helpless women and children, determined to fight until they were killed. As many women as could commenced swimming the Mississippi with their children on their back; a

number of them were drowned, and some shot before they could reach the opposite shore." (p. 115) [7]

Black Hawk's heart broke when he heard the news of what had happened during this murderous river crossing, and his conscience was burdened by his not being there with his people. Black Hawk surrendered at Prairie du Chien to General Zachary Taylor, with more than a dozen other warriors, his sons Whirling Thunder and Roaring Thunder among them. General Taylor put them under the custody of a young Lt. Jefferson Davis.

On September 21, 1832, Keokuk and the Meskwaki chief, Wapello, signed over six million acres of land west of the Mississippi in what is now eastern Iowa to the US government at a nominal, non-negotiable purchase price as a condition of what became known as the Black Hawk Treaty, punishment for waging war against them. The land was surveyed and sold to White settlers and eventually to immigrants, the majority of whom were from Germany, primarily from Schleswig-Holstein the homeland of my paternal lineages. As settlers poured across the Mississippi River, the Sauk and Meskwaki were relentlessly pushed farther westward, far past the treaty land, until finally, in 1842, they were forced to sell their reservation lands and move to Kansas.

This was the juncture between Black Hawk's destiny and my family history that I had been seeking to find—and it filled me with grief. This moment of dispossession was the lynchpin that connected the stories of an Indigenous people and White settlers—the Sauk nation and my ancestors—that when removed, appear as separate histories. But there is no separation; their histories are, in fact, inextricably bound together.

In my first reading of *Black Hawk's Autobiography,* I wondered why he seemed so willing to be chastised by the US Army for his resistance. After his arrest, he and his fellow prisoners were paraded in public, but more like celebrities than criminals. People came out to see them on the steamboat taking them east. Portraits were painted by White men of Black Hawk and his warriors, images now on view at the Smithsonian. The American military lauded him as a great warrior who had just been on the wrong side of the battle. He met President Andrew Jackson in the capital. They took him to the theater, but it was Black Hawk who was onstage.

After Washington, DC, Black Hawk was sent to Baltimore, Philadelphia, and New York City. In New York he went to Castle Island where he might have seen German immigrants on their way to go live on his land. His captors wanted him to know that he could never have won against them and to take that message home with him. I feel like they unnecessarily rubbed his nose in his defeat.

I reconsidered my initial judgement about Black Hawk having given in too easily. He was no doubt glad to be alive and wanted to see his wife and their children again—and his beloved Mississippi River. Negotiating peace is complicated. I know why he defended the beautiful land that I walked on almost 200 years later. I still am in awe that his commitment to what he saw as right was such that he was willing to give his life to defend it. He was sixty-five years old when he went into battle that last time, still vital and courageous. I respect his passion and strength.

Between 450 and 600 Sauk and other Indigenous people died in the Black Hawk War. If Black Hawk had not led his people into battle, would the US have stayed east of the river and been less eager to acquire Indigenous land in Iowa? Of course not. If he and his people had just crossed over the Mississippi with Keokuk, without a fight, there would have been pressure soon enough for all Indigenous nations to sell their lands west of the Mississippi, bit by bit. *The Americans wanted it all.* Our manifest destiny.

Seventy-seven American men died fighting Black Hawk's warriors. As with most wars, it gave several young men leadership experience and public recognition. Besides Zachary Taylor and Jefferson Davis, twenty-three-year-old Abraham Lincoln became a squad captain of the militia that showed up for battle before the US Army got there. It was not the last time Lincoln was involved in killing Indigenous people.

In 1862, as president, Lincoln ordered the largest mass execution in US. history, recounted in Layli Long Soldier's poem *38*.[8] Thirty-eight Dakota warriors were hanged in Mankato, Minnesota, the day after Christmas—punishment for their part in the US Dakota War, fought after years of starvation and disease, mistreatment, and abuse of their people at the hands of corrupt Indian agents. Similar to the story of the Black Hawk War, there was internal conflict within the Dakota nation about whether to resist White settler treatment or acquiesce. And also similar to the Black Hawk War, the true nature of the conflict was subverted and hidden from history books for many years.

———❦———

When I read *Black Hawk's Autobiography*, my attention kept landing on the White settlers who pushed their way into Saukenauk, taking what was not theirs. My anger mounted as I kept hearing their voices asking Black Hawk not to resist, to accept the fate of his people. But why should he have? More than a century later, people enraged over state sanctioned police violence are being asked to stop protesting in the streets and just let conflicts work themselves out. Why are the people who have been harmed always asked to be peaceful and play nicely? In examining Keokuk's life, we see the people who comply don't always get the rewards they expect. Though he stayed out of the fight, eventually his people were pushed farther and farther west. Though there is a town named for him, he died landless and penniless.

We might ask why Black Hawk is the one best remembered. I think that Americans loved his resistance and his warrior spirit, even if they wanted the land he went to battle to defend. Somehow, they resolve this logical inconsistency by forgetting the consequences of his defeat and focusing on the warrior. The lesson here perhaps is not to back down. If you obey without resisting, you lose no matter what. If you fight back, you have a chance of winning, and the dignity of standing up for your convictions.

⸻ ⥊ ⸻

How will *our* descendants explain to their children the injustices of today—how Americans stood by and let the border patrol take immigrant children—many of them Indigenous—away from their parents and house them in cages? Or let thousands of Indigenous women and girls disappear without enough moral outrage to make it stop. Our relationships with each other and with the natural world are frayed and unraveling. The troubled waters of injustice keep rolling over everyone, regardless of which political party is in power.

The murder of innocents in the Battle of Bad Axe is a blood-chilling story. It is a story people do not want to tell about their ancestors, even as they venerate the leader of those killed.

What if there had been a story of America where European explorers and White settlers found a way to respect and share territory with the people who inhabited the land before they arrived? My father's life would have been different, and my life and my children's lives would have been different as well. And so would the lives of the Sauk and Meskwaki and their children and their children's children.

And maybe this would be a country of compassion for every human being and respect for the natural world. We cannot change what has already happened. Perhaps, though, settler descendants can own up to our ancestors' past actions and consider how our histories and current lives are bound together with those of Indigenous ancestors and their descendants. And all of us together can find a safer passage across the river.

Rudy walking the paths traveled by Black Hawk a century earlier.
Archival photograph of Rudy at age fifteen in Davenport, superimposed onto a 2020 digital image of Credit Island. A bike ride away
from where my father lived in Davenport and the site of happy

childhood memories. The place where, centuries ago, the Meskwaki and Sauk people traded with French and English people; and a War of 1812 battle site in which Black Hawk and 1000 warriors fought with the British against the Americans.

burial grounds (iowa)

The hand of Yahweh set me down in the midst of the valley, and it was full of bones . . . . Thus, says Yahweh to these dry bones: Behold, I will lay sinews on you, and will bring up flesh on you, and cover you with skin, and put breath in you, and you shall live.

Ezekiel 37

BURIAL GROUNDS ARE spaces dedicated to the memory of loved ones—their bones perhaps the last touchstone of their existence. Coming from a tradition of burying deceased loved ones, the physical presence of their unseen bones in cemeteries calls up memories, real or imagined, beckoning me to experience our lineal bonds. During my visit to Iowa, I sought out the gravesites that house the bones of all my German ancestors who lived and died in Iowa. What I found, also, were stories about the bones of Indigenous people from this place.

My great-great-grandparents, the Muhs, and their daughter and son-in-law, my great-grandparents, the Lindemanns, are buried in rural Walcott. Though the cemetery is small relative to the expansive farm-scape around it, its headstones are spread out in a way that feels spacious. There is no pretense of uniformity among the gravesites. The cemetery is locally famous for a mausoleum for a child whose parents promised that a light would be kept on for her always after death.[1]

I found my ancestors' headstones there quickly by walking around the well-kept lawn, shaded by small stands of regal fir and towering cypress trees. The Lindemanns are buried close to the entrance. Other familiar family names led me to the Muhs' headstone. I took photographs of these family monuments, but also of angel statues and the flat land that opens out forever from two sides of the cemetery with a high sky in the distance as far as I can see.

Looking at the death dates of William Lindemann, it dawned on me for the first time that he died a few months before his daughter, Augusta, married my grandfather William Stock. I wondered if that slowed or hastened their nuptials. As I stood in front of the Muhs' and Lindemann's gravestones, I was thinking about surviving family members who had stood on the same ground before me to pay their respects. I conjured them here, above and below the ground, with flesh and heat.

William and Augusta Stock, my paternal grandparents, are buried in Davenport Memorial Park, a dozen miles east of Walcott, in Davenport. Finding their graves was not as easy as I anticipated. Before we found my grandparents' graves, I found the gravestones for my great uncle Theodor, the American, Ted, and Ted's wife Alvina. We happened onto a section of the cemetery just for babies. It pulled at my heartstrings to see hundreds of tiny heart-shaped markers in one place, and I wondered if the babies would not rather have been buried with their parents. But then I realized that parents are unlikely to have family burial plots when babies die so early in the life of a family. My father's younger brother Clarence died of pneumonia and measles in 1927 when he was two years old, and my father was five. He is buried close to where the family's house was at the time, in the Fairmont Cemetery, not in this burial ground near his parents.

When we saw the flags and military symbols in the veterans' section, I thought my father's brother, my uncle, Henry, might have been buried here after his body had been shipped from Lauzon in the Philippines near the end of World War II. I looked, but didn't find him. Later, I discovered that his body was buried in the Manila American Cemetery and Memorial with over 17,000 other Americans killed fighting in wars in Asia.[2] When I finally found William and Augusta— buried in 1966 and 1972, respectively—I see there is a star under Augusta's name to honor her as a gold-star mother and a flag under William's name, also a symbol of honor for having lost his son in battle.

I have memories of William's and Augusta's deaths. Augusta died seven years after my grandfather. Seven years was the difference between their ages, and so they died at the same age of 74. My grandmother was here on this ground for her husband's burial, and my dad was here for both. I have no idea what any of them thought about life after death. Their burials were much in the same tradition as those of their ancestors in northern Germany.

My father attended both of their funerals, but only my father, who made quick trips, each time alone. Being more pragmatic than emotional, he probably did so because he thought it would be too expensive or complicated to get the whole family to Davenport from where we lived in North Carolina. I doubt any of his siblings had an opinion about whether we should have been there with him. They were glad that he came.

My grandparents' shared grave marker was a bit dirty, so I went back to the car to get the wipes we'd been traveling with. I cleaned the marker as best I could. I remembered reading stories in elementary school social studies books about special days in Asian cultures to honor ancestors and clean ancestors' gravesites. I didn't understand why at the time, but when I saw my grandparents' marker with bird droppings on it and pieces of trash nearby, it made sense. A dirty marker felt wrong to me. I was glad for the chance to show my respect to them in this way and felt some regret that I cannot do this regularly because I live so far away. Since returning home, I began to make it a practice to clean my parents' double headstone, located nearby, when I go to visit it.

I brought three stones from the shores of Fehmarn, Germany, my grandfather's birthplace, to leave here. Picking up the stones in the Baltic Sea was done on a whim. I may have been inspired by Patti Smith's descriptions of paying homage to great writers and artists by visiting their gravestones and leaving small mementos. I did not want to leave the stones on a dirty marker. I debated whether to dig them into the ground next to the marker or place them on the marker, knowing that eventually they will roll away with the wind or rain. I left them free to move but took a photograph to document that they were there. I had three more stones that I later left on my father's gravesite.

I spent a few minutes there in contemplation of all the things that brought William's and Augusta's bones to this final place of rest. And to think about Augusta's parents and grandparents buried in Walcott. I reached across time, and in this place, held them in my heart and thanked them for their part in the life I live.

Thousands of years before my ancestors arrived on land near the Mississippi River, Indigenous people began burying their loved ones in communal gravesites near where I found my grandparents interred. Indigenous burial mounds were protective structures built around the deceased where they were laid on the ground, usually more than one at a time, and piled with basketfuls of dirt over the top. They were built on blufftops overlooking water on one side and villages or on terraces beside them on the other, creating undulating landscapes surrounding their seasonal settlements.

These mounds were first discovered when they were accidentally excavated by nineteenth century settlers plowing farmland. Afterward, burial mounds in Iowa and all along the Mississippi River were searched for and dug up on purpose, looted, and vandalized. Eventually, archeologists began studying these sites systematically for information about the ancient mound-builder cultures. Though no one really knows what happened to the mound-builders, the bones found by these early scientists, along with possessions laid out beside them, told them stories about who these ancient people loved, where they traveled, and what they considered precious and worthy of taking to the next life[3].

⸫⸫⸫

The design, construction, and contents of the mounds excavated by White nineteenth century archeologists were thought by them to be too sophisticated to have been part of Native culture, which they unapologetically labelled as "savage." Mound-builders, these theorists posited, came from an earlier race of people from one of the more "advanced" Old World civilizations, such as Greece or Egypt. They built these structures and left artifacts from their own cultures in them. The theory did not explain how these precocious people arrived or why they had disappeared—perhaps mound-builders had been exterminated by the more recent Native "savage" people, who the settlers themselves were trying to eradicate.[4]

The theory was debunked when it was discovered in the 1870s that fraudulent artifacts were manufactured to convince the skeptical members of the Smithsonian Division of Mound Exploration of the theory's veracity. These experts questioned a specific report from the Davenport Academy; under investigation, subsequent secret testimony made by whistle blowers disclosed that the report was the result of a series of hoaxes and cover-up efforts, unbeknownst to the archeologist leading the study. This incident became known as the Davenport Conspiracy and haunted the reputation of the Davenport Academy, now known at the Putnam Museum and Science Center, for many years.

⸙

At the same time communal burial grounds were being discovered by settlers, so were the remains of more recent Native people buried in single cemetery plots, often dug up by scientists and collectors to be used for experiments or put on display like carnival sideshows. A particularly famous incident was the theft of the remains of the famous Sauk warrior Black Hawk.

Black Hawk died in October 1838 and was buried on a friend's farm in Davis County, Iowa, on the northern bank of the Des Moines River. His remains were stolen in July 1839 by James Turner, who planned to exhibit the warrior's skeleton for profit. Black Hawk's two sons, Nashashuk and Gamesett, asked Robert Lucas, governor of the Iowa Territory at the time, to have their father's remains returned.

Governor Lucas had them retrieved. One version of the story goes that, with permission of the sons, he had them held at the Burlington Geological and Historical Society. Its building burned in 1855, however, destroying the bones beyond any possibility of recognition. In an alternate but no less problematic narrative, the governor gave the recovered bones to a physician, Enos Lane, who then passed them on to another doctor named McLaurens, who later moved to California. Black Hawk's bones were found by workers repairing

McLaurens' former house. According to this version, his bones were then re-buried in a potter's grave in the Aspen Grove Cemetery in Burlington, Iowa. Whichever of these stories is correct, there is now a Black Hawk marker in the Iowaville Cemetery on the Des Moines River, near where he was initially buried.[5]

The disrespectful handling of Indigenous people's remains in Iowa and elsewhere into the twentieth century was stopped, in part, due to Native resistance in Iowa. In 1969, the state Department of Transportation accidentally disturbed an old pioneer cemetery. They reburied 26 non-Native bodies found there but sent the one Native body to the University of Iowa for research. When Native Maria Pearson (Running Moccasins) learned of this differential treatment of Native and non-Native bones, she demanded an interview with the governor, which eventually led to the 1976 Protection of Human Remains and Sacred Sites. This first state law of its kind outlines procedures for investigation and re-interment of all remains accidentally disturbed. The Indian Advisory Council was created within the Office of the State Archeologist to ensure compliance.

In 1990, the US Congress enacted the Native American Graves Protection and Repatriation Act requiring federal agencies to inventory Native American human remains, burial artifacts, sacred objects, and objects formerly owned communally by tribes. Once inventoried, everything must be returned to its affiliated tribe. Greater care is given in the disposition of ancient remains, and collaboration between White archeologists and Native communities has become standard practice in this process.[6]

Numerous state-protected mound-builder sites along the Mississippi River are open to the public in Iowa and Illinois. I wanted to visit them during my visit to Iowa to get a more personal experience of what they are like, and how they might stir my imagination about Indigenous life before my ancestors arrived. I hoped for some beauty to photograph as well. I consulted the archeologist at the Putnam Museum about which mounds I should visit. She told me that the Albany Mounds and the Toolesboro Mounds were closest. "I especially love the Albany Mounds," she said. "I've done field work there, and I believe the land there is very similar to the way it looked when the mound-builders lived nearby."

⸺⸺⸺⸺

The Albany Mounds were discovered on the eastern side of the Mississippi River in Albany, Illinois, an hour's drive from Davenport. The preserve that now protects 36 of these burial sites abuts a residential area and farmland; the picnic shelter at the entrance is within sight of someone's backyard. Wide swaths of grass have been cut away from the botanically diverse meadows covering the ground above and between the sloping hills that mark the mounds. Faded signs provide information about the natural world of the preserve. This site was quiet and somewhat secluded. A sense of calmness pervaded. We saw only one or two people during our several-hour stay, which included a picnic lunch.

I began taking photographs as we started walking around the mounds. How wide an angle did I want to shoot? The distant horizon was such an expanse, I worried about losing detail. When I shot close enough for detail, I lost the big picture. A dilemma I faced when taking photographs of Walcott's corn and soybean fields. The world is both those things. The story I want to tell is both of those things. More sky or more land? I took in the images all the ways that I saw them, knowing there was more than I even could see. I didn't over-think it while I was out in it. I tried to capture all in the information I could for constructing a visual narrative when I had a better grasp of the whole.

Grasses, small white wildflowers, deep pink thistle, goldenrod, and blackberry brambles were all there, and so many kinds of shrubs entangled with each other in the meadows in many variations of greens and shapes and heights. Insects buzzing and birds singing and small silent rabbits. Beauty all around. And the sky above—clouds vaguely threatened rain that never showed up. The broad paths took us a circuitous route around the mounds, many forks in the road, choices to make.

We came to witness a landscape inhabited by human beings long ago. Mound-building disappeared in the first few centuries in the common era, roughly when Christianity became a religion of Empire. The beauty of these meadows alone evokes connection to Spirit. The bones of humans held by this ground hold sacred stories of human relationship.

We chose one trail and then another, thinking they would re-connect to a central route, that it would all make sense in the end. We walked through the middle of meadows, with stands of sumac, locust, and so many flowing grasses on the edges with tall, stately hardwood trees on the outside borders. Acres of farmland are within sight on the far side of these mounds. We came to a place where we thought we had wrapped around to the beginning of the trail but saw from a posted map, we had not. An impending storm made the air sticky; I felt hot and cranky about being twice as far from the car as I had thought. My irritation was startled out of me when a deer jumped up out of the tall grass. Once we got back in the shade of the trees, most of them older than I am, I found more ease, and once again I was in peaceful communion with this place.

———————

To visit the second preserve, we drove several hours south of the river near Davenport, then west, toward Louisa County, Iowa, and the Toolesboro Mounds. Along the Iowa River we passed endless farm-land, juxtaposed against concrete factories and industrial plants and more people living in impoverished conditions than we had seen else-where in Iowa—old trailers, mostly. The farm work looked highly mechanized, so we wondered who all these people worked for—and assumed it was the concrete factory. We learned later there are meat processing plants nearby as well.

Beyond the rangers' office (closed for the Covid-19 quarantine) were two round hills—the only Toolesboro mounds visitors can view. They were carpeted with uniformly short, bright green grasses, blan-keted by tiny white clover, smaller and more distinctly shaped than the ones in Albany. It seemed a long drive to see only these two small mounds with little else around. But, I realized, in getting here, we saw some of Iowa we would have not seen otherwise. Always the journey.

⌘

While visiting both mound sites, I keep thinking of the Bible story of the "dry bones." Yahweh reminds the Jewish people, then exiled in Babylon, of the dry bones of their ancestors slain as they marched through an unprotected valley—bones picked clean by scavengers, exposed, left as a sign of their enemies' disrespect. Through the prophet Ezekiel, Yahweh promises to release the Israelites from their captivity in Babylon, a release that will bring them to life as one people in a community of faith, as if he were breathing life back into a lifeless body. A resurrection. Yahweh asks only for their steadfast faith. Re-reading this story after my visit to Iowa, I learned that it orig-inated on the other side of the world at almost the same historical time that the mound-builders began burying their dead.

⌘

Returning from our visit to the mounds, we stopped in the world of life and breath to get gasoline and coffee. I stepped out of our car, drawn to the words "This too shall pass," inscribed in the thick dust on the large window in a Blimpie's sandwich shop next to a Dunkin'

Donuts kiosk. Two twenty-something men were parked next to us. In jeans and t-shirts, they were sweaty, and their clothes bore dirt stains from working construction or in the fields. I felt self-conscious about finding this quote in the dirty window photo-worthy and wanted them to leave so I could take a photograph unobserved.

One guy left. I got tired of waiting, so I went ahead and took the picture. The other guy noticed me but not my camera. He started talking about the heat and humidity. As we discussed the coming rainstorm, I mentioned I was surprised to see irrigation machines turned on when the rain seemed imminent. He said the storm had stalled out and probably wouldn't come. He was chatty and friendly, and it was nice to talk to someone so casually. As we spoke though, I realized I had not put on my mask; he was not wearing a mask, either. *Shit.* We were more than six feet away from each other, but was that enough? Is it *always* going to be like this—second-guessing the risk of human connection?

—⊶⊷—

After our visit there, I read that in the Toolesboro mounds, archeologists found small, narrow, copper pins surrounding the buried remains, set vertically into the clay subflooring. In the Albany mounds, pins made from a trumpeter swan's bones were found in a similar configuration around a burial pit. Both the copper and bone pins, it is believed, secured some sort of shroud, a cloth or skin to cover the dead. Historians believe that the burial arrangement—the preparation of clay floors, position of bodies, placement of the pins and bird bones—reflects a belief in the Algonquin and Sioux origin story of the Earth Diver.[7]

According to this story, water spirits that resemble riverine birds or mammals, such as otters or muskrats, were sent into a watery universe to bring up some primordial muck or mud from the ocean's bottom—to use it to create land by securing it between the sea and sky with anchors or weights. Ceramics shaped like water panthers, otters, beavers, turtles, frogs, and ducks, as well as the skeletons of these animals, have been found in mounds in both these sites. Perhaps the dead in these mounds were buried with these Earth Diver symbols in hopes of breathing life back into the bones of loved ones who had died, even if in the bodiless dream world beyond our own.

———⊶⊷———

Within a specific time and place, the actions of my ancestors set in motion events that breathed life into my existence. I traveled to this physical space to breathe life into their dry bones. I am glad for the places where I know these bones are protected, where I can find them. People who lived on this land thousands of years ago put the bodies of their deceased loved ones into the ground for safe memory-keeping, same as mine, deserving the same protection and respect.

May it be so.

Walcott Cemetery. *Walcott, Iowa, June 2020.* These are the grave markers for my great-grandparents Bertha Muhs and William Lindemann. Bertha's parents, Catrina Stoltenberg and Peter Muhs, are buried up the driveway and on the right. Cornfields for as far as one can see surround the graveyard straight ahead and to the left. I know my grandparents and great-grandparents walked this ground. It verifies their existence to me, their names chiseled in stone. As a connoisseur of cemeteries, I found this one lovely—small, with many different styles of lovely headstones, not too crowded, lots of trees, and a few angels (the more angels the better, in my opinion).

part four
gracelands

coming home—bethel (north carolina)

"Know that I am with you and will keep you wherever you go, and will bring you back to this land."

Genesis 28:15

BITTER WINTERS and the isolating terrain of the Appalachian Mountains made living hard for my ancestors in western North Carolina. Abundant summers and deep family ties made it hard for them to leave. Both sides of my mother's family began moving there from other places in North America after the American Revolutionary War. They settled on land that became available to them after the violent removal of Cherokee people whose territory it had been previously. Descendants of my settler forebears, for over a dozen decades, did not leave the mountain land where they were born.

Until, that is, my mother's generation began moving away. Though even as she and her siblings left for an elusive bigger world, Mother continued to long for a breath of crisp mountain air, the feel of fresh, crystalline snow, the gurgle of rapid waters tripping over river rock, and the sparkle of the first fireflies of summer. These were the never-ending sirens, calling her back and back and back again. And now I hear them and am pulled back to this place of childhood memories. I wanted to take another look at what I thought I had known about myself as part of her family in light of all that I had learned on my ancestor journey of the previous several years.

ᴧᴧᴧ

The town closest to where Mother grew up was Waynesville, but if you asked her where she was from, she would say "Bethel." This is the mountain community where she was born and raised, where she went to Bethel Baptist Church, Bethel Elementary School, and graduated from Bethel High School, where my grandparents lived most of their married lives, now a township in Haywood County, halfway between Waynesville and Canton.

It is not surprising to me that this Appalachian community, where signs announce, "Jesus is Lord of Haywood County," would be given a place name from the Old Testament. Bethel was at the crossroads between Israel and Judah, where Isaac's son Jacob sleeps one night after he runs away from his brother Esau. There he dreams of a ladder that ascends into heaven. At the top of the ladder, Jacob encounters God, who tells him, "The land on which you lie, I will give to you and your offspring. . . . Know that I am with you and will keep you wherever you go, and will bring you back to this land." When Jacob wakes up, awed by his experience of the divine, he consecrates the spot where he was sleeping, naming it Bethel, the house of God. He keeps his vow to return to worship God in this place when his journey is over.[1]

ᴧᴧᴧ

The farmhouse that was my grandparents' home, where a young Californian couple with young children now resides, fronts the two-lane US Highway 276, also called Pigeon Road. At one time the surrounding twenty or so acres were used as farmland by my grandparents, D.D.[2] and Ethel York. They were covered with fields of vegetables and flowers and a small apple orchard, but also a pasture with a barn for cows, a pig pen, and chickens.

I knew this land and this house as a child. It was where we stayed when we came to visit, sleeping in the bedrooms my mother and her siblings shared as they grew up. It is where I helped pick beans and strawberries, climbed apple trees, fed the pigs, and sometimes went out to into the pasture to bring in the cows for milking. It is where my cousins and I ran around the yard, caught fireflies in the summer, had watermelon seed-spitting contests, where we strung green beans with my grandmother on the porch, had after-church Sunday meals and whole family Thanksgiving dinners. I continued to visit the place for as long as my grandfather lived there, which was until he was ninety-five years old—long after I became an adult. It has been the geographic anchor in my life. It was only in the past several years, as I began my ancestor search, that I learned complicated stories about this land.

This land did not come easily to my grandparents. After many years of living on and working rented land, my grandfather eventually had a job selling Singer Sewing Machines that earned him enough money so he and my grandmother could buy a tract. They built a small house on it where they lived contentedly for several years. And then the stock market crashed. My grandfather's income disappeared. He told what happened to my aunt Dorothy on a recording made in 1988 when he was 88.

"One morning I got up and learned that the worst Depression that's ever happened to this country, in the '30s, had come on, but then in a week or two I couldn't sell a machine, I couldn't collect for what I had sold. I was on a strict commission. I kept trying and doing my best I could, but things kept getting worse and worse and worse. Well, what I owed for my house was financed through a friend, a wonderful man who owned buildings in Clyde [small town near Waynesville] and Canton and I went to him. 'I can't pay, I just can't, I don't have it.' I worried along that way for a year or so. Finally, I told him. I said, 'You'll just have to sell my home to get my money.' And it was up for sale, sold at the courthouse . . . The man sold my house and after a day or two, somebody knocked at the door, and I went to the door and there stood my previous landlord a few years before that. A big smile on him and cigar in his mouth. He said, 'Deed, you can move now, this is my house, you can get out.' So I was so sorry for my wife, as much as it hurt me, I was hurt for her more."

My grandparents and the three small children they had at the time, the youngest of them my mother, had to move and once again had to pay rent for a house to live in and land to work. During the leanest of times, my grandfather dug up stumps from trees cut down for timber or pulp and sold the stumps for firewood at ten cents a truckload. Eventually he was able to do some truck farming and later found work as a mechanic at the Wellco shoe factory in Waynesville.

⋌⋌⋌

I listened to the recording of my grandfather years after he passed away. It broke my heart to hear these hard stories in his voice that I knew so well. I could not imagine why it had taken so long for me to listen to these cassettes, though I know it was the hubris of youth and the illusion that I was too busy, had too much else to do to take care of my family and make a living. It grieved me that I could not talk to Granddaddy about them, that now after his death I understood so much better all that he did for his family and community, and me. I was glad, however, that my aunt Dorothy gave this gift to her family, and that I did eventually listen to these tapes. The stories he told gave me a new affection for him—and my grandmother—beyond the respect I had for them as elders. This newfound understanding of them fueled my interest in learning more, entangling me even more deeply with this place.

⋘

As they were growing up, my mother and her siblings worked on the farm when they were not in school, but they were never kept out of school because of farm work. My mother packed sweet potato slips for market, milked cows, made butter, watched the babies, and killed chickens (when they had them) for dinner. She could also cook and sew. They all went hungry sometimes, and even decades later, she never overcame the fear that there might be a time again when there was not enough.

Deed and Ethel were able to get back the title to their land in 1941 when my mother was in high school. The house I always knew as my grandparents' house was built then on that land, dismantled piece by piece in Waynesville and reassembled in reverse-order on their lot. They always had a garden there and kept cows and pigs and chickens, even when Granddaddy was earning money years later selling Pfaff sewing machines from a store in town. Three decades later, when I was in junior high school, they renovated the house and improved the mud-floor basement so that Granddaddy could move his sewing machine shop from Main Street to their house.

My grandparents gave my mother and her siblings each an acre of land when they got married. In their 30s, Mother and Daddy built a brick house on their land. It was our base camp while we continued to move from place to place for Daddy's job, where we stayed when visiting my grandparents, and it was where they eventually lived after Daddy retired. Mother and most of her siblings purchased extra tracts from Granddaddy and Grandmother as a way of helping with their parents' retirement finances. My grandparents and all their children are now deceased, and most of the original twenty acres has been sold, but two cousins and I still maintain title to a few acres of it.

АΛΛ

I did not want to let my ties to my grandparents' farm go, though earlier in my life, I would not have predicted feeling that way. I never longed for these mountains the way my mother did. I understand now, however, that the mountains were always a part of who I was, deeply woven into the fabric of my existence. When my aging parents sold their house in Bethel to move closer to me in Chapel Hill, I acquired title to their second tract with the idea I would build a small house on it eventually, though I did not think I was likely ever to move there permanently.

I kept talking to my relatives about building a house there as a way of keeping the idea alive, like the way one rolls a sip of good wine around in one's mouth to keep the flavor present. People around me were impatient for me to quit talking and actually build one. Building a house required time and money that I didn't feel like I had. At the time of this visit, even with more time, the money part was still a mystery to me. But the vision of a small dwelling there continued to tug at my soul. I was stuck on the money part of it, but I hoped this would become clearer if I kept moving toward the light of my vision. And, now that my husband was semi-retired and had more time, I drew on his energy to help work my way through this.

And there was also a matter that required some negotiation with others. Those who lived around my acre changed from kin to non-kin, mostly. I needed either a culvert across a creek or a right of way across another's property. I was shy about asking for something from non-family neighbors and also slow to engage with family I had not talked to recently, wary of stepping into relationship landmines not of my own making. Coming to Haywood County as the destination in my ancestor journey provided me with the motivation and opportunity to introduce myself to the new people and re-engage with family to discern the best way forward. Could these conversations actually heal old family wounds? I told myself not to expect too much.

⋙

My mother's mountain families were Kuykendalls and Yorks. My immigrant ancestor investigations focused more on my grandmother's lineages (Kuykendalls and Blacklockes/Blalocks) than on the Yorks because I had more information about them. The York lineage presumably was from England, but I was never able to identify the first direct York ancestors to leave England. In my grandfather's maternal lines, I found that most families (Millers, Burnetts) came from England in the mid to late 1600s or early 1700s and most got to North Carolina via Virginia, but also from Pennsylvania, Maryland, and Connecticut.

I could have picked any other family line to follow and found interesting stories to tell, but there wasn't enough time to tell them all. I chose the ones you have read about thus far. What all my maternal lineages had in common, including the Dutch Kuykendalls and English Blacklockes/Blalocks, is that their families eventually found their way to western North Carolina to live on land that once gave shelter and sustenance to members of the Cherokee nation.

ᴧᴧᴧ

I did not know much about Indigenous people in America as a child, and what I did know or believe was mostly what I had learned about Cherokee people while spending my summers in or near my grandparents' house here. And to be honest, I can't remember much of that. I knew of the nearby town of Cherokee where real Indians lived then, and now. People frequently found arrowheads in their fields or in the woods and because of that I surmised that Cherokee had lived more spread out on the land before my ancestors got to the mountains. There were conversations about Indians among my family members, but I don't remember what was said. Sometimes people talked about people who had Cherokee blood. The only Cherokee I ever saw were in Cherokee, selling souvenirs by the side of the road.

Sometime around age nine or ten, I saw the outdoor drama, *Until These Hills*, performed in Cherokee, North Carolina, as it still is, every summer. Written by a White playwright, Kermit Hunter, and at the time I saw it, enacted by mostly White cast members playing Cherokee people, the play portrayed Cherokee history from contact with DeSoto in 1540 up to the nineteenth century tragic removal of most Cherokee. Known as the Trail of Tears, it was a forced march from the southeastern United States to what is now Oklahoma in which an Indigenous nation lost its beautiful mountain land and "half the sixteen thousand Cherokee men, women, and children rounded up and force-marched in the dead of winter"[3] lost their lives[4].

My memory of the play is vague, but it no doubt taught me more Cherokee history than I had known before. It was not something I understood very well; nor did it seem very connected to my reality. It was more like a Bible story about people long ago and faraway. There is another story, however, that I had never heard growing up, that not many people know, even now. There was no outdoor drama portraying what came to be known as the Rutherford Trace. The brutal facts of how this land was taken from the Cherokee a century before the Trail of Tears and opened the way for people like my ancestors to settle there are heartbreaking to hear.

ᗺᗺ

The Cherokee people who settled what is now known as southeastern North America trace their lineage from or through South America and Mexico. There are several theories about exactly how they got to the Appalachian Mountains 10,000 years ago, several thousand years after the Celts got to Britain. Cherokee historian Robert Conley believes that his ancestors likely migrated north through Mexico, stopping for a time in the northeast and eventually moving back southward, settling in present day southeast America. This scenario is based on the Iroquoian roots of the Cherokee language and lifeways thought to be heavily influenced by the Eastern Woodlands culture of the northeast.[5]

After Spaniard explorer Hernandez DeSoto's first recorded European contact with Cherokee people in 1540, the Cherokee developed and sustained trade relationships with the French and the English. In the seventeenth century, Cherokee people lived in Middle Towns in the North Carolina colony, Valley Towns in the South Carolina and Georgia colonies, and in Out or Overhill Towns in what is now Tennessee and Kentucky.[6]

Smallpox decimated the Cherokee population over several epidemics in the late seventeenth through the mid-eighteenth centuries, killing seven to ten thousand people, weakening their ability to resist colonial intrusion into their territories. Cherokee leaders' trust of the European traders eroded because of this. Some of their own traditional beliefs began to unravel as the remedies known and used by their medicine men tended to exacerbate the disease rather than cure it.

Cherokees first ceded land to the British invaders in 1721 and then again in 1755 as a way of paying for goods they desired with what they believed was a resource abundant enough to meet everyone's needs. They learned soon enough, however, that settlers' desire for land would never be sated.

The Cherokee were allies of the British in the French and Indian Wars. When the British were victorious over the French in 1763, however, there was intense pressure from American settlers to establish themselves on land that extended from the Appalachian Mountains to the Mississippi River. This was land ceded to the English by the French in the Treaty of Paris, land the Cherokee considered *their* territory, not Britain's. Hoping to avoid fanning the flames of conflict between settlers and Indigenous people, the English government prohibited White settlement on these newly acquired lands under the Proclamation of 1763.

England also wanted to prevent settlers from trading raw goods with other countries or growing food for commercial purposes. Believing they would have a difficult time monitoring trade activity of settlers beyond the mountains also motivated their attempt to block colonists from moving westward. The Proclamation, however, did little to stop settlers from encroaching into what was supposed to be Indian territory, resulting in continual aggression and retribution.

I had never really considered the transition from loyal British subject to American revolutionary as anything other than an obvious desire for democracy over tyranny (as had been taught to me in school), until I discovered that it was Virginia's landed gentry—and George Washington, in particular—who felt most of the pain of the Proclamation's restrictions. They—and he—had been speculating on Britain's newly acquired lands since the 1740s in anticipation of making money off it after victory over the French.

Participation in the French and Indian War by elite colonists was more motivated by their expectation of getting rich(er) from selling land in the Ohio Valley than by loyalty to the British government. Washington had invested heavily in these land futures and believed the limitations on westward movement in the Proclamation of 1763 discriminated against elite colonials wanting to alleviate personal debt through profitable landholdings. This money-making opportunity, he believed, was especially owed to veterans of the French and Indian War, such as himself. Historians cite the creation of this policy as a clear ideological break between colonial elites and the Crown, though it seems to me to have more to do with capitalism than with democracy.

Settlers who ignored the Proclamation and entered Cherokee territory created enormous pressure on Cherokee leaders to sell them land, though actually it was illegal for the Cherokee to sell it. To mitigate potential aggression from White people, the Cherokee "voluntarily" ceded almost 50 square miles over several transactions from 1758 to 1762, thinking each time would be the last. This constant short-term acquiescence ended when a younger generation of Cherokee warriors felt they could no longer tolerate settler encroachment.

The Treaty of Sycamore Shoals, in which Cherokee leaders, as an act of accommodation, illegally sold twenty million acres to White settlers, created a profound rupture between Cherokee elders and a younger generation of warriors, most notably, Dragging Canoe. He spoke out passionately against his elders making this transaction.

"Nations have melted like snowballs in the sun. We never thought the white man would cross the mountains, but he has, and has settled on Cherokee land. We hoped that the white men would not be willing to travel beyond the mountains. Now that hope is gone. They have passed the mountains and settled on Cherokee land. Should we not therefore run all risks and incur all consequences, rather than to submit to further laceration of our country? Such treaties may be all right for old men who no longer hunt and fight. As for me, I have my young warriors about me. We will have our land."[7]

⋀⋀⋀

I did not know how emmeshed the Cherokee were in the rising conflict between colonists and the British Crown until I began making a conscious effort to learn about Cherokee history. I had never heard of Dragging Canoe, nor had any idea about the brutal destruction of towns by White settlers, people I had grown up thinking of as the good guys in the battle against English tyranny. Nor did my cousin Nadia know this history until she learned about it from a second cousin of ours, Charles Miller. What he told her so gripped her that she spent ten years of researching and writing *A Demand of Blood*[8] to bring it to light. It was from Nadia that I first learned about the Rutherford Trace. And with deeper digging into the story of it, I was shocked by a profound time-transcending personal connection. It is a story of trauma and grief.

⋀⋀⋀

Settlers never stopped pushing their way over the boundary drawn in the Proclamation of 1763, and the Cherokee (understandably) never stopped retaliating for the theft of their land. American colonists believed that the conflict with the Native nations needed to be resolved before they could successfully rid themselves of British rule, in part because of Native alliances with the British. Even the Declaration of Independence called for the extermination of the "merciless Indian savages." As I learned the true settler colonial history of America, it became clear that "liberty and justice for all" was not really what the signers of The Declaration of Independence had ever meant —not for kidnapped and enslaved Africans, not for men who did not own land, and not for women. But *especially* not for Indigenous people who they wanted gone.

In retaliation for their continuing intrusion into the shrinking Cherokee territory, in the summer of 1776, only days after the signing of the Declaration of Independence, Dragging Canoe and his warriors attacked and killed at least 200 settlers in western North Carolina. In this summer of "fear, confusion, and swirling rumors," a few historians suggest that some attacks against settlers may even have been carried out by White people trying to incite settlers into further action to extinguish the Cherokees' presence and obtain their land.[9]

In August 1776, a colonial militia of 2,700 men gathered for that very purpose at Davidson Fort, now known as Old Fort, in the eastern part of the current McDowell County, just east of Buncombe County. On September 1, General Griffith Rutherford led 2,400 of these men out of the fort on a mission known as the Rutherford Trace. The day-to-day logistics of this campaign were documented in a journal by William Lenoir.[10] The locations identified along the militia's route recorded by Lenoir are described here in terms of present-day geographical landmarks. I know some of them well.

The militia crossed the Blue Ridge Mountains east of Black Mountain and marched down along the Swannanoa River and crossed over the French Broad River. They continued west past the small town of Enka, down Hominy Creek and into Canton, turned up by the Locust Field Cemetery, and headed toward the Bethel community on state highway 110 and turned left onto US 276. They marched up the east side of the Pigeon River and crossed Silver Bluff.

Here. Right here. Where they turned left off of 110 and travelled on the land along what is now called Pigeon Road, past where my mother had grown up and where my grandparents had farmed and where I was thinking about building a small house. *Right here* they crossed to Silver Bluff. At the time the soldiers marched down this path, it was still open Cherokee territory—the Cherokee towns were farther west.

I have traveled this route by car hundreds of times without any knowledge it was traveled centuries ago by a militia on their way to exterminate Cherokee towns.

My cousin tells me that Rutherford's men were following a road known to be a Native trade route. Many Cherokee had passed through this land over centuries, if not millennia.

Rutherford's men continued over the mountain and camped out at Sulphur Springs in what became Waynesville. They marched on through Balsam Gap, down Scott's Creek on to Sylva, onward to the Tuckaseegee River, and then finally getting close to the destination of their malevolent intent, the Cherokee Middle Towns.

On September 8, they entered the Cherokee town of Watauga. It was difficult to keep reading this history, to realize the extent of the cruelty of their actions once they arrived. They cut down all the crops, killed the livestock and a couple of Cherokee men who were around. They burned every house to the ground. My stomach turned inside out at the sounds I heard in my head of animal and human screams of agony, and the heat I felt from flames licking the sides of the buildings. The words I heard in my mind were wickedness, iniquity, and soul-numbing sin.

Their brutality was relentless. Rutherford's militia moved to the next town and then every Cherokee town after that along the Tuckaseegee and the Little Tennessee Rivers, destroying each one the same way. They took some residents as prisoners to sell as slaves, and they shot, killed, and scalped others. In one town they forced all the women into one house and burned them alive. Evil actions that could not be undone. Could these deeds come from any other place but disturbed minds, part of a disturbed culture? And what about afterward? Were the men involved visited by nightmares for the rest of their lives? And yet, isn't this what nation-states keep sending young people into war to do, to live with?

According to Lenoir's journal, the colonial militiamen were surprised by how large the towns and crop fields were and at the abundance of food stored in them. They also were surprised to be met by so few warriors, possibly because Middle Town warriors had left to join forces with Overhill Towns being attacked by the Virginia militia under the command of General William Christian. And yet they were ruthless.

A South Carolina militia led by General Williamson had made plans to meet Rutherford's men at the Cherokee town of Nikwasi (located in present-day Franklin, NC) on September 10. The connection was missed, but Rutherford's men decimated Nikwasi on their own. The two militias were, for a time, each setting towns ablaze on parallel paths.

On September 26, men from the separate militia finally met up. Rutherford was greeted with a 13-cannon salute by Williamson in recognition of Rutherford's massive destruction of the Cherokee Middle Towns. Together, the two generals decided it was too late in the year to push farther west and risk getting caught in bad weather with exhausted soldiers and low supplies. Each militia took the route home previously traveled by the other and continued to lay waste to any town that had been missed by the other militia. Historians estimate 55 to 70 towns were destroyed. This is more life destroyed than I can bear to imagine.

The Cherokee people in western North Carolina who survived the raids became a nation of refugees with no housing or food that winter. No one knows how many people died. Some towns were eventually rebuilt; many were abandoned. The pain of it crushed the souls and hardened the hearts of those left behind. Cherokee elders eventually sued for peace with the "American" rebel patriots in North Carolina and surrounding states. Two treaties of 1777 divided the negotiations over two geographic regions. The treaties verbally humiliated the Cherokee who survived the fighting as the colonists demanded land for peace. Over half a million acres were ceded to colonists in those treaties.

ᨊᨊ

There were few deaths among the colonial forces during their attacks because there were so few warriors in the Middle Towns to fight back.

The campaign took a heavy death toll, nonetheless, on the hard trip home. Many died of exhaustion or disease. How, I wonder, could they also not be ruined by a sickness in their souls for the evil they had perpetrated?

The concept of "soul wounds" explained in Louise Dunlap's book, *Inherited Silence*, aptly describes what I imagined they must have experienced, and what lives on in the land they crossed. A soul wound, according to Native psychotherapist Eduardo Duran, is self-inflicted psychic damage experienced by the perpetrator as a result of hurting others[11].

How deep were their soul wounds? Could they even sleep with memories of the screams of women and children burning to death? What demons followed the survivors home and were passed down to their descendants—as they are in every war ever fought? Don't we all understand that we hurt ourselves when we hurt others? If the truth about original wounds is suppressed, subsequent generations suffer without knowing why. I hope that by telling this story, I can give festering wounds a chance to heal in the light of day.

⅄⅄⅄

Many of the White Rutherford Trace survivors found themselves fighting together again four years later, but against the British, at King's Mountain. Rutherford himself was captured and later freed by British forces. Many of the original militia returned to settle the lands opened up after the American Revolutionary War—lands they had traveled across during the Rutherford Trace and found so beautiful.

In 1796, a man named David Allison received a grant for 250,240 acres that included most of what would become Haywood County in 1808.[12] He was thus the first White person to lay claim to the land, though there were decades of disputes among White men over the ownership of these acres. This land, including the land where my grandparents farmed and I spent so many summers, holds more heartache than I could have imagined, and the question on my mind was what I might do to help heal generations of wounds for both Cherokee descendants and my ancestors.

ᗩᗩᗩ

When I began this final leg of my ancestor trip to western North Carolina with my husband in October 2021, our first stop was to visit my cousin Nadia. It was Nadia who helped me several years before to get started researching our grandparents' lineages, beginning with the Kuykendalls. I had been meaning to get in touch with her to share some of what I had been learning about our ancestors, but I had hesitated, I'm not sure why. Her genealogy skills were way more sophisticated than mine. What if she found a mistake? I also worried that she might think I was intruding on her work.

Before my trip to Waynesville, however, she reached out to *me*. I got an email from her about a new book she had written, *Murder in the Mountains*; she asked me to be on a social media launch team. One of the murder victims she wrote about is our great-great-grandfather, Eli John York. Her previous book, *Demand of Blood*, is about the Cherokee War of 1776 and very relevant to my visit.

When I accepted her request to help with her book launch, she asked about my research on the Dutch ancestors—her research is more focused on the Kuykendall generations closer to our own—and she accepted my offer to send her my chapters on the Kuykendalls. In turn, we accepted her offer to be her houseguests when we were in the mountains.

She knows every documented detail of the Cherokee War of 1776, including the story of the Rutherford Trace, by heart. She told me, "I feel that if I had not written *Demand of Blood*, this story would have been lost. People would not have known what had happened to the Cherokee before the Trail of Tears."

I told her that with little previous knowledge of this story, the information in her book had been a lot to absorb the first time I read it. But now that I was reading it again, after spending time learning about Indigenous genocide and removal, I had more context for understanding what had happened.

We discussed how the broad themes of the story played out nearly every place Europeans came to settle in this country—but so few people know what really happened in the places they live now. Nadia believes Dragging Canoe was really the hero in the Cherokee story, even though, in the end, he was not able to keep the settlers off the land he loved. I learned more Cherokee and family history than I could actually process within the short time we stayed with her and her husband, Hugh. I was happy to reconnect with Nadia, and we continued to stay in touch.

ᏊᎷᎷ

On our way from Nadia's house to Waynesville, where we spent most of the rest of the trip, we took a couple of detours to see mounds that mark remnants of old Cherokee Middle Towns. The largest and most accessible is the Nikwasi mound in the middle of what is now downtown Franklin. This outcropping is utterly strange in this location. I was reminded of the mounds in Iowa and Illinois in shape and color, but instead of being part of rolling hills, it rose up alone, in stark contrast to the commercial buildings around it.

At the core of communal life in Nikwasi, and all Cherokee towns, was the idea of "the right way," a way of life that was characterized by harmony and balance. Community responsibility and sacrifice were essential elements of their lives in small towns built around a structure called the townhouse, built over a mound like this one. A sacred fire was kept lit here, and decisions were made by democratic consensus.

What was once the spiritual center of an Indigenous community was now, as part of downtown Franklin, surrounded by mundane artifacts of the twenty-first century—telephone lines, stop lights on one corner, cinder block buildings that house the 828 Café, Abby's Angel CBD Dispensary, and a BP station. The historical plaque in front of the Nikwasi mound mentions the name of one person, a White man. Nothing about the land being soaked in the blood of a massacre. History erased.

⋙

The next morning in Waynesville, I moved through a checklist of tasks I needed to accomplish before I decided whether or not to build a small cabin on the land I now held title to. My first stop was to introduce myself to the couple who would be my neighbors if I built up here. I knew their names from Haywood County's real estate database. We knocked on Karen and George's front door around 10 am. A man with white hair, a kind face, and silk blue eyes opened the door.

As it turned out they were on their way out, but it was good to meet them in-person and Karen gave me the telephone number of someone who could help clear the lot enough so I could get a survey done. I promised to keep them apprised of whatever we did going forward.

We walked down to the lot. There were some old apple trees my cousins and I used to climb when we were children. We walked down to the bottom of the field where the stream was running, but I was disappointed to see that torn paper and empty glass and plastic bottles lay along the road. As I stood facing away from the road, I envisioned a house on the slope of the hill.

I called Herman, whose name and number Karen had given me,

and he agreed to meet us there at 5 pm that same day to give us an estimate for the work. Already, I was further along my decision-making process than I had been in a decade. A small shift in momentum. I still had more on today's to-do list, however.

ᴧᴧᴧ

We headed back into Waynesville to the county courthouse. On the road into town, I noticed for the first time a historical marker that I have passed hundreds of times before that says "Rutherford Trace" across the top. It was impossible to slow down enough to read what it says, but now I knew the story.[13] So much hidden in plain sight.

Before this trip to the mountains, I began learning how to navigate Haywood County's Register of Deeds online. I wanted to see how far back it was possible identify names of people who held title to the land I was contemplating building on, but I got stuck before I went very far. At the courthouse, I asked for some help in the registrar's office and discovered I was searching under the wrong category. The paper deeds are all there as well, bound and accessible to the public. I sat down at a desktop computer and began my backward search through time.

The story unfolding resonates with the story that my grandfather told my aunt Dorothy. From most recent to furthest past:

- My father's purchase of a second tract of land, the one I hold title to now, from Granddaddy in 1967,
- Granddaddy's purchase of land from Claude Kinsland in 1941,
- Claude Kinsland's purchase for $5,000 in 1931 after foreclosure during the Depression,
- Grandaddy's original purchase from Fred and Celia Davis in 1925, and

- the Davis's purchase from Neppie and D.M. Penland in 1922.

Neppie Penland is Neppie Kinsland Penland, sister of Claude Kinsland, and her land had been passed down to her from her father, W.S.[14] Kinsland who, in 1890, at age 40, purchased a larger tract of land from L.P. and Sarah Long.

As the years go backward, the deeds went from typewritten documents to handwritten ones. They got fainter and the handwriting harder to read. The configuration of the tracts of land changed over the years and it became difficult to figure out exactly where my tract was located. I stopped with the last item, knowing that the Longs' purchase came from David Allison's initial land grant. And I knew whose land it was before that.

After my computer search, I went into the archive room and pulled out the huge hardbound books of deeds identified on each document. I put my hands on the very papers that my grandparents' had both signed. I imagined them as younger adults than when I knew them. I thought about them as they got dressed to come to the courthouse to sign papers, sitting side-by-side. I remembered similar events in my own young adulthood, and I now understood them a little differently —not the old people I knew when I was a child, but as real people, young people with hopes and dreams, in their 20s, 30s, and 40s, as they first purchased the land, lost it, and then got it back again. I felt an intimate kinship with them as their experiences resonated with mine.

⋏⋏⋏

Before I left the registrar's office, I stopped by the front desk again. "I noticed that Clifford Sechser's survey company that did the last survey on my property is out of business. Can you suggest someone else for me to call to get a survey updated?

"Oh," said the patient woman who helped me with the computer search, "Cliff died a few years ago. All his files transferred over to Kevin Ensley. You can call him. He should be able to help you."

When I called later, Ensley's assistant put us on a waiting list. New construction was booming at the time, and he said it would take several months to get this done, but at least I was on the list.

⋏⋏⋏

After lunch we visited places on the other side of Waynesville: Camp Branch Creek and Allen's Creek. My grandfather talked about them on the oral history recordings as places he lived as a small boy. I had only associated my grandfather and his parents with Bethel, where they all lived when I was a child and since the 1930s. I wanted to see these other places geographically close to Bethel and significantly distinct in my grandfather's memory.

Granddaddy's family moved to Camp Branch in Waynesville when his father, Will York, got a job working for his brother-in-law as a pipefitter helping put in Waynesville's first water line along Allen's Creek, around 1908. Granddaddy recounted memories of walking with his sister Florence into a classroom for the first time in a school here, feeling completely out of place. He also remembered the first time he ever went to church, when his grandmother Vicie Reece York took him to Allen's Creek Episcopal Church. He recalled that the minister, Dr. Pruitt, preached a sermon about Jesus casting demons out of swine. At age 88, he said on the recording, "I never did forget it."

Though this area is close to town, it is still relatively undeveloped. Allen's Creek flows cleanly under the Piney Mountain Road Bridge and north, across the road from the Allen's Creek Baptist Church. Mountains crop out of the landscape, not so far in the distance on each side of the creek. Camp Branch Creek is east of Allen's Creek. We followed it farther back into the mountain, not really knowing where the Yorks had lived. We found a place to park so we could get out and walk along the creek a bit.

A small, white, wood frame structure with a short cross on top houses the Camp Branch Free Will Baptist Church. It sits next to the creek on a scrap of land with nearly no lawn. The building has been there for a while but is well-maintained. I found it adorable, even as it felt wrong to think that about a house of God.

Free Will Baptists are a whole other kind of Baptist than the ones I grew up among. I thought about the Holy Spirit manifesting itself inside this building every Sunday morning up in these winding mountain roads. Did people speak in tongues here? What demons did Jesus cast out? Could He cast out a few of mine?

A small bridge crosses the creek into a sparsely populated neighborhood. A mountain that we saw from the other side sits behind the houses here. It was late afternoon, clear skies, quiet except the murmur of water flowing under the bridge. A utilities van sat next to our car with workers taking a break from their labors. We hung around until it is time to go to Bethel to meet Herman.

⁂

Herman arrived in a heavy-duty work truck. He was in his 30s or 40s, had dark hair, dark eyes and a short, small-framed, sturdy, and muscular build. He had been working hard all day, but he buzzed with energy. He knew his way around this lot. We showed him the plat and the markers we could find and walked him down past the creek, while deciding exactly what he should cut down and what to do with the debris. He quoted us a price that was a big number, but we could have imagined a bigger one, so we agreed. Best of all, he could do it a week from that day, making it possible for us to see his work and pay him before we headed back to Chapel Hill. After he left, I walked around the lot again, more weight lifted. I leaned even further into the possibility of putting a house here.

⌒⌒⌒

With almost all my property-related tasks completed for the moment, we had a couple of days for hiking. I identified trails around Cold Mountain and the East Fork of the Pigeon River, and around the Sunburst area of the Pisgah National Forest, places where generations of both sides of my mother's family lived.

The Pigeon River weaves these mountains together. It arises from the West Fork and the East Fork, both in Haywood County. They join south of Canton and move north and west, eventually into Tennessee and the French Broad River. My grandfather told this story to my aunt about the naming of the river:

"[A man] sat in Pigeon Gap up here, and watched a covey of pigeons flying through. They were called passenger pigeons; they're extinct now . . . .[the man] went there and watched them fly through the gap . . . I can't remember how long he said it took there were so many of them. It was estimated to be seven, not millions, but seven billion of them I think it was. They were so thick that it darkened the area they were flying through and that is why that is called Pigeon Road, Pigeon Gap and this is called Pigeon River."

I have heard this story about the naming of this river from other people as well and know it to be true. As I heard my mother's voice in my grandfather's mountain cadence, it was as if they both were in the room with me. I was so grateful to my aunt for these tapes, but I'm not sure I ever told her so.

Granddaddy continued this story with details I found particularly fascinating.

[A long time ago before this area was settled] "farmers knew about so many of the pigeons that they would come in here and build lots and bring their hogs. They would camp out here and at night they'd take a stick, the pigeons were so thick on the ground that had come here from elsewhere that they'd just kill 'em by the hundreds and pile 'em in the hog lots to feed their hogs. And they'd fatten their hogs, and they'd come here and kill their hogs and dress them and haul 'em to market in whatever conveyance that had to get them out of here."

ᴧᴧᴧ

The first trail Ron and I went to hike was along the Pigeon River's East Fork, toward the Cruso community. A month earlier, a freak micro-burst storm hit over the top of Cold Mountain and caused massive flooding.[15] I saw photos of the destruction in its immediate aftermath posted on social media, but I was unprepared for the substantial damage that remained on both sides of the river. Buildings torn apart, trailers overturned by the violent flow. A gulley cut deep down the side of a steeply sloped hill, a gaping wound bleeding mud and stone. Construction crews were out cleaning up and repairing what they could. The rushing waters of this storm hit hardest those who could defend themselves the least.

Trails along both sides of the East Fork had been washed out, but they were at least partway walkable when we were there. Trees were down and boulder-sized stones had been re-arranged by the powerful torrents. Brown and yellow leaves hid the path, still covered in some places with inches of mud run-off from higher elevations. Tree roots snuck out from under the leaves and sometimes caught the toes of our leather boots. The trail abruptly ended on a high bluff. We sat ourselves down right where the trail ended to eat our lunch while we listened to the fast water symphony rising up from below.

After a bit more exploration of nearby trails, we took a slightly different route back to Waynesville. I wanted to see what damage was done to the Dix Creek[16] area where the Kuykendalls lived. Dix Creek is a branch of the East Fork. We didn't see anything like what we had seen earlier. We turned down Joeberry Lane, a long driveway named after my great-grandfather, and all the trailers and houses in front of Cold Mountain seemed intact. I wondered if I was just not seeing damage farther into the mountain, but I also did not want to drive any more up the dirt road and risk invading someone's privacy—or raising their ire.

⋏⋏⋏

We continued down the Dix Creek Road, stopping at the Mt. Zion Baptist Church cemetery where so many Kuykendalls, Blalocks, and Deavers are buried. We also stopped at the Bethel Cemetery afterward. I'd been both places before, but I felt the need to check on my ancestors. It settled me as I walked these grounds.

Bethel Cemetery is not far away from Dix Creek, across Pigeon Road from Bethel Baptist Church where my mother and grandparents were members. I went there with my grandparents sometimes. Mother and I would sit in the same pew as my grandmother, while my grandfather sat with the other deacons in the "Amen corner," that part of the sanctuary in country churches where the men of the church could be heard affirming various parts of the sermon with an audible "amen," not so different than finger snapping at a poetry slam. It was my mother's job to keep the cousins quiet. There was to be no giggling in God's house. No speaking in tongues in this church, either.

Unlike the more suburban (and I thought, more sophisticated) churches I usually went to, there was no baptismal font inside this church, because people who got saved around here were baptized in the Pigeon River.

Bethel Cemetery sat high up on a hill. As I looked out from this vantage point, I realized for the first time, that as the crow flies, my grandparents' house and farm were not so far from where the Kuykendalls lived on Dix Creek. I thought of the story my grandfather told of taking my grandmother, when they were first married, in a horse and buggy down the old road to see her parents. They'd have made a right turn just about half a mile from here, and then another one not too much farther on.

As I faced Pigeon Road and the church from the top of the hill, I saw Cold Mountain (made famous by Charles Frazier's book of the same name) [17] behind the church. A *ways* behind the church, as they say around here. Today on this hill, I found for the first time the gravestone of Etheldred Blaylock, the great-grandfather of my grandmother Ethel Kuykendall York, both of them descendants of ancestor Thomas Blacklocke who left England to immigrate to Virginia.[18] Etheldred lived in Bethel and worked there as a carpenter, except for the years he was fighting as a Confederate soldier in the Civil War. And I saw the family plot of the Kinslands who, I only recently had learned, owned my grandparents' land before they did.

The past travels down this road in front of me between the cemetery and the church. Before it was called Pigeon Road, before my grandparents or the Kinslands owned any of the nearby land, it was the road General Rutherford marched his troops over on their way to annihilate the Middle Town Cherokee people.

∧∧∧

Thus far, I have written nothing about my ancestors' connection to another problematic aspect of America's history, the kidnapping and enslavement of Africans, but this is the place to do so. At the time of this visit to Bethel, I knew only of one ancestor who ever extracted labor from an enslaved person: Abraham Kuykendall. Abraham was possibly the most well-known person in the history of my family, and I am not altogether proud to call him kin. To my embarrassment, I heard his name lauded on television in a story about how he had become the historical darling of a certain bizarre splinter group of neo-conservatives. He was, for a time, the sheriff of Buncombe County, and the county enslaved a man who reported to Abraham. I had thought there were few enslaved people in the mountains, and assumed Abraham was the only ancestor with any relationship to the kidnapping and enslavement of Africans. I thought maybe I could take a "pass" at reckoning with ancestral legacies, but I know now, this is not true.

For one thing, I realized that I had ancestors who fought on both sides of the War Between the States, meaning some of them fought to defend the practice of slavery. Thus, some of my ancestors were not innocent of perpetuating this peculiar institution, nor of harms that have followed since the Reconstruction era. But also, I learned that there were several plantations in Haywood County that employed slave labor before the American Civil War, and one of them was owned by a great uncle to Etheldred Blalock, Elijah Blalock. Fifty or more of the people who worked on Elijah's plantation are buried in unmarked graves in the same cemetery where Etheldred is buried. The land for the cemetery was given to the Bethel community by Elijah with the stipulation that the enslaved people who had worked on his plantation be buried there when they passed. Now more than a century later, White people in the community are seeking to repair relationships with the descendants of these people. I am just beginning to think about how to engage in this community effort. I am stunned that I had never heard any of this story when I was growing up. Did my mother even know?

~~~

During the 1910s, massive amounts of timber were cut down to feed the nearby paper mills powered by the energy of the Pigeon River. A railroad route was cut through the mountains to haul the wood to its destination. The Sunburst community, south of Bethel along the East Fork played a major role in this industry. My grandfather worked as a sawyer at one of these in his late teens. The mill provided a bunkhouse for the men who worked there. On the weekends my grandfather stayed with relatives on his father's side who lived in the area, the Reeces. It was in Sunburst that he went to a revival and was "saved." It was also in the nearby Burnett Siding Baptist Church that he met my grandmother Ethel Kuykendall. Her family lived not so far away, but in the opposite direction of the sawmill.

With my grandfather's stories still ringing in my ears, we made our way to see Sunburst Falls in the Pisgah National Forest. We were somewhat distracted by men in camouflage pants and jackets and orange hats and vests with rifles, whose vehicles took up most of the limited parking spaces available. We pulled into a space behind a white, oversized pick-up truck. A young man in hunting attire startled us as he suddenly appeared from behind the truck. In front of us was another man holding a walkie-talkie and a rifle. He walked over to our car and peered in with a half-frown on his face. We lowered the window.

"Hello. What's up? Is something wrong?"

"No," he said.

His soft, pink face was sparsely covered with an auburn beard. Curls of the same color pushed out from under his orange hunting cap. He continued, "I thought you wanted to tell me something. Like maybe you'd seen a dog hit on the road."

That's random, I thought, but answered, "No, we just want to go look at the falls, and this seemed the closest place to park. Any problem parking here?"

There wasn't.

We crossed the road to get to the spectacular cascades and climbed around them as much as we could and still feel safe. We felt the power of the water spilling down over eons-old upended granite slabs.

When we got back to the car, the walkie-talkie guy was still there. I said, "So what are y'all huntin'?" I noticed that my accent had become steadily more mountain during this trip.

"Bear," he said.

"Think you'll get one?" I asked, trying to engage him, though it felt the like the lame attempt it was.

He shrugged me off. He knew I didn't live around there. He pegged me as a tourist from God-knows-where. As he turned his face back to the woods, he said, "You never know."

I told this story to Nadia later over the phone. She said, "Sunburst is bear-hunting country. The Reeces were big bear hunters." Maybe the walkie-talkie guy was a distant cousin.

After viewing the falls, we were up for some hiking. The signs that marked the trail entrances were obscured by thick foliage. We made our way to where we thought we were supposed to start and found an extremely steep path in dense forest up the side of the mountain. We expected to find a more level trail when we got to the top. It was gorgeous under the canopy, but we quickly realized that the incline was more challenging than we expected. I was more concerned about the trail going down than the one going up. Ron went a bit farther on his own to check it out, and he found that it was a long way until it flattened out. Our lack of orange clothing was also on my mind. We stopped and awkwardly ate our lunch. We heard water in the distance. We also heard gunshots. As we climbed back down the trail, we saw a doe bounding full speed out across the road. "Bambi's mother!" we said in unison to each other, afraid for her.

ᴧᴧᴧ

We drove west to Kentucky and Ohio for the weekend to visit friends there. On our way back Sunday afternoon, we got a call from Herman, the guy who was supposed to clear the lot the next day.

"Is something wrong? I thought we were going to meet you out there in the morning."

"There's no problem," he said. "It's all finished."

"What?" I asked.

"It was supposed to rain tomorrow and Tuesday, so we got it done this weekend."

I felt two ways about this, but I decided to just be happy about it. "Wow. We are still about 30 minutes away from there. Can you stay a bit? We'll check it out and then settle with you."

"Yes, no problem. We are doing some other work for your neighbors while we are here."

We found Herman hanging out with a larger, scruffier, much older man who often worked with him. Praises for their work flowed easily from my lips. The previously unkempt field got a badly needed haircut and a shave. The gnarled, dead apple trees were gone, along with the brambles. Lovely younger trees now stood out along the ridge line about halfway down the field. Everything felt lighter, clearer.

Herman chipped up the fallen wood and left it on the ground. Down by the creek, the trash and debris were now more noticeable, however, and some of the organic matter had fallen into the water. I made a mental note that we needed to come back in the morning with a rake and some garbage bags to liberate the creek bed from anything keeping the waters from flowing or the grounds from their true beauty. I felt protective of this place. I cautiously began to believe that I would build a place here that I could share with others. If I could have turned cartwheels, I would have.

ᴧᴧᴧ

We came back the next morning with clean-up tools in hand. Before we started clearing the garbage along the roadside, I attended to the creek. It is not wide, but it took me a very long stride to get over. More than once I landed in the water as I leaped across; my old hiking boots were baptized with creek mud. A sacrament.

A couple of concrete blocks in the creek, at about the place where my lot ends and my cousin's begins, were put there as a dam by my uncle a couple of decades ago. I pulled out rusted sheets of metal that may have been part of the dam or that just got caught there. The concrete was broken up also. I pulled out as much as I could to let the water go.

Fragments of branches and underbrush cut down or cut back during the past two days made their way into the water. Some of it was tangled in grasses growing out of the eroded perimeter, slowing down the stream. I used my small rake to pull as much of it out as I could while squatting on the edge. To avoid losing my balance and toppling into the breach, I stretched myself out flat, belly-down, perpendicular to the creek, with my head and arms hanging over to reach the debris I want to remove.

And there it was. I felt it in my whole body, the warm embrace of the ground below me. *I am* welcomed *here, I am welcomed* here, on land where I can look out over and see my granddaddy's front porch. I am content. A peace that passes understanding. I felt settled. Yes, settled, that contentious word.

I could not un-march Rutherford's militia past this place, but in that fleeting moment, I believed that, somehow by being here, I could do something to heal old wounds.

I can honor my ancestors as I continue my journey to discern what can be done to repair past atrocities. This is where it all came together for me, my genius loci. The land's blessing has made this a sacred space for me.

Home.

Bethel. From left to right, top to bottom. Will and Lonie York (my maternal grandfather's parents); Joeberry and Bertha Kuykendall (my maternal grandmother's parents), D.D. and Ethel York (my maternal grandparents) standing in their driveway, the field behind them, and farther back, Cold Mountain; and my grandfather D.D. York and great-grandfather Joeberry, standing behind me in my grandparents'

driveway, their house to the right. I'm about 5 years old in this photograph.

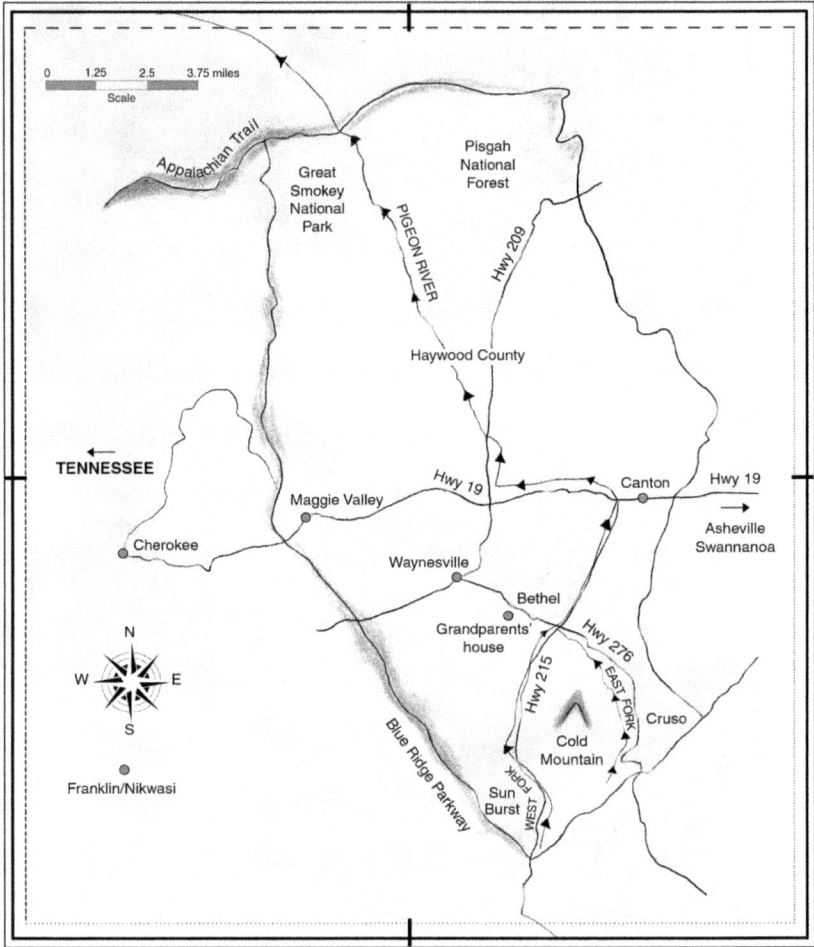

Map of Haywood County, North Carolina

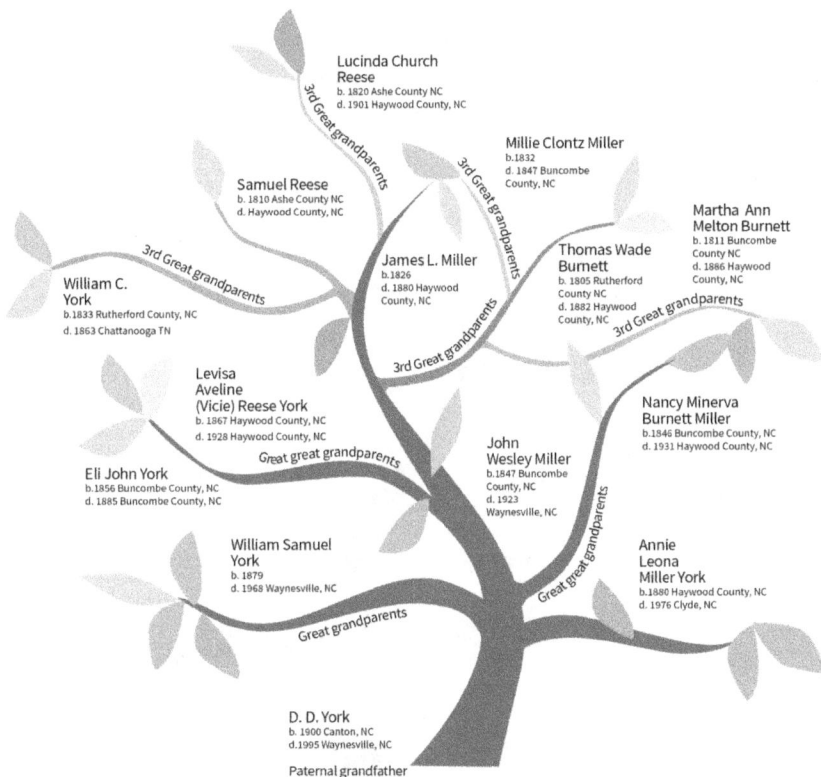

Lucinda Church
Reese
b. 1820 Ashe County NC
d. 1901 Haywood County, NC

3rd Great grandparents

Millie Clontz Miller
b.1832
d. 1847 Buncombe
County, NC

3rd Great grandparents

Samuel Reese
b. 1810 Ashe County NC
d. Haywood County, NC

Martha Ann
Melton Burnett
b. 1811 Buncombe
County NC
d. 1886 Haywood
County, NC

William C.
York
b.1833 Rutherford County, NC
d. 1863 Chattanooga TN

3rd Great grandparents

James L. Miller
b.1826
d. 1880 Haywood
County, NC

Thomas Wade
Burnett
b. 1805 Rutherford
County NC
d. 1882 Haywood
County, NC

3rd Great grandparents

3rd Great grandparents

Levisa
Aveline
(Vicie) Reese York
b. 1867 Haywood County, NC
d. 1928 Haywood County, NC

Nancy Minerva
Burnett Miller
b.1846 Buncombe County, NC
d. 1931 Haywood County, NC

Great great grandparents

Eli John York
b.1856 Buncombe County, NC
d. 1885 Buncombe County, NC

John
Wesley Miller
b.1847 Buncombe
County, NC
d. 1923
Waynesville, NC

Great great grandparents

William Samuel
York
b. 1879
d. 1968 Waynesville, NC

Annie
Leona
Miller York
b.1880 Haywood County, NC
d. 1976 Clyde, NC

Great grandparents

D. D. York
b. 1900 Canton, NC
d.1995 Waynesville, NC

Paternal grandfather

Family tree for my paternal grandfather's lineage

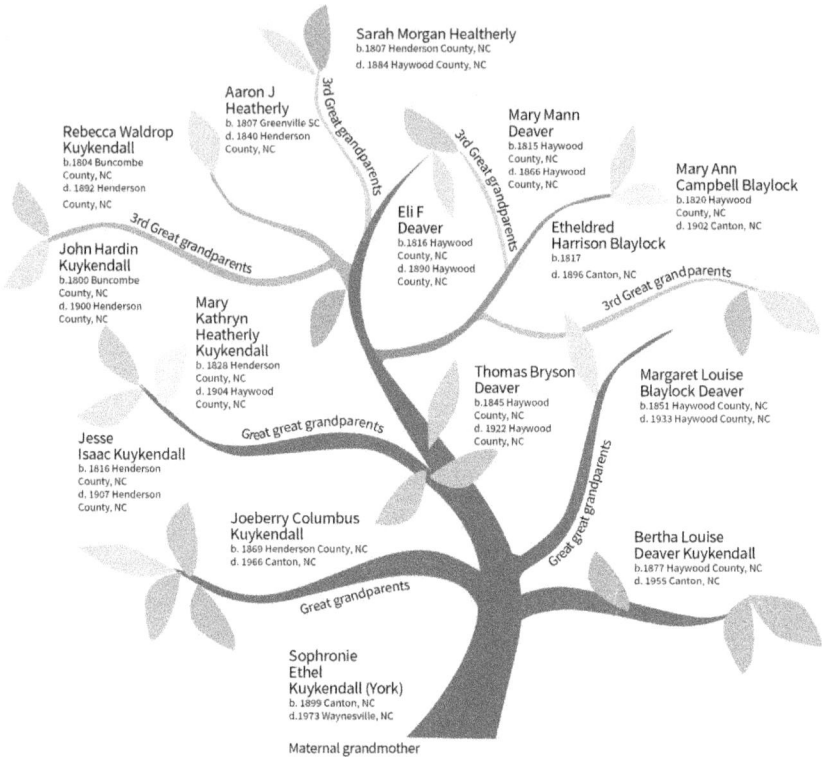

Sarah Morgan Healtherly
b.1807 Henderson County, NC
d. 1884 Haywood County, NC

Aaron J Heatherly
b. 1807 Greenville SC
d. 1840 Henderson County, NC

3rd Great grandparents

Rebecca Waldrop Kuykendall
b.1804 Buncombe County, NC
d. 1892 Henderson County, NC

Mary Mann Deaver
b.1815 Haywood County, NC
d. 1866 Haywood County, NC

3rd Great grandparents

Mary Ann Campbell Blaylock
b.1820 Haywood County, NC
d. 1902 Canton, NC

Eli F Deaver
b.1816 Haywood County, NC
d. 1890 Haywood County, NC

Etheldred Harrison Blaylock
b.1817
d. 1896 Canton, NC

3rd Great grandparents

John Hardin Kuykendall
b.1800 Buncombe County, NC
d. 1900 Henderson County, NC

Mary Kathryn Heatherly Kuykendall
b. 1828 Henderson County, NC
d. 1904 Haywood County, NC

Thomas Bryson Deaver
b.1845 Haywood County, NC
d. 1922 Haywood County, NC

Margaret Louise Blaylock Deaver
b.1851 Haywood County, NC
d. 1933 Haywood County, NC

Great great grandparents

Jesse Isaac Kuykendall
b. 1816 Henderson County, NC
d. 1907 Henderson County, NC

Great great grandparents

Joeberry Columbus Kuykendall
b. 1869 Henderson County, NC
d. 1966 Canton, NC

Bertha Louise Deaver Kuykendall
b.1877 Haywood County, NC
d. 1955 Canton, NC

Great grandparents

Sophronie Ethel Kuykendall (York)
b. 1899 Canton, NC
d.1973 Waynesville, NC

Maternal grandmother

Familiy tree for my maternal grandmother's lineage

grace land

IN MUCH THE same gentle way I felt my ancestors pull on my shirtsleeves more than five years earlier, beckoning me into their lives, they quietly leaned over my shoulder and whispered into my ear, "It is time to move on."

A surprise and a release. And just a bit sad. I had become used to having them in my thoughts, bending my life around a desire to tell their stories. I felt assured, however, that moving on did not mean I was abandoning them—or they me. My journey taught me so much about the contexts and particularities of their lives and times and showed me the abundant table they set for me and the rest of their descendants—and also the price of that abundance for others. Their stories enriched my life with new meaning, new purpose, and created an intimacy with them that will stay with me always.

⸎

Yes, I had been hanging on, not sure if I was ready to put this story into the world. After visiting the last ancestor destination, Waynesville, my efforts focused on photographs, layering multiple images of family and landscapes together into single ones, an acknowledgement of their deep roots into these homelands. These new pieces found their way into a solo exhibit, Landscapes of Ancestral Migration, at a local gallery. Visitor responses to the show gave me new confidence in myself as a visual artist and confirmed that my ancestors' stories resonated with other people.

It was, perhaps, at that juncture that I tightened my grip on this storytelling project when it was, in fact, time to loosen it. My store of landscape and vintage photographs is vast, and they touch my heart so deeply. I began working methodically on new art—so sweetly it held me as I spent hours editing an image of one set of grandparents or another to add to yet another field or seascape, potentially tethering me to the project indefinitely. Then one day, I took an enormous family photograph album off the shelf to find a few photographs I had not yet digitized. I meticulously turned every page and absorbed every image.

I closed the book after the last page and felt the physical sensation of saturation, of enough. My heart knew it was time to let go. Not to slam on the brakes, but to ease up on the gas as I rolled to a stop at the next intersection. I teared up a bit as I thought of this surrender; I had come to love these people—ancestors I had known and ancestors I had not—because I had heeded their call to look more deeply into their lives.

Completing this part of my quest did not completely sate my sentimental hunger for the Thanksgiving dinner of my memory. In the end, however, it gave me more than what I asked for. I filled in empty spaces around the outlines of people and stories little known to me before. Following the trail unfolding for me a step at a time, I began to understand my ancestors as real people. Similarities between their lives and mine surprised me and comforted me. I discovered much about how my life was shaped by theirs. Seeing my life arising out of the intersections of all their decisions and movements, I understood my story entangled with theirs and found myself reckoning with my responsibilities to them and to the wider world.

And my feelings about the parents, grandparents, and great-grandparents I had known but who had now passed changed in a way that strengthened my connection with them, even after their deaths. I was able to love them differently than before and give them more grace because I understood them better. This was particularly true for my mother. I am a bit wistful that this compassion did not arrive sooner, but I am grateful that it did appear.

And, I have sat down to real Thanksgiving dinners with living, breathing, extended family, reunited in our interest in family stories.

I felt a new calling to attend to the present moment. Though not abandoning it entirely, I had pulled away from the present to investigate the past. It was time to use all that I learned to intentionally move forward into the here and now with new knowledge of what I had been given and what I owed. There was more repair to make, more justice to work for, and more beauty to shine a light on.

I recently dug into beautiful dark soil to plant two chestnut trees on the two-acre tract of that land—formerly part of my grandfather's farm—where finally I am building a cabin. Every moment on that land makes me feel like I belong to it, that I am beckoned by it. I want to be worthy of it, to become "naturalized" to that place, a process Potawatomi scientist and writer, Robin Wall Kimmerer describes in *Braiding Sweetgrass*:

Being naturalized to a place means to live as if this is the land that feeds you, as if these are streams from which you drink, that build your body and fill your spirit. To become naturalized is to know that your ancestors lie in this ground. Here you will give your gifts and meet your responsibilities. To become naturalized is to live as if your children's future matters, to take care of the land as if our lives and the lives of all our relatives depend on it. Because they do. [1]

❈

As I got to know my ancestors, I came to believe that they loved and cared for the lands they lived on; this place in particular, they were naturalized to. Some family members may have been more rootless, as I have felt sometimes. This land has nurtured other people's ancestors, and it still holds past trauma. Soul wounds lie in this ground, in need of healing. Now, however, at the end of my ancestor journey, *this* land calls me home, to honor it by taking care of it because of what I now know, and as if lives depend on it.

❈

The next part of my journey requires an open heart and ongoing discernment with others with whom I have common cause. Lately, I have found a community of like-minded descendants of European settlers who wish to repair what was broken so long ago, beginning with a recognition of histories hidden from view. As more stories are told, more communities of trust can be built. I believe it is through this land and the opportunities it provides me that I can make amends and settle debts incurred. *I do not yet know exactly how this will happen.* I am pulled toward healing the land as a first step. It will not be a quick fix, but a process, the work of the rest of my lifetime. As I put one foot in front of the other, a path will continue to unfold.

Is there something your ancestors may be calling to you to do?

———⊶⊷———

Genealogy helped me find my ancestors, the stories of their lives, and whole worlds in which they lived. I saw them as part of a bigger sweep of history that showed me my connections with them that also took me deeper into my life. I found some strange comfort in knowing that the social upheaval and what seems like madness in the current world is nothing new. Human lives have always been shaped by more forces than anyone can see or understand as they are being lived. As I pulled on the threads of history in my ancestors' stories, these threads wove themselves into my story as well. I found my place in the world, feeling less fragmented, less isolated, and part of a whole.

notes

Preface

1. David Whyte. "Seeking Language Large Enough" Interview by Krista Tippett *On Being with Krista Tippett*. April 7, 2016; updated May 26, 2022. Transcript. https://onbeing.org/programs/david-whyte-seeking-language-large-enough/.

1. Time Out of Time

1. Jane Goodall, *Reason for Hope: A spiritual journey* (New York: Warner Books, 1999), Chapter 12, iBooks.

2. Setting Out and Moving Forward

1. The genealogy site I began with was www.geni.com. I eventually purchased a membership to have greater access to materials, including the www.myheritage.com. www.findagrave.com was instrumental to working from present backward for my great-granddaddy Kuykendall's family. Eventually, I also joined www.ancestry.com which arguably has the best links to supporting documents and photographs.
2. Jacob followed the Dutch custom of using his father's name as his second name. The use of the surname "Kuykendall" is described later in the book.
3. https://www.geni.com/people/Jacob-van-Kuykendall/6000000001531267023.
4. For example, some information on Jacob indicates that he and Stynte had three daughters and one son, the first daughter born before they left Amsterdam. Others say he had two daughters and a son, all born in New Netherlands. When I looked closely at the birthdate of the daughter supposedly born in Amsterdam, also named Stynte, I realized that she would have been born almost a year before Jacob and Stynte got married, in January 1638. How could that have been possible in the place and times in which they were living? Even if Stynte had gotten pregnant out of wedlock, she would have gotten married before the birth to avoid the punishing stigma that would have followed.

   One of the contributors to Jacob's genealogy site noted, however, that there was another couple in Amsterdam with the same names who married the year before my Stynte and Jacob. A previous researcher may have confused the two couples and assumed that baby Stynte belonged to my ancestors. I was convinced by the greater plausibility of the less dramatic story. This seemingly small difference in a profile history, two daughters versus three, actually had significant implications for how I came to understand Jacob's and Stynte's lives.
5. Nancy Pearl and Jeff Schwager. Interview with Jane Hirshfield. *The Writer's Library*. (Harper One, 2020), 246, 248.

6. All of Helen Rountree's books were luscious invitations to explore the natural world of the Chesapeake Bay area. I began with Helen Rountree, Wayne Clark, and Kent Mountford. *John Smith's Chesapeake Voyages 1607-1609*. Charlottesville, VA: University of Virginia Press, 2008 and eventually also read *The Powhatan Indians of Virginia: Their Traditional Culture*. Norman, OK: University of Oklahoma Press,1988, and Helen Rountree and Thomas Davidson. *Eastern Shore Indians of Virginia and Maryland*. Charlottesville, VA: University of Virginia Press, 1997.

7. https://podcasts.apple.com/us/podcast/the-red-nation-podcast/id1482834485 provides an example of this.

8. Louise Dunlap. *Inherited Silence: Listening to the Land, Healing the Colonizer Mind*. New York: New Village Press, 2022.

3. What it Means to Leave a Place

1. Six months later, I got a staph infection again (I don't know why), but penicillin was now in pill form, so no hospitalization was necessary.

4. The Good Daughter

1. Betty Friedan. *The Feminine Mystique*. New York: WW Norton, 1963.

5. Borderlands (England)

1. Malcolm Gaskill, *Between Two Worlds: How the English Became Americans* (Basic Books, 2014), xix, 16;

2. Gaskill, *Between Two Worlds*, 20-21.

3. This opinion is influenced greatly by Manda Scott whose similar opinion I have heard spoken often on her weekly podcast, *Accidental Gods*. https://accidentalgods. life/our-podcast/

4. Webster, *The Roman Invasion of Britain*, 36-40.

5. In 60 CE the Inceni warrior queen, Boudicca, brought their slow progress to a temporary halt. Enraged by the Roman's theft of her land and rape of her daughters, led a revolt by a tribal coalition, burning down Colchester, St. Albans, and London down to the ground. How had I not heard before of this real-life feminine Celtic hero, Boudicca? I discovered her story while listening to a podcast about something else entirely and then tracked down information about her on the internet. I paused my academic historical research to read *Dream of the Eagle*, historical fiction written about Boudicca by Manda Scott. This book imagines the cultural and spiritual world of Indigenous Britons that stirs my heart in different way than works of archeology and historiography. I also read more scholarly books (e.g., *Boudica: The British Revolt Against Rome* by Graham Webster; *Boudica Britannia: Rebel, War-leader, and Queen* by Miranda Aldhouse-Green; and *Boudica* by Vanessa Collingridge), surprised by how many were out there resurrecting her from near oblivion. The Romans sacrificed the people living in the burning towns in order to attack Boudicca's forces.

6. Eric Apperly, The Romans in Cumbria: An Overview, 2020, https://www.cumbria countyhistory.org.uk/sites/default/files/county-info/romans_in_cumbria.pdf; Henry Summerson, *Carlisle Castle* (English Heritage Guidebooks, 2017), 23.

7. Nicholas Higham, *The Carvetii*. (Sutton Publishing Ltd., 1991), 9-11.

8. Hawes, *The Shortest History of England*, 9.

9. Barry Cunliffe, *The Ancient Celts* (Oxford University Press, 1997), 190-196; Green, Miranda, *Celtic Myths*, (British Museum Press, 1993), 50-51, 56-78; Gary Bitcliffe, *The Spine of Albion*, 2016, video, https://www.youtube.com/results?search_query= belinus+line.

10. Scholars debate whether this happened through horrific death and destruction to existing peoples and places and near complete replacement of the previous popula- tions or whether a Saxon elite minority gradually took control of land that had been recently neglected by the ruling Romans—with little resistance from the descen- dants of the Britons who remained. DNA testing and land use studies bolster the latter theory of adaptation among remaining Britons and incoming Saxons. Hawes, *The Shortest History of England*, 12-13.

11. "Anglo-Saxon" denoted Germanic speakers in Britain versus the German-speaking "Saxons" on the continent.

12. Higham, *The Carvetii*, 137-138

13. Henry Summerson, *Carlisle Castle* (English Heritage Guidebooks, 2017), 23.

14. Hawes, *The Shortest History of England*, 70-73, 98-99, 118; David Underdown, *Rebel, Riot, and Rebellion*, (Oxford Press, 1985), 24-25; 34; 40-41.

15. Hawes, *The Shortest History of England*, 100,122; Underdown, *Rebel, Riot, and Rebellion*, 18, 28.

16. Gaskill, *Between Two Worlds*, 6-7. Hawes, *The Shortest History of England*. 122-123; Underdown, *Rebel, Riot, and Rebellion*, 34.

17. Hawes, Shortest History of Britain, 122-123.

18. Border Reivers, Wikipedia. https://en.wikipedia.org/wiki/Border_reivers . David Fischer, *Albion's Seed: Four British Folkways in America*. (Oxford University Press, 2019), 621-629.

19. See the curse: https://www.bbc.co.uk/cumbria/features/2003/07/restoration/ the_curse.shtml.

20. Summerson, *Carlisle Castle*, 13.

21. Summerson, *Carlisle Castle*, 31,33.

22. Summerson, *Carlisle Castle*, 38,40.

23. First published by Robert Frost, *North of Boston* (David Nutt Publishers, 1914). A copy of it can be found online, here: https://www.poetryfoundation.org/poems/ 44266/mending-wall.

6. Finding Thomas Blacklocke on Virginia's Eastern Shore

1. Virginia General Assembly, Joint Committee of the State Library. 1874. Lists of the Living and the Dead in Virginia, February 16, 1623 published in *Colonial Records of Virginia*, 37.

2. All of Helen Rountree's books were luscious invitations to explore the natural world of the Chesapeake Bay area. I began with Helen Rountree, Wayne Clark, and

Kent Mountford, *John Smith's Chesapeake Voyages 1607-1609*. University of Virginia Press, 2008 and eventually also read Helen Rountree, *The Powhatan Indians of Virginia: Their Traditional Culture*. University of Oklahoma Press, 1988 and Helen Rountree and Thomas Davidston, *Eastern Shore Indians of Virginia and Maryland*, University of Virginia Press, 1997.

3. After seeing maps displayed in a local history museum on the Eastern Shore in Cape Charles, I investigated this meteor crash further via these USGS websites. USGS. 1998. The Chesapeake Bay Bolide Impact: A New View of Coastal Plain Evolution. USGS Fact Sheet: 49-98. Washington, DC: USGS. Retrieved from: https://pubs.usgs.gov/fs/fs49-98/ USGS. 1998. The Chesapeake Bay: Geologic Product of Rising Sea Level. USGS Fact Sheet 102-98. Washington, DC: USGS. Retrieved from http://www.virginiaplaces.org/geology/bolide.html

4. Jennings Cropper Wise, *Ye Kingdome of Accawmacke, Or, The Eastern Shore of Virginia in the Seventeenth Century*. Bell Book and Stationery Company, 1911, 12-13; Charles Mann, *1493*. NY: Vintage Books, 2011, 54.

5. Mann, *1493* 67, 74-85.

6. Wise, *Ye Kingdome of Accawmacke*, 54.

7. Mann, *1493 91-94*.

8. Mann, *1493*, 91.

9. Rountree , Clark, and Mountford, *John Smith's Chesapeake Voyages*, 196.

10. Mann, *1493, 85, 89-90*.

11. C Caulfied, *Wills and Administrations of Accomack County, VA, 1663-1800*. 8-9; *Abstracts of the Wills and Administrations of Northhampton County, VA 1632-1802*, compiled by James Handley Marshall, Pictor Press, 1994, 2001. *Northhampton County, VA Record Book, Volume 10, 1674-1678*. Tithe Tables, 93.

12. Rountree and Davidston, *Eastern Shore Indians*, 59-62.

13. Rountree and Davidston, *Eastern Shore Indians*, 67.

14. Rountree and Davidston, *Eastern Shore Indians*, 61.

15. Rountree, Clark, and Mountford, *John Smith's Chesapeake Voyages*, 22.

7. Take Me to the River (the Netherlands)

1. Russell Shorto, *Amsterdam: A History of the World's Most Liberal City*. Random House, 2013, 28.

2. Peter Tonge, How the Dutch shooed the "waterwolf" from the door. *The Christian Science Monitor*. 9 December 1982. https://www.csmonitor.com/1982/1209/120971.html; Jippe Kreuning, "The many faces of the Waterwolf, the Low Countries' greatest friend and foe". *http://www.waterinitiativeforthefuture.org/blog/the-many-faces-of-the-waterwolf-the-low-countries-greatest-friend-and-foe*. 2015.

3. Shorto, *Amsterdam*, 126, 145, 280.

4. Shorto, *Amsterdam*, 128. I also saw a video depiction of such a ride at the National Maritime Museum in Amsterdam in 2019.

5. unknown, St. Lucia's Flood Kills over 50,000 People in the Netherlands, History Pod, 2021. online video. https://www.historypod.net/12/14/14th-december-1287-st-lucias-flood-kills-over-50000-people-in-the-netherlands/ David Hambling, St. Lucia's Storm: The flood that changed the face of the Netherlands, The Guardian, 12 December 2018, online. https://www.theguardian.com/news/2018/dec/12/st-

lucias-storm-the-flood-that-changed-the-face-of-netherlands-europe; Aleksa Vučković, St. Lucia's Flood: The disaster that changed the shape of Europe, 2023, online: https://www.ancient-origins.net/history-important-events/st-lucias-flood-0018127

6. Eric de Paauw, How the Afsluitdijk Barrier Dam Keeps the Netherlands Safe, Lagersmit, 2022. Online.

    https://www.lagersmit.com/blog/how-the-afsluitdijk-barrier-dam-keeps-the-netherlands-safe/ ;

    Oliver McBride, Dutch Fishers to Bring Protest Over Mounting Issues to the Afsluitdijk, The Fishing Daily, 2021. Online.

    https://thefishingdaily.com/european-fishing-industry-news/dutch-fishers-to-bring-protest-over-mounting-issues-to-the-afsluitdijk/;

    Sarah Tekath, How is an artificial mega-dam putting Dutch ecosystems in danger? Euronews, 5/31/2021, online. https://www.euronews.com/green/2021/05/31/how-is-an-artificial-mega-dam-putting-dutch-ecosystems-in-danger.

7. This I see on a replica of an old map of Enkhuizen that I photographed at the museum. The oldest map I can find with this symbol was drawn in 1581.

8. Shorto, *Amsterdam*, 34-37.

9. Considering their wealth depended on no small part on colonial imperialism and kidnapping and enslaving human beings.

10. Shorto, *Amsterdam*, 65-68; U. Blazani. Early History of the Inquisition in the Netherlands. *Academy and Literature, 886*, 283, 1889.

    https://en.wikipedia.org/wiki/Inquisition_in_the_Netherlands https://en.wikipedia.org/wiki.history_of_religion_in_the_Netherlands

11. Shorto, *Amsterdam*, 76-79.

12. Shorto, *Amsterdam*, 83-85.

13. No author, Jacob (Leurtss) Luurszen (abt. 1616 - 1655) Wikitree. https://www.wikitree.com/wiki/Leurtss-1

14. No author, Jacob (Leurtss) Luurszen (abt. 1616 - 1655) Wikitree. https://www.wikitree.com/wiki/Leurtss-1

15. C. Zeldenrust, P. Zijlstra, P. and M. Verstegen. *Wageningen, A guided tour of the inner city*. Rondleidingen Wageningen, 2014.

16. Anne Marten, The Vulwe, The geologie of The Netherlands. Online. Translated by google translate from Dutch to English. https://www.geologievannederland.nl/landschap/landschapsvormen/stuwwal.

17. personal conversation with Gon

18. Zeldenrust, et al. *Wageningen*; and conversation with Gon

19. Zeldenrust, et al. *Wageningen*; and conversation with Gon

20. Zeldenrust, et al. *Wageningen*.

21. Wageningen-The Travel Guide at WikiVoyage; https://en.wikivoyage.org/wiki/Wageningen.

22. Shorto, *Amsterdam*, 30.

23. Shorto, *Amsterdam*, 30.

24. Shorto, *Amsterdam*, 122-123.

25. Paul Otto. *The Dutch-Munsee Encounter in America*, Berghahn Books, 2006, 88-89; Russell Shorto, *Island at the Center of the World*. Random House, 2004, 87; Janny Venema, *Beverwyck: A Dutch Village on the American Frontier*. SUNY Press, 2003, 17-20.

9. Muhheakantuck

1. Shorto, 2013, *Amsterdam, 37.*
2. Evan. Pritchard, *Native New Yorkers: The Legacy of the Algonquin People of New York.* Council Oaks Books, 2002, 12.
3. E. Pritchard, *Henry Hudson and the Algonquins of New York.* Council Oaks Books, 2009, x.
4. Robert Grumet, *The Munsee Indian: A History.* University of Oklahoma, 2009, 9.
5. https://www.haudenosauneeconfederacy.com/who-we-are/.
6. Janny Venema, *Beverwyck: A Dutch Village on the American Frontier.* SUNY Press, 2003, 18. Russell Shorto, *Island at the Center of the World.* Random House, 2004, 87.
7. The following discussion of Native and Dutch similarities and differences regarding beliefs about land use rights is based on Robert Grumet, *The Munsee Indian: A History,* University of Oklahoma Press, 2009, 84-88.
8. Grumet, *The Munsee Indian,* 91-93.
9. Information about Fort Orange, later incorporated as Beverwyck, is derived from Venema, *Beverwyck, 2003* Shorto, *Island at the Center of the World.*
10. This list of foods is from the diary of Adrian van der Donck, *A Description of the New Netherlands,* first published in Dutch in 1656, translated in English in 2003 as Document 096: American Journeys Collection, Wisconsin Historical Society Digital Library Archives, 2003, translated by Jerimiah Johnson, https://www.americanjourneys.org/AJ_PDF/AJ-096.pdf
11. New Netherland Inferior Court of Justice, *Fort Orange Court Minutes 1652-1660.* Accessed at the New Netherlands Reading Room, NY State Library, Albany, NY
12. New Netherland Inferior Court of Justice, *Fort Orange Court Minutes 1652-1660.* Accessed at the New Netherlands Reading Room, NY State Library, Albany, NY
13. Venema. *Beverwyck, 2003,* 156-9.
14. https://lftantillo.com/len-tantillo-biography.html.
15. Shorto, *The Island at the Center of the World,* 5-6.
16. Descriptions of Kingston and the Munsee Wars are synthesized from the following sources: Grumet, *The Munsee India;* Pritchard, *Native New Yorkers;* Paul Otto. *The Dutch-Munsee Encounter in America,* Berghahn Books, 2006; M Fried, *The Early History of Kingston and Ulster County,* Ulster County Historical Society, 1975.
17. Shorto, *The Island at the Center of the World,* 139-145.
18. https://web.archive.org/web/20110724163429/http://rabbel.nl/nordstrand.html ; https://en.wikipedia.org/wiki/Burchardi_flood.
19. As noted above, I synthesized the history of the Esopus Wars from several sources, but this fact I found in the book, Fried, *A History of Ulster County,* page 38, with my ancestor's name mentioned specifically, as the wife of Jurien Abels Westphal.
20. Stockbridge-Munsee Community Band of Mohican Indians. Our history. https://mohican.com/brief-history/
21. Flad, H. (2002). The Hudson River Valley and the Geographic Imagination. *Watershed.* (1): 45-55;

    Buckingham, M. *Muhheakantuck--Everything Has a Name.* Video http://www.matthewbuckingham.net/muhheakantuck.htm ; NY Department of Environmental Conservation. A River Coming Back from the Grave. Signage next to the Hudson River, Albany, NY. Viewed 13 June 2021.

10. Concealed, Revealed

1. Information pertaining to Syd Solomon was obtained from essays by Michael Auping, George S. Bolge, Gail Levin and Mike Solomon in the exhibit book, *Syd Solomon Concealed and Revealed* published by the estate of Syd Solomon as Artsentry, Inc. in 2016.

11. Daddy's Girl

1. This "it" in my career focused on why people didn't use contraception when they didn't want to get pregnant or protect themselves against HIV when they were at risk. The answers to those questions, as you can imagine, are complicated by social, political, and psychological factors.
2. George Carlson, *1001 Riddles*, The Platt & Munk Co, Inc., 1949.

12. The Land That Could Not Keep You (Germany)

1. Most of the details imagined for my grandfather's emigration experience were based on text of the *Exhibition Guide -- English version. The Emigration Museum. Ballinstadt Hamburg. (obtained during my visit there 6/2019)* and subsequent personal correspondence with archivist Heinz Voderberg. https://www.ballinstadt.de/en/
2. Personal correspondence with Heinz Voderberg, city archivist of Fehmarn Burg on April 25, 2020
3. https://rps.org/news/chapters/germany/2020/2020-september/isle-of-fehmarn/; https://www.ferienhaus-rotdorn.de/english/fehmarn-info/; https://en.wikipedia.org/wiki/Fehmarn.
4. https://en.wikipedia.org/wiki/Fehmarn.
5. http://www.wissers-hotel.de/history.html.

13. Fertile Soil (Iowa)

1. Ma-Ka-Tai-Me-She-Kia Kiak (Black Hawk), *Black Hawk's Autobiography Through Interpretation of Antoine LeClaire*, (American Publishing Company,1912), 62-68; https://www.blackhawkpark.org/tour.php; Lynn Alex, *Iowa's archaeological past. (University of Iowa Press, 2000)*; Chapter 6, iBooks. https://www.facebook.com/MeskwakiNation/videos/321075178942146/ Meskwaki Nation live with Historical Preservation Director Johnathan Buffalo. (Day 2) (August 7, 2020); https://www.facebook.com/MeskwakiNation/videos/313338483349937/?epa=SEARCH_BOX Meskwaki Nation live with Historic Preservation Director Johnathan Buffalo. (Day 1) (August 6, 2020); https://www.blackhawkpark.org/tour.php
2. Ludwig Guldner. *Vascular plants of Scott and Muscatine Counties. Botanical Publication No. 1.* (Davenport Public Museum. Davenport, IO, 1960), 11.
3. Guldner, *Vascular plants of Scott and Muscatine Counties,* 11.
4. Guldner, *Vascular plants of Scott and Muscatine Counties,* 11. The Walcott Historical

Society. *Walcott: The Early Years 1854-1954* (The Walcott Historical Society, 2019), 12.

5. Darcy Mulsbury, "When Agriculture Entered a Long Depression," (posted on darcy-mulsbury.com on 5 March 2020) https://www.darcymaulsby.com/blog/?s=when+agriculture+entered+long+depression

6. Wendell Berry, *The Art of the Commonplace.* (Counterpoint, 2002); Wendell Berry, *Bringing It to the Table: On Farming and Food* (Counterpoint, 2009); Barbara Kingsolver, *Animal, Vegetable, Miracle: A Year of Food Life* (Harper Perennial, 2007). Michael Pollan, *In defense of food* (Penguin Press, 2008). Robin Wall Kimmerer, *Braiding Sweetgrass* (Milkweed Editions, 2013).

7. Johnny O'Hara, Josh Tickell and Rebecca Tickell. 2020. *Kiss the Ground.* Movie produced by Big Picture Ranch. https://kissthegroundmovie.com; Leland Sage, "Rural Iowa in the 1920S and 1930S." *The Annals of Iowa* 47 (1983), 91-103. Available at: https://doi.org/10.17077/0003-4827.8981.

8. R. H. Walker and P. E. Brown P., *Soil Erosion in Iowa. Special Report #2* (USDA, 1936) 3, 35-45.

9. Kingsolver, *Animal, Vegetable, Miracle,* 13-18.

10. https://www.xdsinc.org/farm-at-penny-lane

11. Winona LaDuke, Recovering our land to decolonize our food. In Williams, J and Holt-Gimenez, E (eds) *Land Justice: Re-imagining Land, Food, and the Commons in the United States* (Food First Books, 2017), xi.

12. https://www.pioneer.com/us/about-us/our-history.html; https://www.corteva.us/who-we-are/our-history.html.

13. https://www.meskwaki.org/red-earth-gardens/

14. Wendell Berry, "Renewed husbandry," 2004. In Wendell Berry, *Bringing It to the Table: On Farming and Food.* (Counterpoint, 2019), 94. Full quote: "The industrial program, on the contrary, suggested that it was "uneconomic" for a farm family to produce its own food; the eort and the land would be better applied to commercial production. The result is utterly. Strange in human experience: farm families who buy everything they eat at the store."

15. https://www.fieldworktalk.org

14. Home/Town (Iowa)

1. Tom Loewy, "On the right side of history: Worker describes end to strike at Davenport defense suppliers," *Quad City Times*, March 23, 2022/June 8 2023. Accessed online at https://qctimes.com/news/local/on-the-right-side-of-history-worker-describes-end-to-strike-at-davenport-defense-supplier/article_5aa9c9dd-cbc4-52d2-a886-06250f552968.html

2. Per Jill Hannum, possibly short for "cheroots" because of the cigarettes he smoke?

3. Harry Downer, *History of Davenport and Scott County, Iowa, Vol. 1* (S.J. Publishing Co., 1910), 936. https://archive.org/details/historyofdavenpo01down/page/936/mode/2up.

15. River Crossing (Iowa)

1. Ma-Ka-Tai-Me-She-Kia-Kiak. *Black Hawk's Autobiography Through Interpretation of Antoine LeClaire* (American Publishing Company, 1912); https://en.wikipedia.org/wiki/Credit_Island

2. Ma-Ka-Tai-Me-She-Kia-Kiak, *Black Hawk's Autobiography*, 13, 18-22. https://en.wiki pedia.org/wiki/Black_Hawk_(Sauk_leader);   https://www.blackhawkpark.org/tour.php

3. Ma-Ka-Tai-Me-She-Kia-Kiak, *Black Hawk's Autobiography*, 62-70; https://www.blackhawkpark.org/tour.php

4. James Wilson, *The Earth Shall Weep: A History of Native America* (Grove Press, 1998), 23.

5. It is here I begin the story of the Black Hawk War, synthesized from the following references: Ma-Ka-Tai-Me-She-Kia-Kiak, *Black Hawk's Autobiography*; Patrick Jung. *The Black Hawk War*. https://en.wikipedia.org/wiki/Black_Hawk_War; https://www.history.com/this-day-in-history/black-hawk-war-begins; Nichols, Roger L. "Black Hawk and the Historians: A Review Essay." *The Annals of Iowa 75*, 2016, 61-70. https://doi.org/10.17077/0003-4827.12261;   https://en.wikipedia.org/wiki/Black_Hawk_(Sauk_leader); https://web.archive.org/web/20090815021319/http://lincoln.lib.niu.edu/blackhawk/page2c.html. I will only insert additional endnotes where there is a direct quote from one of these references.

6. Ma-Ka-Tai-Me-She-Kia-Kiak, *Black Hawk's Autobiography*, 78-79.

7. Ma-Ka-Tai-Me-She-Kia-Kiak, *Black Hawk's Autobiography*, 115.

8. In Layli Long Soldier. 2017. *Whereas*. Minneapolis, MN: Graywolf Press, 59-101. Audio recording of reading by author can be heard at: https://soundcloud.com/onbeing/38-by-layli-long-soldier.

16. Burial Grounds (Iowa)

1. The Walcott Historical Society, *Walcott: The Early Years 1854-1954* (Walcott Historical Society, 2016), 80.

2. Record of Henry Stock in Manila; https://www.abmc.gov/decedent-search/stock%3Dhenry.

3. Background information on Albany Mounds and Toolesboro Mounds found in: Albany Indian Mounds Foundation. The Albany Mounds. http://albanymound s.com(6/19/20); Toolesboro Mounds National Historic Landmark found on https://iowaculture.gov/history/sites/toolesboro-mounds-national-historic-landmark

4. Discussion of Moundbuilder Theory and the Davenport Conspiracy found in: Lynn Alex, *Iowa's archaeological past* (University of Iowa Press, 2000), Chapter 2, iBooks.

5. https://web.archive.org/web/20070928065048/http://www.qcmemory.org/Default.aspx?PageId=260&nt=207&nt2=229; https://timesmachine.nytimes.com/timesmachine/1891/09/25/103338220.html?pageNumber=10; https://www.findagrave.com/memorial/2625/chief-blackhawk.

6. The story of Maria Pearson's fight to have Indigenous bones respected and the resulting laws enacted was found in: L. Alex, *Iowa's archaeological past*, Chapter 2, iBooks.

7. Signs of Earth Diver story consciousness in Toolesboro and Albany Mounds and Earth Diver creation story found in: L. Alex, *Iowa's archaeological past*, Chapter 6, iBooks.

17. Coming Home—Bethel (North Carolina)

1. Genesis 28
2. My grandfather's legal name was D.D. York. No one alive knows why it was only initials or why those particular letters. Most people called him Deed.
3. Roxanne Dunbar-Ortiz, *An Indigenous People's History of the United States* (Beacon Press, 2014), 113.
4. Production of Unto These Hills continues through the present. It has been revised twice since I saw it to make it more historically accurate, and Cherokee characters are played by Cherokee actors. *Bender, Albert (December 5, 2008). "Unto These Hills: A Retelling - Now a rescripted version of gripping Cherokee Drama". IndianCountryNews.com. Cherokee, North Carolina.*
5. Robert Conley, *The Cherokee Nation: A History* (University of New Mexico Press, 2005), 5-6.
6. My account of Cherokee history in what is now western NC is a synthesis of the following publications: R.Conley, The Cherokee Nation, Chapters 3-5, 8-9; Nadia Dean, *Demand of Blood* (Valley River Press, 2012), 173-205; ---Proclamation Line of 1763 found at https://www.mountvernon.org/library/digitalhistory/digital-encyclo pedia/article/proclamation-line-of-1763/; Michael Beadle, "Rutherford Trace: Local Historians Examine the Legacy of Shock-and-Awe Revolutionary War Campaign against the Cherokee," *Smokey Mountain News,* August 2006, retrieved online 13 Dec 2021 from https://smokymountainnews.com/archives/item/13169-rutherford-trace-local-historians-examine-the-legacy-of-a-shock-and-awe-revolutionary-war-campaign-against-the-cherokee; NC DNCR, The Rutherford Trace and the Destruction of the Nikwasi. https://www.ncdcr.gov/blog/2013/09/10/the-rutherford-trace-and-the-destruction-of-nikwasi. Roxanne Dunbar-Ortiz, *An Indigenous People's History of the United States* (Beacon Press, 2014), xx.
7. From the diary attributed to Arthur Fairies, South Carolina Department of Archives and History, Columbia, SC. Quoted in N. Dean, *Demand of Blood,* 37-38.
8. N. Dean, *Demand of Blood.*
9. M. Beadle, "Rutherford Trace," online.
10. J.G. de Roulhac Hamilton, ed., "Revolutionary Diary of William Lenoir," *The Journal Southern History,* 6, 2, 247-259. (May 1940). https://www.history.com/topics/native-american-history/trail-of-tears#section_3
11. Duran, Eduardo. Video of Duran's closing keynote remarks: "Forgiving." Filmed in 2013 at Wellbriety. Conference, Washington, DC. Video, 50:52. Youtube.-com/watch?v=D4d2Y3PHJfo. Cited from Dunlap, Inherited Silence, 230.
12. https://www.haywoodcountync.gov/352/Haywood-County-History.
13. I looked it up online. It is one of 9 signs marking various landmarks along Rutherford's campaign. Here is what this one says, "The expedition led by Gen. Griffith Rutherford against the Cherokee, Sept. 1776, passed here, through Pigeon Gap." It was erected in 1954, the year before I was born. https://www.hmdb.org/m.asp?m=11791.

14. W.S. stands for Winfield Scott, for whom Scott County, Iowa is named for his leadership in removing the Sauk and Meskwakis from nearby lands. In 1838, he was asked by President Van Buren to lead the forced removal of Cherokee from the southeast to "Indian country" now known as Oklahoma. W.S. Kinsland was born 12 years later.
15. As the final manuscript of this book was being edited, this same area was hit by Hurricane Helene, bringing tragic damage to this same area and beyond.
16. I learned sometime later that Dix Creek was named after my ancestor Richard Deaver, who lived near the creek. It was initially called "Dick's" Creek, which was then changed to its homonym, "Dix" Creek. Richard was the grandfather to Thomas Bryson Deaver, husband to my great-great grandmother Mary Louise Deaver.
17. Though the story Frazier tells in *Cold Mountain* (Atlantic Monthly Press, 1997), is fictional, there is an Inman family from that area, and I am distantly related on the Kuykendall lineage to that family.
18. Having spent so much time studying English history to understand Thomas Blacklocke's life, I recognize 'Etheldred' as a very Anglo-Saxon name.

18. Grace Land

1. Kimmerer, *Braiding Sweetgrass*, 2013, 214.

bibliography

Aldhouse-Green, Miranda. *The Gods of the Celts*. Gloucester, United Kingdom: The History Press, 2011.

Alex, Lynn. *Iowa's archaeological past*. Iowa City, IA: University of Iowa Press, 2000.

Anbinder, Tyler. *City of Dreams*. New York: Houghton Mifflin Harcourt, 2016

Auping, M., Bolge, G., Levin, G. and M. Solomon.*Syd Solomon Concealed and Revealed*. Sarasota, FL: Artsentry, Inc. (the estate of Syd Solomon), 2016.

Berry, Wendell. *Bringing It to the Table: On Farming and Food*. Berkeley, CA: Counterpoint, 2009.

———. *The Art of the Commonplace*. Edited and introduced by Norman Wirzba.
Berkeley, CA: Counterpoint, 2002.

Buckingham, Matthew. *Muhheakantuck/Everything has a name*. (film), 2008.
https://www.smb.museum/en/exhibitions/detail/matthew-buckingham-everything-has-a-name/

Clark, Medford. *The Early History of Haywood County*, Waynesville, NC: self-published, 1961.

Clarren, Rebecca. *The Cost of Free Land: Jews, Lakota, and an American Inheritance*. USA: Viking, 2023.

Colgrave, Betram. (ed.) *Two Lives of St. Cuthbert*. Cambridge, England: Cambridge University Press, 1985.

Conley, Robert. *The Cherokee Nation: A History*. Albuquerque, NM: University of New Mexico Press, 2005.

Cunliffe, Barry. *The Ancient Celts*. London: Oxford University Press, 1997.

Dean, Nadia. *A Demand of Blood*. Cherokee, NC: Valley River Press, 2008.

Deloria, Vine. *Custer Died for Your Sins: An Indian Manifesto*. NY: Macmillan and Norman, OK: University of Oklahoma Press, 1970, 1988.

———. *God is Red*. Golden, CO: Fulcrum Press, 1994.

Diamond, Jared. *Guns, Germs, and Steel: The Fates of Human Societies*. NY: WW Norton and Company, 1997.

Diaz, Natalie. *Postcolonial Love Poem*. Graywolf Press, 2020.

———. *When My Brother Was an Aztec*. Copper Canyon Press, 2012.

Downer, Harry E. *History of Davenport and Scott County, Iowa, Vol. 1*, Chicago, IL: S.J. Publishing Co, 1910.

Dunbar-Ortiz, Roxanne. *An Indigenous Peoples' History of the United States*. Boston, MA: Beacon Press., 2014.

———. *Not a Nation of Immigrants: Settler Colonialism, White Supremacy, and a History of Erasure and Exclusion*. Boston: Beacon Press, 2021.

Dunlap, Louise. *Inherited Silence: Listening to the Land, Healing the Colonizer Mind*. NY: New Village Press, 2022.

Erdrich, Louise. 2020. *The Night Watchman*. NY: Harper, 2020.

Etchart, Linda. "The role of indigenous peoples in combating climate change." *Palgrave Commun* **3**, 17085 (2017). https://doi.org/10.1057/palcomms.2017.85 .

Estés, Clarissa Pinkola. *Women Who Run with the Wolves: Myths and Stories of the Wild Woman Archetype*, New York: River Wolf Press, 2017, iBooks. My Book.

Estes, Nick. 2019. *Our History is The Future*. Brooklyn, NY: Verso Press, 2019.

Estes, Nick, Melanie Yazzie, Jennifer Nez Denetdale, and David Correia. *Red Nations Rising: From Bordertown Violence to Native Liberation*. Oakland, CA: PM Press, 2021.

Fiorentino, Wesley. 2021. Saint Cuthbert. World History Encyclopedia, 2021. https://www.worldhistory.org/Saint_Cuthbert/.

Fischer, David. *Albion's Seed: Four British Folkways in America*. Oxford and New York: Oxford University Press, 1989.

Flad, Harvey. The Hudson River Valley and the Geographical Imagination. *Watershed*, 2002, (1): 45-55.

Fried, Marc. *The Early History of Kingston and Ulster County, NY*. Kingston, NY: Ulster County Historical Society, 1975.

Friedan, Betty. *The Feminine Mystique*. New York: WW Norton, 1963.

Frost, Robert. "Mending Wall," *North of Boston*. London: David Nutt, 1914.

Gaskill, Malcolm. *Between Two Worlds: How the English Became Americans*. NY: Basic Books, 2014.

Gilligan, Carol and Richards, David A. Darkness Now Visible: Patriarchy's Resurgence and Feminist Resistance. New York: Cambridge Press, 2018.

Giovale, Hilary. *Becoming a Good Relative: Calling White Settlers toward Truth, Healing, and Repair*. Brattleboro VT: Green Writers Press. 2024.

Goodall, Jane. *Reason for Hope: A Spiritual Journey*. New York, Warner Books, 1999, iBooks.

Grumet, Robert. *The Munsee Indian: A History*. Norman, OK: University of Oklahoma, 2009.

Guldner, Ludwig. 1960. *Vascular plants of Scott and Muscatine Counties. Botanical Publication No. 1*. Davenport Public Museum. Davenport, IO. 1960. (QK160.G8) p. 11.

Hämäläinen, Pekka. *Indigenous Continent: The epic contest for North America*. NY: Liveright Publishing Company, 2022.

Harari, Yuval Noah. *Sapiens: A brief history of humankind*. NY: Harper Perennial, 2015.

Hawes, James. *The Shortest History of England*. Exeter, England: Old Street Publishers, 2020.

Hernandez, Jessica. *Fresh Banana Leaves: Healing Indigenous Landscapes through Indigenous Science*, Berkeley, CA: North Atlantic Books, 2022.

Higham, Nicholas. *The Carvetii*. London: Sutton Publishing Ltd., 1991.

Kimmerer, Robin Wall. *Braiding Sweetgrass*. Minneapolis, MN: Milkweed Editions, 2013.

Kingsolver, Barbara. *Animal, Vegetable, Miracle: A Year of Food Life*. New York: Harper Perennial., 2007

LaDuke, Winona. Recovering our land to decolonize our food. In Williams, J and Holt-Gimenez, E (eds) *Land Justice: Re-imagining Land, Food, and the Commons in the United States*. Oakland, CA: Food First Books, 2017.

Long Soldier, Layli. *Whereas*. Minneapolis, MN: Graywolf Press, 2017.

Ma-Ka-Tai-Me-She-Kia-Kiak. *Black Hawk's Autobiography Through Interpretation of Antoine LeClaire*. Rock Island, IL: American Publishing Company, 1912.

Mann, Charles. 2005. *1491: New Revelations of the Americas before Columbus*. NY: Vintage Books, 2005.

———. *1493*. NY: Vintage Books, 2011.

Mengiste, Maaza. *The Shadow King*. NY: W.W. Norton, 2019.

Orange, Tommy. *There, There*. NY: Vintage Books, 2018.

Otto, Paul. *The Dutch-Munsee Encounter in America*. NY: Berghahn Books, 2006.

Pearl, Nancy and Jeff Schwager. *The Writer's Library*. NY: Harper One, 2020.

Percy, Walker. *The Moviegoer*. NY: Knopf Publishers, 1966.

Pollan, Michael. *In Defense of Food*. NY: Penguin Press, 2008.

Pritchard, Evan. *Henry Hudson and the Algonquins of New York*. San Francisco, CA: Council Oaks Books, 2009.

———. *Native New Yorkers: The Legacy of the Algonquin People of New York*. San Francisco, CA: Council Oaks Books, 2002.

Rohr, Richard. Growing up men. Interview with Krista Tippett. *On Being* podcast. April 13, 2017. www.onbeing.org/programs/richard-rohr-growing-up-men/

Rountree, Helen. *The Powhatan Indians of Virginia: Their Traditional Culture*. Norman, OK: University of Oklahoma Press. 1988.

Rountree, Helen and Davidson, Thomas. *Eastern Shore Indians of Virginia and Maryland*. Charlottesville, VA: University of Virginia Press, 1997.

Rountree, Helen, Clark, Wayne, and Kent Mountford. *John Smith's Chesapeake Voyages 1607-1609*. Charlottesville, VA: University of Virginia Press, 2008.

Schiffels Stephen, Wolfgang Haak, Pirita Paajanen, Bastien Llamas, Elizabeth Popescu, Louise Loe, Rachel Clarke, Alice Lyons, Richard Mortimer, Duncan Sayer, Chris Tyler-Smith, Alan Cooper, and Richard Durbin. Iron Age and Anglo-Saxon genomes from East England reveal British migration history. *Nat Commun. 19*; 7:10408. 2016 Jan. doi: 10.1038/ncomms10408. PMID: 26783965; PMCID: PMC4735688/

Scott, Manda. *Dreaming the Eagle*, New York: Penguin Random House, 2003.

Shorto, Russell. *Amsterdam: A History of the World's Most Liberal City*. NY: Random House, 2013.

———. *Island at the Center of the World*. NY: Random House, 2004.

Smith, Paul Chaat. *Everything You Know about Indians Is Wrong*. Minneapolis, MN: University of Minnesota Press., 2009

Summerson, Henry. *Carlisle Castle* (Carlisle, England: English Heritiage Guidebooks), 2017.

The Red Nation. *The Red Deal: Indigenous Action to Save Our Earth*. Brooklyn, NY: Common Notions, 2021.

Tonge, Peter. How the Dutch shooed the "waterwolf" from the door. *The Christian Science Monitor*. 9 December, 1982.

Treuer, David. *The Heartbeat of Wounded Knee: Native America from 1890 to the Present*. New York: Riverhead Books, 2019.

———. Return the National Parks to the Tribes. *The Atlantic*. May 2021. https://www.

theatlantic.com/magazine/archive/2021/05/return-the-national-parks-to-the-tribes/618395/

Underdown, David. *Revel, Riot and Rebellion: Popular Politics and Culture in England* 1603-1660. New York: Oxford University Press, 1985.

Venema, Janny. *Beverwijck: A Dutch Village on the American Frontier*. Albany, NY: SUNY Press, 2003.

The Walcott Historical Society. *Walcott: The Early Years 1854-1954*. Walcott, Iowa, 2016.

Webster, Graham. *The Roman Invasion of Britain*. Totowa, NJ: Barnes and Nobles Books, 1980.

Whyte, David. "Seeking Language Large Enough" Interview by Krista Tippett *On Being with Krista Tippett*. April 7, 2016; updated May 26, 2022. Transcript. https://onbeing.org/programs/david-whyte-seeking-language-large-enough/.

Williams, Justin and Eric Holt-Giménez. *Land Justice: Re-imagining Land, Food, and the Commons in the United States*. Oakland, CA: Food First Books/Institute for Food and Development Policy, 2017.

Wilson, J. 1998. *The Earth Shall Weep: A History of Native America*. NY: Grove Press.

Wise, Jennings Cropper. *Ye Kingdome of Accawmacke, Or, The Eastern Shore of Virginia in the Seventeenth Century*. United States: Bell Book and Stationery Company, 1911.

Zeldenrust, C., P. Zijlstra, and M. Verstegen. *Wageningen, A guided tour of the inner city*. Wageningen, Netherlands: Rondleidingen Wageningen, 2014.

Zimmer, Eric Steven. *Red Earth Nation*. Norman OK: University of Oklahoma Press, 2024.

resources for further study

Indigenous history and current events

Blackhawk, Ned. *The Rediscovery of America: Native Peoples and the Unmaking of US History.* Yale University Press, 2023.

DeLoria, Jr. Vine. *Custer Died for Your Sins: An Indian Manifesto.* University of Oklahoma Press, 1988.

Dunbar-Ortiz, Roxanne. *An Indigenous Peoples' History of the United States.* Beacon Press, 2015.

_____. *Not a Nation of Immigrants.* Beacon Press, 2021.

Estes, Nick. *Our History Is the Future.* Verso Press, 2019.

Nagle, Rebecca. *By the Fire We Carry.* Harper Collins Publishers, 2024.

Treuer, David. *The Heartbeat of Wounded Knee: Native America from 1890 to the Present.* New York: Riverhead Books, 2019.

Zimmer, Eric Steven. *Red Earth Nation.* Norman OK: University of Oklahoma Press, 2024.

Decolonization/What does it mean to make reparations?

Baker, Brea. *Rooted: The American Legacy of Land Theft and the Modern Movement for Black Land Ownership.* One World, 2024.

Clarren, Rebecca, *The Cost of Free Land: Jews, Lakota, and an American Inheritance.* Viking, 2023.

Dunlap, Louise. *Inherited Silence: Listening to the Land, Healing the Colonizer Mind.* New Village Press. 2022.

Giovale, Hilary. *Becoming a Good Relative.* The Green Writers Press, 2024.

Land Justice Futures. *Introduction to Land Justice.* Video. https://www.landjusticefutures.org/video-library/v/r5a7zdx85haj2e85b5rlsgs4hn3jp6

Murphy, Nora. *White Birch, Red Hawthorn: A Memoir.* University of Minnesota Press, 2017.

Williams, Justin and Eric Holt-Giménez. *Land Justice: Re-imagining Land, Food, and the Commons in the United States.* Oakland, CA: Food First Books/Institute for Food and Development Policy, 2017.

gratitude

I am grateful to so many people I encountered and was supported by along the journey of this book, beginning with my ancestors who kept showing up, nudging me along, and keeping me motivated when challenges arose. Thank you to my cousin Nadia for the significant assistance in my genealogy research and also to our distant cousin now passed, Charles Miller, who sent me a summary of information he collected over many years. All the online sources I used are, in fact, crowd-sourced by so many people, and I thank all the distant relatives I will never know who contributed any information that filled in all the pieces of my family story I had not known before.

I am grateful to you Louise Dunlap for being my friend and my entrée into the world of decolonization. Your book *Inherited Silence* modeled for me how to write mindfully about traumatic events. Not only did you take the time to read several chapters of my book and provide feedback, but you introduced me to several organizations of White settler descendants working to make reparations to BIPOC groups in this this country, and into a growing network of other writers on this topic. These were communities I didn't even know when I began this book, but they were communities that enriched my understanding of what I needed to move this book from manuscript into publication. In particular, I am grateful for the Rekindling (and Tending) Ancestral Memory Circle(s) led by Elyshia Holliday and Hilary Giovole, and for all the members of the Decolonial Dames.

Thank you to Jill Hanuum for your developmental editing that challenged me to go deeper into my personal story. Thank you to Simone, Anne, Jane, Shary, Ellen, and Lucila who listened to various versions this book as members of two different writing groups. Thank you also to Ron, Sarah, Robert, and Nadia who read a part of or the whole manuscript before it was accepted for publication. All of you gave me valuable and compassionate feedback.

I became a huge fan of librarians, archivists, and citizen historians while writing this book. I want to thank Stacia Childers at the Accomac Library Genealogy Reading Room; Bob Kernkamp, the archivist in Wageningen, Netherlands with whom I corresponded; Heinz Voderberg, the archivist in Fehmarn, Germany; Kelly Lao from the Immigration Museum in Davenport, Iowa, and Christine Chandler from the Putnam Museum in Davenport; Eric Zimmer for his correspondence about the Meskwaki settlement and sharing a draft copy of his dissertation; Karen Puck, the Genealogy Director for the American/Schleswig-Holstein Heritage Society; Gon van Laar, my excellent tour guide in Waginengen, and Peter Stock my second cousin living in Fehmarn for his responsive emails. Thanks also to the staff attending the New Netherland Reading Room at the New York State Library.

Thank you to Federick Marine for your amazing hand-drawn maps and to Denise Todoloski for your graphics design of the lovely family trees and map borders.

Thank you to the Durham Arts Council for an Emerging Artist Grant in 2020 that covered travel expenses to Davenport, Iowa, and also for allowing me to exhibit photographic work from this project.

Thank you to everyone at Torchflame Books: to Teri Rider for giving me the opportunity to publish this book; Jori Hanna for the beautiful cover and your marketing genius; and to Aleigha Hummel for your thoughtful/thought-provoking editing. Thank you (in no particular order) to friends and family not already mentioned who provided emotional support and encouragement: Jaki, LaHoma, Leigh, Libby, Greg, Jennifer, Max, Kate R., Paul, Lucy, Karen K., my inspiring yoga teacher Martha and all my lovely early morning classmates, and to dear Ann F., for helping me over some bumps in the road.

And last, but definitely not least, thank you to Ron Geary, my partner in literature and life, who provided emotional (and financial!) support along the way, who read multiple drafts and stayed engaged with the story of the book from beginning to end.

about the author

Cindy Waszak Geary grew up in the southeastern United States in the 1950s and 60s. She received a PhD in social psychology from the University of North Carolina. For over 30 years she applied this content knowledge to global health research. This work took her across the United States and around the world to many countries in Africa and Asia. Her travels to new places and different cultures ignited an interest in black and white photography to document her experiences. As she found herself winding down her public health research career after three decades, she had a strong desire to write stories about social justice through the lens of her own experience.

In 2017, she co-authored *Going to School in Black and White: A Dual Memoir of Desegregation*, with LaHoma Smith Romocki. Cindy and LaHoma describe how they, as two teenage girls who lived across town from each other—one black, one white—were altered by a court-ordered desegregation plan for Durham, NC in 1970. She began the investigation that became *Ancestral Landscapes* in 2018.

Cindy currently lives in Chapel Hill, North Carolina, though she also spends time every month in the mountains of North Carolina on land where her maternal grandparents once farmed. When in Chapel

Hill she volunteers at a therapy farm, The Farm at Penny Lane. She also practices yoga, participates in community-based social justice activities, and spends as much time hiking in the woods as possible. She is the mother of two adult children and 'nana' to one grand-daughter.

Connect with her online at:
www.cindywaszakgeary.com
instagram.com/cindywaszakgeary

thank you!

Thank you for reading! If you enjoyed this book, please leave a review on Amazon, Goodreads, BookBub, The Story Graph, or anywhere else you like to track your recent reads. Alternatively, you could post online or tell a friend about it. This helps our authors more than you may know.

   - The Team at Torchflame Books

Follow Torchflame Books for news about our authors and upcoming new releases @TorchflameBooks.

Find your next great read at www.torchflamebooks.com.

continue reading...

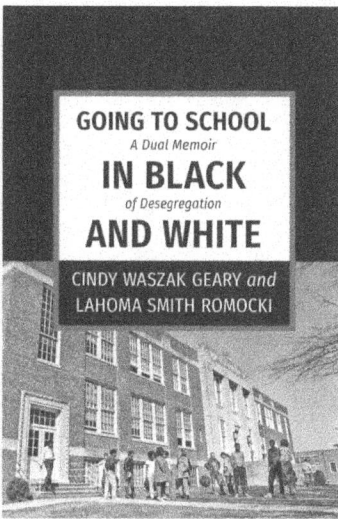

The school careers of two teenage girls who lived across town from each other—one black, one white—were altered by a court-ordered desegregation plan for Durham, NC in 1970. Their intertwined memoir explores race, education, and identity, from school days to careers in public health, reflecting on desegregation's impact and the return to de facto segregation in schools today.

Read Now!

"The challenges of identity, assimilation, achievement, and politics that were faced by Lahoma and Cindy are the same challenges our youth are facing today."

Jaki Shelton Green, poet and NC Literary Hall of Fame inductee

---